Architecture and Feminism

Architecture and Feminism

YALE PUBLICATIONS ON ARCHITECTURE

EDITORS

Debra Coleman | Elizabeth Danze | Carol Henderson

PRINCETON ARCHITECTURAL PRESS

PUBLISHED BY
Princeton Architectural Press
37 East 7th Street
New York, NY 10003
212.995.9620

Printed and bound in the United States

Book design and production editing: Sara E. Stemen
*Special thanks to Caroline Green, Clare Jacobson, Therese Kelly, Mark Lamster,
and Annie Nitschke—Kevin C. Lippert, Publisher*

LIBRARY OF CONGRESS CATALOGING-IN-PUBLICATION DATA
Architecture and Feminism: Yale Publications on Architecture /
editors, Debra Coleman, Elizabeth Danze, Carol Henderson
    p. cm.
Includes bibliographical references
ISBN 1-56898-043-4 (pbk.)
1. Feminism and architecture. I Coleman, Debra, 1959–   .
II. Danze, Elizabeth, 1956–   . III. Henderson, Carol, 1962–   .
IV. Yale University. School of Architecture.
NA2543.F45A73   1996
720'.82—dc20   96-34510
                        CIP

For a free catalog of other books published by
Princeton Architectural Press, call toll-free 800.722.6657

Visit Princeton Architectural Press on the World Wide Web at http://www.papress.com

Contents

Acknowledgments

This book grew from our efforts to create an ongoing forum at the Yale School of Architecture for the discussion of the relationship between architecture and feminism. Originally conceived as the *Yale Journal of Architecture and Feminism*, this endeavor was enthusiastically supported and encouraged by Dean Thomas Beeby. We are especially grateful to him. We also thank his successor, Dean Fred Koetter, for his continued endorsement of this project. Deborah Berke, our faculty advisor, provided invaluable assistance on a day-to-day basis. We could never thank her enough.

Both to cultivate a diverse group of authors, and to promote the idea that architecture and feminism is an important area of study, we issued an open call for papers and projects. In response, we received over one hundred submissions. At the time, this project was still conceived of as a journal, and we believe that one of the reasons for this robust response was the endorsement that the journal's Advisory Board gave to the project. For their time and support, we thank: Diana Agrest, Thomas Beeby, Deborah Berke, Esther da Costa Meyer, Kenneth Frampton, Catherine Ingraham, Barbara Kruger, Mary McLeod, Toril Moi, Linda Nochlin,

Daniela Puppa, Adele Santos, Denise Scott Brown, Norma Sklarek, Susana Torre, Billie Tsien, Jennifer Wicke, and Mark Wigley.

The numerous submissions were reviewed by a dedicated editorial board whose hard work and thoughtfulness were critical to the development of this book. We are grateful to: Larry Chang, Margaret Chisolm, Clay Eicher, Pamela Fischer, Kimberly Jones, Jeanne Lawrence, Courtney Mercer, Robin Osler, Elaine René-Weissman, and Paul Udris. Kimberly Jones and Courtney Mercer deserve special acknowledgment for their contributions to this project at its inception. We also thank all of the people who sent us their work, which, in addition to being interesting, provoked a number of animated discussions.

We owe special thanks to Mary McLeod for her advice, wisdom, and scholarship. We also thank the faculty and staff of the Yale School of Architecture, especially Alan Plattus, Sandra Cloud, and Lorraine Amendola. We thank Angela Giral from Columbia University's Avery Library, and Peter Matorin of Beldock Levine and Hoffman for their special assistance. In addition, thanks are due to Lutfi Özkök and Josef Astor for their exceptional generosity.

We also want to acknowledge the individuals at Princeton Architectural Press whose efforts made the production of this book possible. We thank Kevin Lippert for his interest in our project, and Clare Jacobson and Ann Urban for their initial publication coordination. We are particularly grateful to our editor, Sara Stemen, for her keen oversight and sympathetic assistance.

Finally, for their endless patience and support of what has at times seemed like a unending project, we thank John Blood, Bruce Graham, and Cilla Smith.

Introduction

DEBRA COLEMAN

What is "outside" is not simply the Other—the "not me"—but a notion of futurity—the "not yet". . . . Will what appears as radically Other, as pure exteriority, be that which we refuse and abject as that which is unspeakably "Other," or will it constitute the limit that actively contests what we already comprehend and already are?

—JUDITH BUTLER, "FOR A CAREFUL READING"[1]

The cover of a magazine shows a woman running and then jumping over a small stool. Since she is one of Eadweard Muybridge's specimen-subjects, her movement is captured frame-by-frame; unlike many of his other subjects, however, this woman is completely clothed (this is a *professional* magazine). Muybridge's jumping woman has been borrowed from the pages of his 1887 *Animal Locomotion* in order to perform in the service of the cover story "Women in Architecture: Leveling the Playing Field." In this context the footstool is transformed into a drafting stool, and the woman into a contestant. The stakes? Equity. She is the Susan B. Anthony of the drafting room.

Or is she?

Published in 1995 in the now defunct *Progressive Architecture*, the article "Women in Architecture" is part chronicle, part editorial.[2] It describes in general terms the difficulties women still face as architects and students, and suggests that architecture (as a profession) risks being consigned to the margins of culture unless greater "gender diversity" is achieved within its ranks. Significantly, feminism is never mentioned. Instead, "gender" appears in tandem with words such as "gap," "discrimination," "bias," and "equity" to describe what is wrong with or missing in the architectural profession. But then it's not surprising that a mainstream architectural magazine would choose more user-friendly terms to describe the problems and goals of women in architecture. Feminism, especially as it's often used in mass culture, is an unpopular word, raising as it can the specter of the spinster boomer, the burned-out supermom, the childless career woman, and, of course the man-hater and the lesbian. Even among women, feminism is often misunderstood— and perhaps even a little feared. As reported by Susan Faludi in *The Nation*, when asked if they are feminists, "51 percent of [American] women say yes; when told that a feminist is 'someone who supports political, economic, and social equality for women,' the proportion jumps to 71 percent."[3]

It would be easy to criticize the purveyors of "Women in Architecture" for failing, not so much because of their inability to choose between the goals of feminism and the alternative, the status quo, but because in their inability to *say* "feminism" they dilute or sanitize their message. As a result, this message becomes just another patient—and compromising—reminder of how far the profession has yet to go. The remedies proposed in "Women in Architecture" are, in fact, underwritten by such complaisance. While a few of the suggestions are of the self-help variety ("set your own goals, ask for challenging assignments"), many more rely on the goodwill and authority of the American Institute of Architects, National Architectural Accrediting Board, Equal Employment Opportunities Commission, and universities to change policies and set new standards (under the dubious proposition that giving more power to the already powerful will create more equity). As the article's author notes, there is an even less proactive, if more depressing, approach: "Many people believe that a generation or two must *die out* before a real paradigm shift can occur."[4] But as Laurie Anderson sardonically observed in her song "Beautiful Red Dress," there is an interminable half-life quality to this kind of wait-and-see approach: "You know, for every dollar a man makes a woman makes 63 cents. / Now, fifty years ago that was 62 cents. / So, with that kind of luck, it'll be the year 3,888 before we make a buck."[5]

Despite the statistics regarding the participation of women in architecture—as reported in *Progressive Architecture*, one-third of undergraduate and graduate students, 9.1 percent of regular AIA members, and 8.7 percent of tenured faculty[6]—there is no consensus that feminism is relevant to this still largely masculinist discipline. In fact, many women seeking acceptance in this field disassociate themselves from talk of gender difference in order to escape "being tarred by the brush of female Otherness, of being contaminated by things 'female.' "[7](For example, the notion "woman architect," widely disdained for presupposing an odious distinction between architects and *women* architects, is seen by many as an unavoidable outgrowth of gender consciousness.) Some women worry that feminism will tarnish their architectural careers. Feminism is "too radical," and its opposing nature is unseemly in a field that values a posture of gentility.

Women are often drawn instead to "professionalism" with its "neutral" standards of intellectual rigor, critical objectivity, and excellence. For the aspiring academic or practicing architect, professionalism *by itself* looks like a wholly adequate buttress against gender-based inequity. But as Susan Bordo points out, the promise held out by professionalism— that it is the means for being accepted on an even playing field where we are all simply and equally "human"—is unrealizable within our present system of social relations: "In a culture that is *in fact* constructed by gender duality . . . one *cannot* simply be 'human'. . . . Our language, intellectual history, and social forms are 'gendered'; there is no escape from this fact and from its consequences on our lives."[8] Indeed, it is all too simple to point to those sites within the profession and discourse of architecture where discrimination against women occurs. Consider the list Mark Wigley presents in his essay "Untitled: The Housing of Gender": "The active production of gender distinctions can be found at every level of architectural discourse: in its rituals of legitimation, hiring practices, classification systems, lecture techniques, publicity images, canon formation, division of labor, bibliographies, design conventions, legal codes, salary structures, publishing practices, language, professional ethics, editing protocols, project credits, etc."[9] At each of these sites exclusionary or repressive practices should be challenged—and eliminated. At the same time, focusing too closely on professional *status* can itself be limiting; an emphasis on equity issues can tend toward what Judith Grant has referred to as "corporate feminism" where the "concern is that [women] be liberated into a free market economy where there is no glass ceiling, so that they can make as much money as the men of their classes." From this perspective feminism is about self-interest rather than an interest in "challenging gender per se."[10]

In the end, merely changing the superficial rules of inclusion does not guarantee deep changes in architectural culture; for as Lisa Jardine has pointed out, "having made it" can also register "an acceptance which is *not accompanied* by any alteration in the power relations between women and men."[11] Perhaps this last suggestion points (indirectly) to one of the reasons why feminism, and especially its central aim of eliminating gender injustice, has not taken hold in architectural culture, even though discussions about sexuality and gender seem to be highlighted with more and more frequency within architectural theory venues. In other words, feminist critiques and interventions can be resisted at the same time that an outward tolerance for diversity is sustained—and even promoted. Acceptance along these lines depends on the taming of feminism's political will. It also hangs on at least one question: What role does architectural discourse itself play in preserving gender-based relations of power? Obviously, to ask this is to risk revealing the complicity of architectural discourse in the struggles over the mobility and social space granted to women. By itself, the risk of being "found out" may explain why this discourse is so reticent when it comes to feminism. Is there something else, though, beyond a masking of the *roles* it plays, that makes architectural discourse so impregnable?

In an essay titled "Women, *Chora*, Dwelling," Elizabeth Grosz explores the cultural origins of ideas of spatiality, and proposes a link between "the very *concept* of architecture [and] the phallocentric effacement of women and femininity"[12]—an insight that suggests that the muteness within architectural discourse goes beyond complicity with *external* forces working to maintain current relations of domination. Reading Plato and Jacques Derrida, Grosz shows that the concept of *chora* (Plato's featureless, neutral, but altogether necessary "bridge" between the world of Forms or Ideas and material reality) can be understood as the basis for the engendering of the intelligible world. Grosz also points to the "unacknowledged and unrepayable debt that the very notion of space, and the built environment that relies on its formulation, owe to what Plato characterizes as the 'femininity' of the *chora*." [13]But while the affiliation of *chora* with the concepts of spatiality and femininity is readily acknowledged, in the case of femininity, the connection depends on a refusal of women's tangible qualities. Grosz aligns her argument with Luce Irigaray's reading of the history of philosophy as the erasure of women's autonomy and worth, wherein concepts associated with women and femininity nevertheless continue to serve as a kind of unspoken base for philosophical value. In Grosz's words,

> Irigaray claims that masculine modes of thought have performed a devastating sleight of hand: they have obliterated the debt they owe to the most primordial of all spaces, the maternal space from which all subjects emerge, and which they ceaselessly attempt to usurp. . . . The production of a (male) world—the construction of an 'artificial' or cultural environment, the production of an intelligible universe, religion, philosophy, the creation of true knowledge and valid practices of and in that universe—is

implicated in the systematic and violent erasure of the contributions of women, femininity and the maternal. This erasure is the foundation or ground on which a thoroughly masculine universe is built.[14]

Grosz's analysis points to the absence of the feminine at the very heart of architectural discourse, the result of a maneuver that both precedes and exceeds other gender-based asymmetries at work in this discourse. This absence is not so much a simple act of subordination or an instance of blindness. It is the total eclipsing of the feminine. Following this analysis, just sketching "her" in now is not enough. The issue is not really what architecture lacks, what is overlooked in its conception, what nuances are ignored. Rather, space and place must be reconceptualized. The question is: Will we theorists, critics, students, and practitioners of architecture participate in the work of generating "new perspectives, new bodies, new ways of inhabiting"?[15]

Architecture and Feminism is, then, more of a proposal than a definition of the relationship between architecture and feminism. Instead of the prescriptives "architecture *if* feminism" or "architecture *plus* feminism," we suggest the strategic and speculative "architecture *and* feminism." The link we have in mind would not assuage the inadequacies of architecture (or, for that matter, feminism). Nor would it be limited to the character of an interdisciplinary crossover, with its focus on an exchange of concepts and the creation of "new" ideas. Rather we propose a connection forged out of the desire to produce intertextual work that contests an unjust social order.

What does this work look like? by what methods is it induced? with what languages is it studied?—these questions are best left unsettled. For we imagine a connection between feminism and architecture that only exists to the extent that it is put into play, and, then later, put into play again. This "and," in Linda Singer's words, "keeps open a site for strategic engagement."[16] Its contours must be flexible enough to account for the puzzle of issues and circumstances that are bound to come into focus when these two discourses associate. At the same time, the critical and theoretical work emanating from the space between feminism and architecture should reach beyond the general feminist goal of opposing male dominance and endeavor to be context specific. As Nancy Fraser has written, "Although gender dominance is ubiquitous, in sum, it takes different forms at different junctures and sites, and its character varies for differently situated women. Its shape cannot be read off from one site or one group and extrapolated to all the rest."[17]

Architecture and feminism is, finally, a compact that aspires to weaken the "architecture is art/feminism is politics" dichotomy, and, in the process, reanimate questions about the limits of architectural discourse in the expression of sociocultural and political critique. Employed *now*, in the form of this collection of essays and projects, it operates at a time when the discourses of feminism and architecture are each suffused with uncertainties, as theorists in both fields question whether theoretical foundations are necessary and wonder how utopian hopes might be articulated. Under these circumstances, it is tempting to favor the search for "better" theories over interventions that—with all of their unpredictability—seek to transform current social, cultural, and political conditions. But as Judith Butler has argued, "The lure of a transcendental guarantee . . . is one which seduces us away from the lived difficulty of political life. This urge to have philosophy supply the vision that will redeem life, that will make life worth living, this urge is the very sign that the sphere of the political has *already* been abandoned."[18] For those of us who do our work within the bounds of architectural discourse, it remains to be seen whether or not we are ready to venture *something else*.

NOTES

1. Judith Butler, "For a Careful Reading," in *Feminist Contentions: A Philosophical Exchange*, Seyla Benhabib, et. al. (New York: Routledge, 1995), 142–43.

2. Abby Bussel, "Women in Architecture: Leveling the Playing Field," *Progressive Architecture* (November 1995): 45–49, 86.

3. Susan Faludi, "Who's Calling Whom Elitist?" *The Nation* 262, no. 2 (8/15 January 1996): 28.

4. Bussel, "Women in Architecture," 86 (emphasis added).

5. "Beautiful Red Dress," by Laurie Anderson, © 1989 Difficult Music. Reprinted with the permission of the author.

6. Bussel, "Women in Architecture," 45, 46, 86.

7. Susan Bordo, "Feminism, Postmodernism, and Gender-Scepticism," in *Feminism/Postmodernism*, ed. Linda J. Nicholson (New York: Routledge, 1990), 149.

8. Ibid., 152.

9. Mark Wigley, "Untitled: The Housing of Gender," in *Sexuality & Space*, ed. Beatriz Colomina (New York: Princeton Architectural Press, 1992), 329.

10. Judith Grant, *Fundamental Feminism: Contesting the Core Concepts of Feminist Theory* (New York: Routledge, 1993), 188.

11. Though Lisa Jardine makes this point in the context of feminist psychoanalytical theory, her observations about institutional politics can be applied to the discipline of architecture as well. Lisa Jardine, "The Politics of Impenetrability," in *Between Feminism and Psychoanalysis*, ed. Teresa Brennan (London: Routledge, 1989), 63.

12. Elizabeth Grosz, "Women, *Chora*, Dwelling," in *Postmodern Cities and Spaces*, ed. Sophie Watson and Katherine Gibson (Oxford: Blackwell Publishers, 1995), 47.

13. Ibid., 48.

14. Ibid., 55.

15. Ibid., 57. See also Grosz's citation of Irigaray: "In order for [sexual] difference to be thought and lived, we have to reconsider the whole problematic of *space* and *time* . . . A change of epoch requires a mutation in the perception and conception of *space-time*, the *inhabitation of place* and the *envelopes of identity*." (55)

16. Linda Singer's thoughts about the nature of strategic conjunctions are useful in this context. In an essay exploring the possible relationship between feminism and postmodernism, she wrote: "'The 'and' is a place holder, which is to say, it holds place open, free from being filled substantively or prescriptively. . . . To try to fix that space by mapping it . . . is precisely to miss the point of a conjunction which is also always already nothing." See Linda Singer, "Feminism and Postmodernism," in *Feminists Theorize the Political*, ed. Judith Butler and Joan W. Scott (New York: Routledge, 1992), 475.

17. Nancy Fraser, "Pragmatism, Feminism, and the Linguistic Turn," in *Feminist Contentions*, 159. "Every arena and level of social life is shot through with gender hierarchy and gender struggle. Each therefore requires feminist theorization. Each, however, is also traversed by other, intersecting axes of stratification and power, including class, 'race'/ethnicity, sexuality, nationality, and age—a fact that vastly complicates the feminist project."

18. Judith Butler, "For a Careful Reading," in *Feminist Contentions*, 131.

Everyday and "Other" Spaces

One of the primary preoccupations of contemporary architecture theory is the concept of "other" or "otherness." Members of the so-called neo-avant-garde—architects and critics frequently affiliated with publications such as *Assemblage* and *ANY* and with architecture schools such as Princeton, Columbia, SCI-Arc, and the Architectural Association—advocate the creation of a *new* architecture that is somehow totally "other." While these individuals repeatedly decry utopianism and the morality of form, they promote novelty and marginality as instruments of political subversion and cultural transgression. The spoken and unspoken assumption is that "different" is good, that "otherness" is automatically an improvement over the status quo.

While the formal and ideological allegiances of these advocates vary considerably, most fall into two broad categories. The first consists of self-identified proponents of deconstruction in architecture, who seek to find an architectural equivalent or parallel to the writings of Jacques Derrida. This group includes the so-called deconstructivists Peter Eisenman, Bernard Tschumi, Andrew Benjamin, Geoff Bennington, Mark Wigley, and Jeffrey Kipnes.[1] The second category is a diverse group of critics and theorists without any collective identity but who are all adherents of Michel Foucault's notion of "heterotopia." These include Anthony Vidler, Demetri Porphyrios, Aaron Betsky, Catherine Ingraham, and Edward Soja.[2]

The desire for "otherness," shared by these two groups, raises a series of questions concerning theory's political and cultural role that have been largely unexplored in recent architectural debate. To what extent is this preoccupation with "otherness" a product of critics' and practitioners' own identity and status? Does it elucidate or support groups considered socially marginal or "other"? Are there positions in architecture outside these two tendencies that address concerns of "otherness" relevant to "ordinary" people—those for whom the avant-garde has little significance?

The deconstructivists have argued that Derrida's notion of *différance* (a word play on "differ" and "defer") challenges the canons of architecture, such as function, structure, enclosure—in other words, that his claim that meaning is infinitely deferred and has no extra-linguistic beginning or end undermines any notion of architectural truth or foundation. Proponents, such as Eisenman and Wigley, value the disclosure of this instability as an end in itself. They claim that by revealing how binary oppositions such as form and content or structure and decoration are inscribed within a seemingly fixed, hierarchical structure and then eroded by the second or subordinate term in the opposition, the value system of architecture itself is eroded and put into flux. The second term is then seen as a condition of possibility for the whole system. For the most part, these theorists view the "secondary," the "other," as something largely internal to architecture. They assert that binary oppositions in architecture can be undone, or dismantled from within, through an investigation of the object. In his essay "En Terror Firma: In Trails of Grotextes," published in 1988 (the year of the Museum of Modern Art's *Deconstructivist Architecture* exhibition), Eisenman makes this explicit:

> Textual or textuality is that aspect of text which is a condition of otherness or secondarity. An example of this condition of otherness in architecture

is a trace. If architecture is primarily presence—materiality, bricks and mortar—then otherness or secondarity would be trace, as the presence of absence. . . . This other architecture. . . this second text will always be within the first text and thus between traditional presence and absence, between being and nonbeing.[3]

FIG. 1 Peter Eisenman (in collaboration with Richard Trott), Wexner Center for the Visual Arts, The Ohio State University, Columbus, Ohio, 1980–86

Eisenman's discourse is itself slippery, and the buzz words change every six months: "presence of absence," "grotesque," "monstrous," "the fold," "weak form," "slim mold," "anti-memory," and, most recently, "ungrounding the desire for grounding." With the possible exception of the writings of his palimpsest phase, coincident with the design of the Wexner Center (FIG. 1), his rhetoric, whether structuralist or poststructuralist, has consistently proclaimed architecture as "independent discourse." In his essay "The End of the Classical, the End of the Beginning, the End of the End" (1984), he asserts that architecture is "free of external values—classical or any other; that is, the intersection of the *meaning-free*, the *arbitrary*, and the *timeless* in the artificial."[4] Bernard Tschumi has made similar claims in his oft-published account of La Villette (FIG. 2). Although Tschumi alludes to intertextuality and applauds programmatic juxtaposition and experimentation, he asserts that "La Villette . . . aims at an architecture that *means nothing*, an architecture of the signifier rather than the signified, one that is pure trace or play of language."[5] Otherness is confined here to form (language) and textuality, refusing any reality outside the object (text).

As I have argued elsewhere, several of these deconstructivist practitioners have based their political claims on this strategy and its discourse.[6] Using words such as "unease," "disintegration," "decentering,"

FIG. 2 Bernard Tschumi, Parc de la Villette, Paris, 1983–85

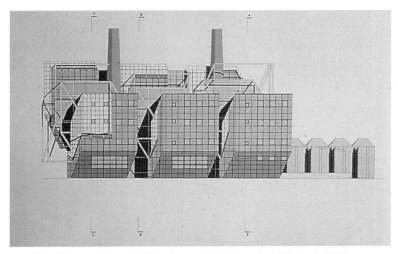

FIG. 3 Peter Eisenman, Carnegie-Mellon Research Institute, project, Pittsburgh, 1988

"dislocation," and "violation," they have stated that their work subverts the status quo through formal disruptions and inversions within the object. Describing his Carnegie-Mellon Research Institute (FIG. 3), Eisenman writes, for instance,

> The presence of a 40' frame over a 45' solid leaves the outline of the 40' N-cube as a trace on the surface of the 45' cube. In this way the fallibility of man is seen as undercutting the hyperrationality of the forms of knowledge systems, leading to a new and complex condition of the beautiful.[7]

In other words, while such architecture forsakes the modern movement's political agenda, including the transformation of productive processes and institutional boundaries, it now gains political power simply through the cultural sign, or, more precisely, through revealing the disintegration of that sign. Newness and "otherness"—traditional claims of the avant-garde—are largely an issue of formal strategy.

Although this tendency in architecture has found its most important theoretical source in Jacques Derrida's philosophy of deconstruction, other contemporary architecture critics have linked this new fragmented architecture (and what are sometimes considered its historical precedents, such as Piranesi's *Carceri* or *Campo Marzio*) with Foucault's more politicized concept of "heterotopia"—literally, "other places."[8] Here the notion of "other" refers to that which is both formally and socially "other." Difference is a function of different locations and distributions of power, as well as formal or textual inversion. "Other" is therefore not always an issue of "within" but of arenas outside of or marginal to our daily life.

Foucault gives his most complete discussion of heterotopia in his essay "Des Espaces autres," a lecture that he delivered at a French architecture research institute in 1967 and which was not published in English until 1985.[9] Since it was written as a lecture, it lacks Foucault's usual rigor; his argument seems loose, almost conflicted at times, as if he were groping for examples. But it is also his most comprehensive discussion of

FIG. 4 Thomas Wright, Kirkdale House of Correction, near Liverpool, 1821–22

FIG. 5 Libéral Bruand, Hôtel des Invalides (a hostel for wounded soldiers), Paris, 1670–77

physical space,[10] and its very looseness may account for its influence in recent architecture discourse.

In "Des Espaces autres" Foucault distinguishes heterotopias from imaginary spaces—utopias—and from everyday landscapes. He proposes that certain unusual or out-of-the-ordinary places—the museum, the prison, the hospital, the cemetery, the theater, the church, the carnival, the vacation village, the barracks, the brothel, the place of sexual initiation, the colony—provide our most acute perceptions of the social order (FIGS. 4, 5). These perceptions might derive either from a quality of disorder and multiplicity, as in the brothel, or from a kind of compensation, a laboratory-like perfection, as in the colony, which exposes the messy, ill-constructed nature of everyday reality (FIGS. 6, 7). Many of the spaces cited, such as the prison or asylum, are exactly the arenas that Foucault condemns in his institutional studies for their insidious control and policing of the body. In this essay, however, his tone is neutral or even laudatory of those "other" spaces. Foucault suggests that these heterotopic environments, by breaking with the banality of everyday existence and by granting us insight into our condition, are both privileged and politically charged. He asserts that they "suspend, neutralize, or invert the set of relationships" that they designate.[11]

What are explicitly omitted in his list of "other" spaces, however, are the residence, the workplace, the street, the shopping center, and the more mundane areas of everyday leisure, such as playgrounds, parks, sporting fields, restaurants, and cafés. (Cinemas, paradoxically, are both excluded and included as heterotopias.) Indeed, in his emphasis on isolated institutions—monuments, asylums, or pleasure houses—he forsakes all the messy, in-between urban spaces that might be considered literally heterotopic. For most contemporary architecture critics, the political ambiguity and two-sided nature of Foucault's notion of heterotopia (its diversity or its extreme control) has been ignored. Following Foucault's alluring account of Borgese's Chinese encyclopedia in *The Order of Things*, they interpret the concept simply as incongruous juxtaposition, all too frequently equating Foucault's notion of "otherness" with Derrida's concept of *différance*.[12] With a kind of postmodern ease, critics have created a heterotopic tableau of these theories seeking to undermine order.

However, my objective here is not to expound upon the distinctions between Foucault's and Derrida's versions of poststructuralism in terms of

FIG. 6 E. Angelou, Prostitute in a French brothel during the Belle Époch, Stereoscopic photograph, ca. 1900

FIG. 7 Joseph Marrast, Palais de Justice, Place Lyautey (now Place de la Ligue Arabe), Casablanca, 1916

architecture, although at times distinctions will be made. Nor is there the opportunity to expand on the philosophical differences in the meaning of the word "other," namely the differences between Sartre's reworking of a Hegelian other in existentialism and Lacan's notions of split subjectivity and linguistic drift.[13] Though certainly significant in philosophical and literary discourse, these distinctions, for better or worse, are typically blurred in architecture theory. The subject of this essay is a more basic issue: What are some of the limitations of a political and social vision of architecture that so exclusively focuses on "otherness," "disruption," and "break," and thus posits its political role as negation?

"GETTING A BIT OF THE OTHER" (WITH A DEBT TO SUZANNE MOORE)[14]

A paramount problem in poststructuralist theory generally and contemporary architecture theory specifically is the omission of any connections between an abstract notion of "other" and women's actual social situation—connections that would seem to follow from their proponents' initial preoccupations. As critics have frequently noted, the positions taken by both Derrida and Foucault (and, one might add, the sometime poststructuralists Roland Barthes and Jacques Lacan) have much in common with feminist theories, especially in their rejection of a universal subject, originary essence, and the notion of objective truth—too often the viewpoint of the white Western male. In fact, one of the most continually repeated refrains in poststructuralist theory is the reassertion, indeed celebration, of the secondary or marginal that had been previously repressed. Focusing more specifically on a Derridean/Lacanian strain of poststructuralism (and momentarily leaving aside Foucault's more social model), femininity becomes "lack," "absence," the "unconscious," "that which cannot be represented"—in short, the "other." It would appear, following this line of thought, that an architecture that seeks to represent "the presence of absence," an "other" architecture, might be about women.

But how can be an absence be about anyone? And is "other" genuinely an "other," or is it simply the all-too-common perspective of a repressed masculine discourse? These two questions—the first raising issues of subjecthood, the second alluding to the homogenizing quality of "otherness"—point to the difficulties some feminist theorists have had with aspects of Derrida's and Lacan's legacy. As Nancy Hartsock has asserted:

> Why is it, exactly at the moment when so many of us who have been silenced begin to demand the right to name ourselves, to act as subjects rather than objects of history, that just then the concept of subjecthood becomes "problematic."[15]

The frequent equation of woman with "lack" recalls Luce Irigaray's caustic critique of psychoanalysis as part of phallocentric culture. Is "woman" the unconscious, as Lacan claims, or does a woman have one?[16] Do women have any positive identities apart from masculine models? What are women's own desires and social realities? For many women architects, the critical point is not just the undermining of binary oppositions, but the denial of women per se. Can you play Eisenman's game if you're not permitted to play, or not even recognized as a potential player? Or more importantly, can you create *different* games—new forms and spaces—if your very existence is denied? Must the rejection of essentialism imply absence?

Paradoxically, the poststructuralist rejection of masculine hierarchies has tended to essentialize all that is "feminine." All women become subsumed into the category of Woman, which then embodies all that is mystical, dark, and otherworldly. For deconstructivist architects, if they recognize the issue of Woman at all, to enter this "dark continent" is in itself transgressive. Whereas modernism's universal subject excluded women, poststructuralism's celebration of "otherness" presents another problem: Too often it consigns women to being the means of constructing the identity of men.[17] It is no accident that Peter Eisenman pays homage to *Blue Velvet*, in which women exist primarily as choices for men, as their "other."[18] However aesthetically alluring and richly ambiguous the film, part of its appeal for men (especially "with-it" men) is that they can have "their sex, their myths, their violence, and their politics, all at the same time."[19] Instead of celebrating the avant-garde's desire for "otherness," architects and critics might investigate the desires of those multiple others, those actual, flesh-and-blood women. The feminine is experienced differently, at different times, in different cultures, by different people. The point is not just recognizing "difference," but all kinds of difference.

Foucault's conception of "other" (*autre*) stands apart from Lacanian and Derridean models in that it suggests actual places and actual moments in time. It acknowledges that power is not simply an issue of language. And this insistence on seeing institutions and practices in political and social terms has been welcomed by many feminist theorists.[20] Yet,

FIG. 8 A café on a colonial street, Algiers, 1985. Although this photo postdates French control, it shows how Foucault's description of the colonies as "perfect, meticulous, and well-arranged" ignores not only pre-existing settlements, but also the everyday habitation of colonial buildings and boulevards.

one of the most striking aspects of Foucault's notion of heterotopia is how his concept of "other" spaces, in its emphasis on rupture, seems to exclude the traditional arenas of women and children, two of the groups that most rightly deserve the label "other" (if by now one can abide the term's universalizing effect). Women have a place in his discussion primarily as sex objects—in the brothel, in the motel rented by the hour. (And what might be even harder for most working mothers to accept with a straight face is his exclusion of the house as a heterotopia because it is a "place of rest.") Foucault seems to have an unconscious disdain for aspects of everyday life such as the home, the public park, and the department store that have been provinces where women have found not only oppression but also some degree of comfort, security, autonomy, and even freedom. In fact, the writings of Foucault and some of his architecture-critic followers (most notably, Mike Davis)[21] display an almost callous disregard for the needs of the less powerful—older people, the handicapped, the sick—who are more likely to seek security, comfort, and the pleasures of everyday life than to pursue the thrills of transgression and "difference." In applauding the rest home, for instance, as a microcosm elucidating social structures, Foucault never considers it from the eyes of the resident. Insight seems to be the privilege of the powerful.

Another major, and all-too-obvious, problem is the exclusion of minorities, the third world—indeed, most non-Western culture in architects' discussions of "other." Some of the same issues surrounding the end of subjectivity and the tourism of "otherness" raised with regard to women are relevant here.[22] One of the most paradoxical aspects of Foucault's notion of heterotopia is his example of the colony. Although the concept of the "other" has had a powerful influence since World

War II on third-world political and cultural theorists (from Frantz Fanon to Edward Said),[23] Foucault himself never attempts to see the colony through the eyes of the colonized (FIG. 8), just as in his earlier institutional studies he avoids the prisoner's viewpoint in his rejection of experiential analysis.[24] In philosophical and literary deconstruction, a major claim for political validity is the notion of dismantling European logocentricism. Yet despite this embrace of "otherness" in some of its theoretical sources, poststructuralist tendencies in architecture posit a notion of "other" that is solely a question of Western dismantling of Western conventions for a Western audience. Again, "other" seems confined exclusively to a Western avant-garde. And once more, deconstructivist currents and the unconscious biases of Foucault appear to converge in architecture discourse.

Thus far, this argument about the exclusion of "others" in the concept of "other" has been restricted to theoretical propositions that have at best—perhaps fortunately—only marginal relation to the architecture produced by these practitioners, or by those that have been loosely grouped with them (such as Zaha Hadid, Daniel Libeskind, and Coop Himmelblau).[25] And by no means is the negative tone of these remarks meant to disparage the incredible aesthetic energy and invention of many of these designs (FIGS. 9, 10). What is disturbing is the link between theory and the architecture culture surrounding this theory. In the United States the focus on transgression in contemporary architecture circles seems to have contributed to a whole atmosphere of machismo and neo-avant-garde aggression. The theoretical language of deconstructivist theory is violent and sharp; the architecture milieu is exclusive—like a boys' club. One is reminded how often avant-gardism is a more polite label for angry young men, sometimes graying young men. All too frequently, lecture series and symposia have at best a token representation of women—and no African Americans or non-Western architects from anywhere but Japan. One of the most telling examples was the first "Anyone" conference, staged at the Getty Center at immense expense. Among the twenty-five speakers, at a conference supposedly about the multiplicity, diversity, and fluidity of identity, there were only two women; and the

LEFT: FIG. 9 Zaha Hadid, Moonsoon Restaurant, Sapporo, Japan, 1990
RIGHT: FIG. 10 Coop Himmelblau, view of entry, Funder Factory 3, 1988–89

men were all white American, white European, and Japanese.[26] In fairness, it should be noted that this exclusionary attitude is not the sole province of the deconstructivists. American and European postmodernists and proponents of regionalism are equally blind to the issues of the non-Western world beyond Japan. Most recently, the same charge might be brought against the Deleuzean "de-form" nexus, despite its rhetoric of continuity and inclusion.[27]

These blatant social exclusions, under the mantle of a discourse that celebrates "otherness" and "difference," raise the issue of whether contemporary theorists and deconstructivist architects have focused too exclusively on formal transgression and negation as a mode of practice. Undoubtedly, the difficult political climate of the past two decades and the economic recession of the late 1980s and early 1990s in the United States have contributed to the profession's hermeticism (namely, its rejection of constructive political strategies and institutional engagement), but the consequences of this retreat are now all too clear. Are there other formal and social options—options beyond transgression and nostalgia, deconstructivism and historicist postmodernism—that embrace the desires and needs of those outside the avant-garde?

EVERYDAY LIFE

The seduction and power of the writings of Derrida and Foucault, and their very dominance in American academic intellectual life, may have encouraged architects and theorists to leave unexplored another position linking space and power: the notion of "everyday life" developed by French philosopher Henri Lefebvre from the 1930s through the 1970s and by cultural theorist Michel de Certeau shortly thereafter.[28] A peculiar synthesis of Surrealist and Marxist notions, Lefebvre's concept of everyday life might be best understood as a series of paradoxes. While the "object of philosophy," it is inherently nonphilosophical; while conveying an image of stability and immutability, it is transitory and uncertain; while unbearable in its monotony and routine, it is festive and playful. It is at once "sustenance, clothing, furniture, homes, neighborhoods, environment"—material life—but with a "dramatic attitude" and "lyrical tone." In short, everyday life is "real life," the "here and now," not abstract truth.[29] De Certeau in his book *The Practice of Everyday Life* (*L'Invention du quotidien*, 1980) gives the notion of everyday life a somewhat more particularist, less Marxist cast, stressing the localized and transitory qualities of daily existence.

In contrast to Foucault, both these theorists not only analyze the tyranny and controls that have imposed themselves on "everyday life," but also explore the freedoms, joys, and diversity—what de Certeau describes as "the network of antidiscipline" within everyday life.[30] Their concern is not only to depict the power of disciplinary technology, but also to reveal how society resists being reduced by it, not just in the unusual or removed places but in the most ordinary. And here, they place an emphasis on consumption without seeing it as solely a negative force, as some leftists have, but also as an arena of freedom, choice, creativity, and invention. De Certeau, who dedicated his seminal work *The Practice of Everyday Life* to the "ordinary man," is strangely silent on the issue of women (except for one female *flâneur* in his chapter "Walking the

LEFT: FIG. 11 F. V. Poole, "London Receiving Her Newest Institution," 1909
RIGHT: FIG. 12 "Shopping with Hubby," c. 1935

City").[31] Lefebvre, however, despite moments of infuriating sexism and disturbingly essentialist rhetoric, seems to have an acute understanding of the role of the everyday in woman's experience and how consumption has been her demon but also her liberator (FIGS. 11, 12), offering an arena of action that grants her entry and power in the public sphere. This argument has been further developed by several contemporary feminist theorists, including Janet Wolff, Elizabeth Wilson, Anne Friedberg, and Kristin Ross.[32] What these critics share, despite their many differences, is an emphasis on pleasure, the intensification of sensory impressions, the freedom and positive excesses of consumption as experiences that counter the webs of control and monotony in daily life. Here, "other" is not so much a question of what is outside everyday life—events characterized by rupture, transgression, difference—but what is contained, and *potentially* contained, within it. In short, their emphasis is populist, not avant-garde.[33] They articulate a desire to bring happiness and pleasure to many, rather than merely to jolt those who have the textual or architectural sophistication to comprehend that a new formal break has been initiated. Of course, these two goals need not be exclusive.

EVERYDAY AND OTHER ARCHITECTURE

This notion of an "intensification of the everyday"—and even an appreciation of the pleasures of consumption—is not something totally new to architecture or architecture criticism. Groups and individuals as diverse as the Situationists, the Independent Group, Denise Scott Brown and Robert Venturi, and Jane Jacobs have all addressed these issues. Tracing this lineage, however,

FIG. 13 Asger Jorn, *Live the Passionate Revolution*, 1968

requires a critical distance. While some of the attempts to embrace the "everyday" have succeeded, or have at least suggested promising strategies, others now appear ineffectual or regressive, frequently carrying overtones of adolescent rebellion and machismo. Especially in the case of the Situationists, the differences between certain positions—notably, the celebration of shock, transgression, and violence—and deconstructivist theory are not so clear.

The Situationists, indebted to Lefebvre and to whom Lefebvre himself was indebted, proposed a complicated mixture of long-standing avant-garde practices involving negation and innovative strategies emphasizing everyday pleasure and its intensification (FIG. 13).[34] Formally launched in July 1957, the Situationist project might be summarized as "the liberation of everyday life." This involved studying the whole range of diverse sensations that "one encounters *by chance* in everyday life" and then proposing acts, situations, and environments that transformed the

world in those same terms.[35] One of the major Situationist techniques
was *dérive*—literally, "drift"—a kind of mindless wandering in the city
which would open up the existing environment to new considerations.
Guy Debord's *Mémoires*, published in 1959, evoke, through a montage of
assorted quotations, the nature of these new perceptions. The investigations of chance urban encounters, everyday locales (streets, cafés, bars),
and the latent desires and techniques of mass culture (comics, film,
advertising)—all for radical, new ends—convey a milieu more accessible
and literally heterotopic than Foucault's "other" spaces. The Situationists attacked both bourgeois art (high modernism) and earlier avant-
gardist movements, explicitly denouncing the Futurists' "technological
optimism," the Surrealists' "ostentatious 'weirdness,'" and Duchamp's
"gamelike rebellions."[36] But as much as those of their predecessors, their
visions of pleasure are permeated with sexism, a sexism inextricably
entwined with their revulsion from bourgeois family life. They catagori-
cally ignore issues such as domesticity, childcare, reproduction—indeed,
all aspects of women's situation in society; and their insistent allusions to
sex, debauchery, violence, cruelty, and madness suggest a kind of puerile
avant-gardism, one that may have unfortunately left its heritage in the
deconstructivist movement.[37] The *Mémoires* feel, as critic Greil Marcus
notes, "like a drunken sprawl through the encyclopedia of common
knowledge."[38] (A quotation that appears on the first collage is "our talk is
full of booze."[39]) Debord calls women "girls"; and among his "girls" are a
model named Sylvie, a "beautiful wife," and "poor" Ann—the young
prostitute in Thomas De Quincey's *Confessions of an English Opium
Eater*. Here, "other" seems again to be for the benefit of male identity.

The few architecture projects by Dutch painter and architect
Constant are among the most evocative and exhilarating aesthetic visions
of the 1950s, anticipating the formal vocabulary of much deconstructivist
work.[40] The Situationists' designs, in contrast to those of their formal
heirs, are assertively constructive. Debord once claimed that his objective
was to negate negation.[41] Yet, their program presents other difficulties.
Although Constant's utopian scheme New Babylon (FIG. 14), dedicated
to a postrevolutionary society of play, proposes a communal and festive

FIG. 14 Constant, Yellow Sector, New Babylon, 1958

use of space, it also carries peculiarly behavioralist connotations in its attempt to manufacture emotions.[42] What he calls the yellow sector shelters a complete zone of play, including labyrinthine houses for endless adventure; and there is also a deaf room, a screaming room, an echo room, a room of reflection, a room of rest, and a room of erotic play. The project's flexible walls and fluid modes of circulation are supposed to allow inhabitants to change their milieux, but pyschogeography's correlation between physical environment and emotion, and the suffocating sense of there being "no exit" from this brave new world, seem to kill the very freedom of discovery and chance so celebrated by the group. Indeed, New Babylon's programmed indeterminacy eliminates privacy, domesticity, social obligations, and loyalties to locales—most of everyday life as we know it. Notions of drift, so difficult to make architectural, are reduced to a project for an admittedly seductive "gypsy camp."

Less overtly revolutionary and less rooted in philosophy, but with a stronger grasp of daily life as experienced by most, is the work of the Independent Group (IG) in London. In contrast to the Situationists' fascination with vagrants and bars, the participants of the IG examined more "normative" conditions of working-class and

FIG. 15 Eduardo Paolozzi, *Dr. Pepper*, 1948

lower middle-class domestic and commercial life. They embraced American mass culture as a foil to both the deprivations of postwar Britain and the sterility of modernist abstraction, and were especially attracted to an aspect of mass culture that had been largely neglected in the first phase of the modern movement: advertising (FIG. 15). This break with the imagery of Machine Age production was a stand self-consciously proclaimed by Alison and Peter Smithson in their 1956 manifesto: "Gropius wrote a book on grain silos, Le Corbusier one on aeroplanes, . . . But today we collect ads."[43] Nor did the Smithsons overlook the feminine overtones of this new vision of mass culture when they alluded to the "patron's wife who leafs through the magazines."[44] The writings and designs of the Independent Group begin to suggest the double nature of consumption as oppression and liberation, and its particular meaning to women.

The Smithsons' architecture clearly embodies an early critique of avant-garde elitism and its neglect of "everyday" concerns. However inclusive the modern movement's initial objectives, by the 1950s it stood for stylistic formalism and abstract functionalism removed from actual human needs. Reyner Banham dubbed the Smithsons' work an "*architecture autre*"—not because of its iconoclastic marginality, but for its very insistence on banality and realism.[45] Housing, the street (not just the traffic corridor), and the playground were arenas to explore; and if their sensibility of pop humor meant including images of Joe Dimaggio and Marilyn Monroe in a photomontage of Golden Lane's street deck (FIG. 16), the exterior views of this unbuilt housing complex showed

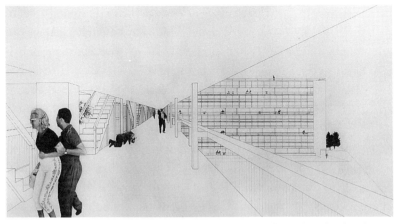

FIG. 16 Alison and Peter Smithson, perspective of the street deck, Golden Lane City, housing project for London, 1952

FIG. 17 Alison and Peter Smithson, Golden Lane City, 1952. Although this project is deeply indebted to Le Corbusier's housing proposals for its heroic scale and ideas of social community, it preserves the fragmented and random urban context of its site, in contrast to the Ville Contemporaine or the Ville Radieuse.

existing urban blight with a poignant realism (FIG. 17). Photographs of
their few built projects included actual inhabitants (children, old people),
not avant-garde drifters. The Smithsons' designs struck a delicate balance between invention and appreciation of the ordinary—a balance that
was undoubtedly appreciated by architects more than the population at
large. While their refusal to compromise may have itself carried elitist
overtones, their inclusive vision began to address (in the sphere of their
profession at least) what Andreas Huyssen has called "the Great Divide"
between modernism and mass culture.[46] However, the IG's embrace of
consumerist culture was not without its own political ambiguity. As
Banham noted, "We dig Pop which is acceptance—culture, capitalist, and
yet in our formal politics, if I may use the phrase, most of us belong firmly on the other side."[47]

Denise Scott Brown (one of the Smithsons' ambivalent heirs) and
Robert Venturi break even more definitively with modernist dogma in
their advocacy of consumerist culture. In their publications, exhibitions,
and teachings of the 1970s (most notably, *Learning from Las Vegas* and
the Smithsonian Institution exhibition *Signs of Life*[48]), they allude to a
world neglected in both modern architecture and Foucault's heterotopic
landscape: the A & P supermarket, Levittown, mobile homes, fast-food
stores—the milieu of ordinary middle- and lower-class people (FIG. 18).
Learning from Las Vegas does contain an overdose of honeymoon motels
and gambling casinos, but in contrast to Foucault's heterotopic spaces or
Anthony Vidler's examples of the uncanny, this landscape is not privileged for its difference or strangeness but taken as part of a continuum of
daily existence. Like the Independent Group, Scott Brown and Venturi
grant the world of women, children, and elderly people—domestic culture—a place in aesthetic culture. Even Dr. Seuss receives homage in
Scott Brown's 1971 *Casabella* essay, with its slogan "Hop on pop."[49]

What has been noted less frequently is that Scott Brown also gives
one of the sharpest, and wittiest, critiques of the machismo underlying
modern architecture and the profession at large. In *Learning from Las
Vegas*, the authors characterize the modern movement as "heroic and
original," "violent, high adventure," "a bunch of angry young men under

FIG. 18 Denise Scott Brown and Robert Venturi, *Signs of Life: Symbols in the American City*, exhibition, Smithsonian Institution, Washington, D. C., 1976

30," "imposing on the whole landscape heroic representations of the masters' unique creations." No less acerbic are their remarks about contemporary architecture in 1970. While the stalwart modern architects of that era are "aging architectural revolutionaries who man the review boards and who have achieved aesthetic certainty," avant-garde designers such as Archigram are the "last, megalomaniac gasps" of a puerile rebellion: "look Ma, no buildings."[50] Scott Brown and Venturi's critique of the heroic gestural designs of the 1960s might apply equally well to more recent deconstructivist works:

> Our heroic and original symbols, from *carceri* to Cape Kennedy, feed our late Romantic egos and satisfy our lust for expressionistic, acrobatic space for a new age in architecture.[51]

Throughout *Learning from Las Vegas* Scott Brown and Venturi convey an intuitive understanding of the problems of universal subjectivity, an

FIG. 19 Venturi and Rauch, Guild House, rear view, 1961

insight that some current architecture theorists would like to claim as their own. They use the term "Man" sarcastically, for example, alluding to the aesthetic experts who "build for Man rather than for people."[52]

However, Scott Brown and Venturi's populism, which seems so removed from the iconoclastic *épater la bourgeoisie* of so much avant-gardism, raises other political issues. While they challenge the stance of heroic originality embedded in so much of modernism, their very preoccupation with the everyday becomes at times precariously close to an endorsement of the status quo (FIG. 19). Must the affirmation of those groups traditionally neglected by the avant-garde necessarily preclude substantial invention and change? And does "ordinary" necessarily have to be ugly or mundane? In short, one yearns for a bit more "other"—another other, a new vision emerging from their very sensitivity to the everyday.

Arguably, the most influential critic to stress issues of the "everyday" in architecture was a non-architect, Jane Jacobs (FIG. 20), whose 1961 book *The Death and Life of Great American Cities* (published nearly a decade before *Learning from Las Vegas*) had a powerful impact on a whole generation of social and architecture critics that emerged in the 1960s and 1970s.[53] While the book preceded the advent of modern feminism in the United States and does not make gender a specific issue, Jacobs's urban landscape comes, as Elissa Rosenberg has argued, explicitly from a woman's experience.[54] A domestic perspective is critical to Jacobs's development of the idea of mixed use. This proposal is not only an attack on modern architecture's functional segregation but an implicit challenge to the traditional split between domestic and public life.[55] Jacobs deliberately rejects theoretical models

FIG. 20 Jane Jacobs at a neighborhood bar, c. 1963

and relies on empirical observation to examine how space is actually used. Of the individuals discussed in this essay, she comes closest to realizing de Certeau's plea for an account of cities, not from the bird's-eye view, but from the experience of the pedestrian, the everyday user. And the terrain she describes is very different from that traversed by Baudelaire's *flâneurs*, from Foucault's prisons and brothels, or from the Situationist bars and gypsy encampments. What is evoked in her descriptions of New York City's West Village and Boston's North End is an informal public life: the world of the stoop, the neighborhood bakery, the dry cleaning establishment, and, most importantly, the street (FIG. 21); and with these come new subjects—mothers in the park, children, grocers, and newsstand attendants. In contrast to Foucault and Mike Davis, who are preoccupied with policing and control (a reflection, I would argue, of their own unspoken subjecthood as men, relatively strong men), Jacobs is

FIG. 21 Hudson Street, Greenwich Village, New York City, 1993. Although Jane Jacobs has decried the changes in the West Village over the past three decades, the neighborhood still retains much of the vitality and diversity she applauded.

concerned with freedom and safety for children, elderly people, and those most vulnerable to attack. She grants a public meaning to domestic life— one that refuses a segregation of the sexes as well as of functions.

This is a vision that shares much with postmodern thought: an interest in blurring categories, in diversity, in understanding and enjoying a genuinely heterotopic milieu. Jacobs's detailed and vibrant picture of daily urban life opens the door for a critical reevaluation of social and functional divisions that are embodied in the physical form of modern economic development. But there is also a nostalgia and a conservative dimension to her interpretation of Hudson Street as a natural order. Her depiction of the city as a "self-regulating system" overlooks the positive potential of human agency and cultural transformation, and despite her acute analysis of many aspects of daily life, the book offers few insights into confronting the connections between space and power.[56]

"OTHER" ARCHITECTURES

What I have tried to do in this brief survey is to point to another series of concerns that have somehow been forgotten in the plethora of recent theoretical writings surrounding deconstructivism. These examples are cited not as endorsement but as territory for rethinking. On the positive side, they offer models of architectural production that counter notions of both cultural elitism and isolated artistic rebellion, finding a stratum of creativity and invention in more familiar terrains. They explore—with different degrees of success—the gap between architecture and what people make of it, seeing its occupants no longer simply as passive consumers or victims but also as vital actors contributing a multiplicity of new images and modes of occupation. Although these groups and individuals cannot provide a framework for political action (nor would any except the Situationists claim to), they articulate a range of concerns neglected in traditional political analyses and theoretical critiques. Most optimistically, these architecture positions embody new social and cultural formations. Yet it must also be stated that any facile rehabilitation of the "ordinary" readily becomes problematic. There is, of course, no "common man," just as there is no universal "other." Despite Lefebvre's and de Certeau's recognition of the polymorphous fluidity of the "everyday," populist tenets frequently homogenize and subsume stratifications of power, such as class, gender, and race, in the fray of contemporary architectural practice and polemics. The "ordinary" becomes a rationalization for market forces and passive consumption; "common sense" becomes a means to avoid the rigors of ideological critique. However progressive and radically generative the proposals of Scott Brown and Jacobs were at their inception, the subsequent history of postmodern architecture, and its easy compliance with the boom forces of the 1980s, invites caution. Indeed, the blatant commodification of postmodernism fueled the attraction to deconstructivism's subversive claims.

But that time has passed, and now deconstructivism itself faces co-option (FIGS. 22–24). Transgression and shock have themselves become part of commodity culture (grunge, deconstructionist clothing, the "junky" look, MoMA exhibitions, Decon coffee-table books); deconstructivist practitioners are firmly entrenched members of the cultural establishment. In this light, it appears that a reconsideration of everyday life might serve as an antidote not only to the solipsism and implicit biases

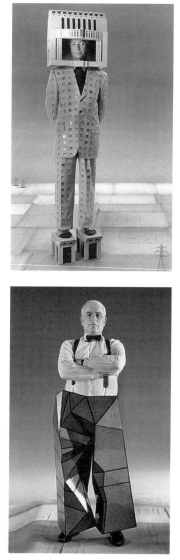

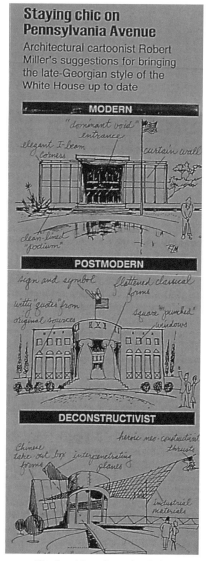

FIGS. 22 AND 23   "Skyscraper Couture," photographs by Josef Astor of Michael Graves (top) and Peter Eisenman (bottom), which appeared in the July 1996 *Vanity Fair*

FIG. 24   "Staying chic on Pennsylvania Avenue," a cartoon by Robert MIller, appeared in *U.S. News and World Report* in July 1988, in an article covering the *Deconstructivist Architecture* exhibition at the Museum of Modern Art.

in much contemporary architecture theory but also to the commodification of "avant-garde" rebellion.

Recently, there have been a few signs of a shifting mentality in American architecture. "Politics"—feminism, issues of gay and lesbian identity, race, ethnicity—have themselves begun to gain a certain fashionability in academic circles, though often in the framework of previous Derridean currents. It would seem these developments too might gain in vitality and breadth by a reconsideration of themes such as consumption, mass culture, and popular taste. Are there politically and aesthetically constructive positions beyond pure negation? Can buildings and urban space also be seen in terms of pleasure, comfort, humor, and emotion? Are there "other" architectures to explore—ones that are less hermetic and more engaged in individuals' emotional and physical lives?

AFTERWORD

It is always safer for an architecture critic to avoid showing exemplary or instrumental images; not only does it save the critic from embarrassment (the examples rarely seem to live up to the grandiose claims), but it also invites closure. Nevertheless, I would like to propose—modestly—two urban places that I believe escape the mechanisms of discipline, and not primarily through negation or transgression. They are cited here neither as social prescriptions nor as formal models, but simply as places that might suggest other urban tactics. Both sites, perhaps not coincidentally, were designed in part by women, women not exactly at the forefront of the avant-garde culture (one early in her career, the other later). Both sites are populist, and highly popular with ordinary people. One is humorous, witty; the other is deeply contemplative involving participation. The first is Niki de Saint-Phalle and Jean Tinguely's Stravinsky Fountain adjacent to Centre Pompidou in Paris (FIGS. 25, 26). The second is Maya Lin's Vietnam Veterans Memorial in Washington, D.C.(FIGS. 27–29). They present possiblilties of architectural space beyond conformity or disruption, both everyday and other.

FIGS. 25 AND 26 Niki de Saint-Phalle and Jean Tinguely, Stravinsky Fountain, near Centre
Pompidou, Paris, 1983

FIGS. 27-29 Maya Lin, Vietnam Veterans Memorial, Washington, D. C., 1981-82.

NOTES

1. By now, the publications of this group are numerous. Among the most notable are: Philip Johnson and Mark Wigley, *Deconstructivist Architecture* (New York: Museum of Modern Art and Boston: Little, Brown, 1988); Andreas Papadakis, Catherine Cooke, and Andrew Benjamin, eds., *Deconstruction: Omnibus Volume* (New York: Rizzoli, 1989); and Mark Wigley, *The Architecture of Deconstruction: Derrida's Haunt* (Cambridge, Mass.: MIT Press, 1993). Needless to say, any label, such as "deconstructivist" is reductive; not only do the positions of individual proponents vary, but they have also changed over time. Nonetheless, all the individuals cited have frequently published their writings and designs under the rubric of "deconstruction" or "deconstructivism."

2. See Anthony Vidler, *The Architectural Uncanny: Essays in the Modern Unhomely* (Cambridge, Mass.: MIT Press, 1992); Demetri Porphyrios, *Sources of Modern Eclecticism: Studies of Alvar Aalto* (London: Academy Editions, 1982); Aaron Betsky, *Violated Perfection: Architecture and the Fragmentation of the Modern* (New York: Rizzoli, 1990); Catherine Ingraham, "Utopia/Heterotopia" (course description of class given at Columbia University), in *Deconstruction III*, ed. Andreas Papadakis, Architectural Design Profile No. 87 (London: Academy Editions, 1994); and Edward Soja, *Postmodern Geographies: The Reassertion of Space in Critical Social Theory* (London: Verso, 1989). To the best of my knowledge, Porphyrios's book, based on his Princeton doctoral dissertation, was the first architecture publication in the English-speaking world to cite Foucault's notion of heterotopia. Anthony Vidler was his doctoral advisor. Although Vidler does not specifically mention heterotopia in *The Architectural Uncanny*, he cites Foucault on numerous occasions and adopts David Carroll's notion of "paraesthetics," which is indebted to Foucault. See David Carroll, *Paraesthetics: Foucault, Lyotard, Derrida* (New York: Methuen, 1987). In several publications, Manfredo Tafuri also alludes sympathetically to Foucault's notion of heterotopia, and Tafuri's interpretation of Piranesi's work as encapsulating the crisis of Enlightenment reason reveals certain parallels with Foucault's claims for heterotopic environments. See especially Manfredo Tafuri, " 'The Wicked Architect': G. B. Piranesi, Heterotopia, and the Voyage," in *The Sphere and the Labyrinth: Avant-Gardes and Architecture from Piranesi to the 1970s*, trans. Pellegrino d'Acierno and Robert Connolly (Cambridge, Mass.: MIT Press, 1987). The complexity of Tafuri's project of ideological demystification and its multiplicity of intellectual sources, however, separates his interest in Foucault from the instrumental applications of many architecture critics.

3. Peter Eisenman, "En Terror Firma: In Trails of Grotextes," *Pratt Journal of Architecture*, no. 2 (Spring 1988), rpt. in *Deconstruction: Omnibus Volume*, 153.

4. Peter Eisenman, "The End of the Classical, the End of the Beginning, the End of the End," *Perspecta*, no. 21 (1984): 166.

5. Bernard Tschumi, *Cinégramme Folie: Le Parc de la Villette* (Princeton: Princeton Architectural Press, 1987), vii. This essay has been frequently republished, most recently in Bernard Tschumi, *Architecture and Disjunction* (Cambridge, Mass.: MIT Press, 1994). Although the essay was significantly rewritten in this last publication, it retains the quoted passage.

6. Mary McLeod, "Architecture and Politics in the Reagan Era: From Postmodernism to Deconstructivism," *Assemblage*, no. 8 (February 1989), 50–51.

7. Peter Eisenman, "Carnegie-Mellon Research Institute," in *Deconstruction: Omnibus Volume*, 172–73. In a 1992 interview Eisenman makes the nature of his "critical" position explicit: "My desire is to displace from within, from the center." See Alan Balfour et al., "Conversation with Peter Eisenman," in *Cities of Artificial Excavation: The Work of Peter Eisenman, 1978–1988*, ed. Jean-François Bédard (Montreal: Centre Canadien d'Architecture and Rizzoli, 1994), 128.

8. Italian philosopher Gianni Vattimo also uses the notion "heterotopia," though in a different manner from Foucault. For Vattimo, "heterotopia" alludes to the plurality of norms that distinguishes late-modern art (since the 1960s) from modern art. Gianni Vattimo, "From Utopia to Heterotopia," in *Transparent Society*, trans. David Webb (Baltimore: Johns Hopkins University Press, 1992), 62–75. Vattimo's writings have influenced European architecture debate, but have had little impact on American architecture theory.

9. Michel Foucault, "Of Other Spaces: Utopias and Heterotopias," in *Architecture Culture 1943–1968: A Documentary Anthology*, ed. Joan Ockman with Edward Eigen (New York: Columbia Books of Architecture and Rizzoli, 1993), 420–26. The paper was first delivered at the Centre d'études architecturales, Paris, March 1967. A brief account of the essay's publishing history is given in Ockman, 419.

10. Despite Foucault's interest in institutions and his insistent use of spatial metaphors, discussions of physical urban space such as cities, streets, and parks are rare in his work. Philosopher Henri Lefebvre charged, probably legitimately, that Foucault was more concerned with a metaphorical notion of space—"mental space"—than with lived space, "the space of people who deal with material things." See Henri Lefebvre, *The Production of Space*, trans. Donald Nicholson-Smith (Oxford: Blackwell, 1991; orig. Fr. ed., 1974), 3–4. Besides his paper "Les Espaces autres," Foucault's most concrete discussions of physical space can be found in interviews from the last decade of his life. See, for instance, "Questions on Geography" (1976) and "The Eye of Power" (1977), in *Power/Knowledge: Selected Interviews and Other Writings 1972–77*, ed. Colin Gordon (New York: Pantheon Books, 1980); "Space, Knowledge, and Power" (1982) in *The Foucault Reader*, ed. Paul Rabinow (New York: Pantheon Books, 1984); and, especially, "An Ethics of Pleasure" in *Foucault Live (Interviews, 1966–84)*, ed. Sylvère Lotringer (New York: Semiotext(e), 1989), 257–77. In this last interview, Foucault distinguishes architects from doctors, priests, psychiatrists, and prison wardens, claiming that the architect does not exercise (or serve as a vehicle of) as much power as the other professionals. Foucault's own class status and power is revealed when he states, "After all, the architect has no power over me. If I want to tear down or change a house he built for me, put up new partitions, add a chimney, the architect has no control" (267). Surely, few occupants of public housing projects or nursing homes could or would make the same statement.

11. Foucault, "Of Other Spaces," 421–22.

12. Michel Foucault, preface to *The Order of Things: An Archeology of Human Sciences* (New York: Vintage Books, 1970), xv–xx. Foucault's notion of heterotopia outlined in his oft-quoted preface

from 1966 is more abstract than that given in his 1967 essay. In the earlier account, Foucault describes heterotopias as "impossible to think"—spaces without "site" which challenge the order and the language that allow "words and things . . . to 'hold together' . . . [They] desiccate speech, stop words in their tracks, contest the very possibility of language at its sources." Architects have largely ignored the fluidity and radicality of Foucault's concept in *The Order of Things* (as well as its theoretical shortcomings), adopting it as a catch-all term for postmodern plurality and as a means to validate discordant geometries and fragmented forms. See Porphyrios, *Sources of Modern Eclecticism*; Georges Teyssot, "Heterotopias and the History of Spaces," *A+U* (October 1980): 80–100; and Stanley Allen, "Piranesi's *Campo Marzio*: An Experimental Design," *Assemblage*, no. 10 (December 1989): 77. A more nuanced historical application is provided by Georges Teyssot in "Heterotopias and the History of Spaces," *A+U* (October 1980): 80–100. Teyssot distinguishes between Foucault's epistemological and spatial notions of heterotopia but does not elaborate on the tnesions between them.

13. For concise accounts of the "problem of other," see Vincent Descombes, *Modern French Philosophy*, trans. L. Scott-Fox and J.M. Harding (Cambridge: Cambridge University Press, 1980) and Elizabeth Grosz, *Sexual Subversions* (Sydney: Allen and Unwin, 1989), 1–38. For a discussion of the "problem of other" and its relation to gender and colonial/postcolonial theory in the context of architecture, see Zeynep Çelik and Leila Kinney, "Ethnography and Exhibitionism at the Expositions Universelles," *Assemblage*, no. 13 (December 1990), esp. 54–56.

14. Suzanne Moore, "Getting a Bit of the Other: The Pimps of Postmodernism," in *Male Order*, eds. Rowena Chapman and Jonathan Rutherford (Oxford: Wichart, 1988), 165–92. I am indebted to this strong and witty argument for articulating some of my own long-standing frustrations with the masculine biases of some poststructuralist theory.

15. Nancy Hartsock, "Rethinking Modernism," *Cultural Critique*, no. 7 (Fall 1987), 187–206. Similarly, Andreas Huyssen asks "Isn't the 'death of the subject/author' position tied by mere reversal to the very ideology that invariably glorifies the artist as genius? . . . Doesn't poststructuralism, where it simply denies the subject altogether, jettison the chance of challenging the *ideology of the subject* (as male, white, and middle-class) by developing alternative and different notions of subjectivity?" Andreas Huyssen, "Mapping the Postmodern," in *After The Great Divide: Modernism, Mass Culture, Postmodernism* (Bloomington: Indiana University Press, 1986), 213. See also Frances E. Mascia-Lees, Patricia Sharpe, and Colleen Ballerino Cohen, "The Postmodern Turn in Anthropology: Cautions from a Feminist Perspective," *Signs* 15, no. 1 (1989): 15.

16. Irigaray argues that Lacan's revision of Freud is even more constraining for women than his predecessor's biological model, where anatomy served as proof/alibi for the differences between the sexes. She reminds us that language presents its own prison, given that its laws "have been prescribed by male subjects for centuries." Irigaray further charges that Lacan seeks woman out only "as lack, as fault or flaw," and that "it is inasmuch as she [woman] does not exist that she sustains the desire of these 'speaking beings' that are called men." Luce Irigaray, "Cosi Fan Tutti" (1975), in *This Sex Which Is Not One*, trans. Catherine Porter (Ithaca: Cornell University Press, 1985), 87, 89. See also Moore, 190.

17. Already in 1949, Simone de Beauvoir in *The Second Sex* argued that men gained their own identity as subjects by constructing woman as the "other." Simone de Beauvoir, *The Second Sex*, trans. H. M. Parshley (New York: Knopf, 1952).

18. This was a major theme in the three lectures that Eisenman delivered at Columbia University in the spring of 1991 (March 25, March 28, April 1, April 4), entitled "Weak Form: Architecture in a Mediated Environment."

19. Norman K. Denzin, "*Blue Velvet*: Postmodern Contradictions," *Theory, Culture and Society* 5, no. 4 (1988): 472. In Denzin's essay this passage alludes to "postmodern individuals," but his assertion seems most relevant to male viewers.

20. Although many feminists have appreciated Foucault's analyses of power and his emphasis on the body as a target of disciplinary practices, some feminists have criticized him for failing to provide a normative basis for action and for bypassing the problem of political agency. See especially Nancy Fraser, *Unruly Practices: Power, Discourse and Gender in Contemporary Social Theory* (Minneapolis: University of Minnesota Press, 1989). For other feminist interpretations of Foucault, see Irene Diamond and Lee Quinby, eds., *Feminism and Foucault: Reflections on Resistance* (Boston: Northeastern University Press, 1988) and Jana Sawicki, *Disciplining Foucault: Feminism, Power, and the Body* (New York: Routledge, 1991).

21. Mike Davis, *City of Quartz: Excavating the Future in Los Angeles* (London and New York: Verso, 1990). This aspect of Davis's eloquent and moving text has been largely ignored by critics.

22. Kristin Ross's observation about the struggles of colonized peoples parallels the quotation of Hartsock cited earlier: "Precisely at the moment that colonized peoples demand and appropriate to themselves the status of men . . . French intellectuals announce 'the death of man.'" Kristin Ross, *Fast Cars, Clean Bodies: Decolonization and the Reordering of French Culture* (Cambridge, Mass.: MIT Press, 1995), 163.

23. Recently, postcolonial critics such as Homi Bhabha and Gayatri Spivak have challenged the manichaeism or binary logic implicit in Fanon's and Said's understanding of colonial identity. See especially Homi K. Bhabha's essay "The Other Question: Stereotype, Discrimination and the Discourse of Colonialism," in *The Location of Culture* (London and New York: Routledge, 1994) for a critique of phenomenology's opposition between subject and object—and its extension into the discourse of colonialism as a rigid division between colonizer and colonized.

24. Although one can be sympathetic to Foucault's wish to avoid speaking for others, his magisterial tone and his refusal to acknowledge voice and perspective in his early institutional studies give the impression that he is stating universal truths, despite his own demystification of conventional Enlightenment truths. Too often his exclusion of certain "others" (for instance, his medical study gives only the briefest reference to issues of reproduction and women's health) results in myopia.

25. Certainly, La Villette and the Wexner Center, the two iconic built projects most cited by deconstructivist theorists, are enjoyed by women and children as much as men, with the possible exception of the predominantly female staff at the Wexner, who are squeezed into extremely tight quarters.

26. One of the women speakers, Maria Nordman, limited her remarks to a request that the windows be opened to let in light and that the method of seating be decentralized; she chose to sit in the

audience during her presentation. *Anyone* (New York: Rizzoli, 1991), 198–99. A third woman—Cynthia Davidson, the editor of *Anyone*—might arguably be included in the list of participants, although this publication does not provide a short biographical statement for her, as it does for the speakers. Subsequent *ANY* events have included more women, perhaps in response to public outrage, but minority architects have yet to be substantially involved. In the 1994 catalogue of Eisenman's architecture, *Cities of Artificial Excavation*, none of the eight authors are women, nor are any of the seven interviewers. Just as scandalous is the track record of the evening lecture series at Columbia University's architecture school (an institution that prides itself on being avant-garde). Not once in the past six years has the semester series included more than two women as speakers; and there have been no African Americans.

27. On another occasion I hope to address the masculine assumptions underlying this new current in architecture theory, which seems to have its greatest energy in New York, and almost exclusively among young men. While Deleuze and Guattari reject the bipolarity latent in much Derridean thought and are more materially grounded, their "becoming—animal, becoming—woman" again suggests their (*male*) desire. As in Foucault's work, what is neglected in their exhilarating vision of fluidity and flow (for instance, domesticity, children, the elderly) is telling, and strikingly reminiscent of the machismo of some male leaders of the New Left in the 1960s.

28. The notion of "everyday life" can be a frustratingly amorphous concept, and Lefebvre's intensely dialectical approach, combined with his rejection of traditional philosophical rationalism ("truth without reality"), makes it all the more difficult to decipher. His encompassing vision of daily life contrasts sharply with Foucault's concept of heterotopias as isolated and removed spaces. Although Lefebvre's and de Certeau's notions of everyday life both counter Foucault's bleaker, more paranoid vision of disciplinary controls, it must also be acknowledged that there are important differences between the two theorists which become more pronounced after 1968. More than de Certeau, Lefebvre acknowledges the tyrannies, monotonies, and inertia of daily existence as well as its spontaneous moments of invention and festival. Although in the wake of 1968 de Certeau frequently alluded to "*quadrillage*" and the disciplinary surveillance of mass society, by 1980 his vision was more optimistic—indeed idealistic—seeing daily life primarily as endlessly creative, useful, and efficacious. See Henri Lefebvre, *Everyday Life in the Modern World*, trans. Sacha Rabinovitch (New Brunswick, N.J. and London: Transaction Publishers, 1984); Henri Lefebvre, *The Production of Space*; Michel de Certeau, *The Practice of Everyday Life*, trans. Steven Rendall (Berkeley: University of California Press, 1984); and Michel de Certeau, *Heterologies: Discourse on the Other*, trans. Brian Massumi (Minneapolis: University of Minnesota Press, 1986).

29. Lefebvre, *Everyday Life in the Modern World*, 17-22.

30. De Certeau, *The Practice of Everyday Life*, xv. When he uses this phrase, de Certeau cites in a footnote Lefebvre's work on everyday life as a "fundamental source."

31. In his introduction there is also one parenthetical reference to a housewife shopping in a supermarket (ibid., xix). Although de Certeau discusses many activities in which women are central—leisure, consumption, cooking—he rarely considers these subjects in terms of their particular implications for women. Nonetheless, his interest in resistance and in minority positions and his

insistence on the specificity of place and the particularity of subject positions makes his writing especially relevant to those groups whose creative activities and tactics of resistance have been traditionally obscured.

32. See Janet Wolff, *Feminine Sentences: Essays on Women and Culture* (Berkeley: University of California Press, 1990), esp. 34–50; Elizabeth Wilson, *The Sphinx in the City: Urban Life, the Control of Disorder, and Women* (Berkeley: University of California Press, 1991); Anne Friedberg, *Window Shopping: Cinema and the Postmodern* (Berkeley: University of California, 1993); Kristin Ross, introduction to *The Ladies' Paradise,* by Émile Zola (Berkeley: University of California Press, 1992); and Ross, *Fast Cars, Clean Bodies.* Of the critics cited here, Ross is the most indebted to Lefebvre, and, like Lefebvre, she stresses consumption's double-sided nature. For an insightful discussion of consumption and women's role with regard to architecture, see Leila Whittemore, "Women and the Architecture of Fashion in 19th-century Paris," *a/r/c,* "Public Space," no. 5 (1994–95): 14–25.

33. In contrast to a lineage of French theorists prior to 1968, I am not opposing popular culture to mass culture; rather, like de Certeau, I see them as increasingly synonymous.

34. Despite the Situationists' obvious debt to Lefebvre, by the mid-1960s they were frequently critical of Lefebvre, accusing him of presenting an "appearance" of freedom in place of an "authentic" experience. Lefebvre continued to praise Constant's projects in his writings, but by 1960 Constant himself had left the Situationists due to his differences with Debord about the role of artistic production. The best overview of the Situationists can be found in the catalogue of an exhibition sponsored by the Institute of Contemporary Art in Boston, *On the Passage of a few people through a rather brief moment in time: The Situationist International 1957–1972,* ed. Elisabeth Sussman (Cambridge, Mass.: MIT Press, 1989). Peter Wollen's essay "Bitter Victory: The Art and Politics of the Situationists" is especially useful. See also Sadie Plant, *The Most Radical Gesture: The Situationist International in a Postmodern Age* (London and New York: Routledge, 1992), and Ken Knabb, ed. and trans., *Situationist International Anthology* (Berkeley: Bureau of Public Secrets, 1981 [orig. publication date, no copyright]; 2nd print. 1989).

35. Ivan Chtcheglov, "Formulary for a New Urbanism," 1953, in *Situationist International Anthology,* 4.

36. Guy Debord, "Report on the Construction of Situations and on the International Situationist Tendency's Conditions of Organization and Action," 1957, in *Situationist International Anthology,* 18, 19.

37. Some of the themes of Bernard Tschumi's early writings and projects (transgression, lust, violence, murder) recall those of Situationist works. See, for example, *Space: A Thousand Words* (London: Royal College of Art Gallery, 1975); *The Manhattan Transcripts* (New York and London: St. Martin's Press/Academy Editions, 1981); and *Questions of Space,* Text 5 (London: Architectural Association, 1990). It should also be noted that Tschumi acknowledges Lefebvre as a source in his writings of the early and mid-1970s.

38. Greil Marcus, in *On the Passage . . .* , 127.

39. Ibid., 128.

40. Constant's full name was Constant Nieuwenhuys. In 1953 he collaborated with Dutch architect Aldo Van Eyck on a color-space installation. The most complete account of Constant, including a

selection of his writings, is Jean-Clarence Lambert, *Constant: Les Trois Espaces* (Paris: Editions Cercle d'Art, 1992). Despite the obvious influence of Constant's work on Tschumi and other so-called deconstructivists, the Situationists are not mentioned in the Museum of Modern Art's catalogue *Deconstructivist Architecture*.

41. In an article written with Gil J. Wolman, Debord states: "It is necessary to go beyond any idea of scandal. Since the negation of the bourgeois conception of art and artistic genius has become pretty much old hat, [Duchamp's] drawing of a mustache on the *Mona Lisa* is no more interesting than the original version of that painting. We must now push this process to the point of negating the negation." Guy Debord and Gil J. Wolman, "Methods of Detournement," *Les Lèvres nues*, no. 8 (May 1956), rpt. in Knabb, ed., *Situationist Anthology*, 9.

42. Constant, "New Babylon," in *Programs and Manifestoes on 20th-Century Architecture*, ed. Ulrich Conrads, trans. Michael Bullock (Cambridge, Mass.: MIT Press, 1970), 177–78; Constant, "Description de la zone jaune," *Internationale situationniste*, no. 4 (June 1960): 23–26. See also the suggestive commentary by Anthony Vidler, "Vagabond Architecture," in *The Architectural Uncanny: Essays in the Modern Unhomely*, 212–13 and Hilde Heynen, "New Babylon: The Antinomies of Utopia," *Assemblage*, no. 29 (April 1996), 24–39.

43. Alison and Peter Smithson, "But Today We Collect Ads," *Ark* 18 (November 1956), rpt. in David Robbins, ed. *The Independent Group: Postwar Britain and the Aesthetics of Plenty* (Cambridge, Mass.: MIT Press, 1990), 185.

44. Ibid., 186. It is perhaps not coincidental that women played an active, if less overtly public, role in the Independent Group. Mary Banham wrote: "The women, all young and some with children, believed most strongly of all. We threw our best efforts into the ongoing discussion; opened our homes to provide the places; worked on publicity; designed and installed exhibitions; and talked, listened, and wrote." Mary Banham, 1990, in "Retrospective Statements," *The Independent Group*, 187.

45. Reyner Banham first used the term "*une architecture autre*" in his essay "The New Brutalism," *Architectural Review* 118, no. 708 (December 1955): 361.

46. Andreas Huyssen, *After the Great Divide*.

47. Reyner Banham, "The Atavism of the Short Distance MiniCyclist," *Living Arts* (1963); rpt. in *The Independent Group*, 176. In the preceding paragraph, Banham makes it clear that "the other side" is "in some way Left-oriented, even protest-oriented."

48. Robert Venturi, Denise Scott Brown, and Steven Izenour, *Learning from Las Vegas* (Cambridge, Mass.: MIT Press, 1981 [orig. 1972, 2d. ed. 1977]) and *Signs of Life, Symbols in the American City*, Smithsonian Institution, Renwick Gallery, February 26–September 30, 1976. While Scott Brown and Venturi stress the intensely collaborative nature of their writing (Denise Scott Brown and Robert Venturi, interview by Mary McLeod and Stanislaus von Moos, March 18, 1996, Philadelphia), the populist strains and sharpest polemical passages attacking architects' machismo and heroic posturing are more reminiscent of Scott Brown's independent writings than of Venturi's. One would never characterize these passages as part of a "gentle manifesto" (Venturi's own description of *Complexity and Contradiction*).

49. Denise Scott Brown, "Learning from Pop," *Casabella*, nos. 359–360 (December 1971); rpt. in Robert Venturi and Denise Scott Brown, *A View from the Campidoglio* (Cambridge: Icon Editions, Harper and Rowe, 1984), 32. Many have argued that Scott Brown and Venturi's populism is compromised by their irony and "pop" sensibility, especially in a project such as the Guild House, where symbolism sometimes seems more a product of aesthetic provocation than of a sensitivity to the occupants' own sensibilities or needs. Nonetheless, Scott Brown and Venturi's appreciation of mass culture and attention to lower- and middle-class taste has served as an important antidote to the modern movement's aesthetic strictures.

50. Venturi, Scott Brown, and Izenour, *Learning from Las Vegas*, 165, 149.

51. Ibid., 148.

52. Ibid., 154.

53. Jane Jacobs, *The Death and Life of Great American Cities* (New York: Vintage Books, 1961). Jacobs is quoted in *Learning from Las Vegas*, 81.

54. Elissa Rosenberg, "Public and Private: Rereading Jane Jacobs," *Landscape Journal* 13, no. 2 (Fall 1994): 139–44. I am indebted to Rosenberg's insightful reading of Jacobs for several significant points in my analysis of *The Death and Life of Great American Cities*.

55. Ibid., 139.

56. Ibid., 143–44. See also Thomas Bender, "Jane in the Cities," *The Nation* 238, no. 21 (2 June 1984): 678.

The Knowledge of the Body and the Presence of History—Toward a Feminist Architecture

DEBORAH FAUSCH

What are the possibilities for a feminist architecture? Or for a feminist architectural history, theory, or criticism? In order to begin to answer these questions, it is first necessary to address certain general issues in feminist theory. If, as many feminist writers have argued, it is impossible, or at any rate dangerous, to define a feminine "nature,"[1] it remains true that without any essential(ist) definition of the feminine—of the female, of woman—it becomes impossible to claim any viewpoint or issue as feminist, except in the contingent sense that where oppression, exploitation, objectification, or marginalization of women occurs, there a feminist position can be taken. This line of reasoning provides for clear lines of action, but much muddier theoretical positions. It can lead to useful alliances with other revolutionary philosophies such as Marxism and poststructuralism. To conceive feminism in this way is also, however, to run up against all of the problems of defining the female as the Other of the normative male, so that feminism becomes derivative of a dominant masculine vision—penis envy in a more subtle form.[2]

To push this analysis to its conclusion is to reveal "the feminine" to be a metaphor in our society, a counter in the game of language, a label applied with ideological intent to certain aspects and practices of human being and action, so that designating a practice as "feminist" can be done only metaphorically. On the other hand, to abandon all gendered discourses as false or useless leads back to the trap of subsuming the universal or unmarked under the male. Eschewing essentialism, then, deprives not only the patriarchy but feminism of an important tool to think with. In *Discerning the Subject*, Paul Smith has considered this double bind in terms of the definition of the feminist subject and has advocated a double stance, fluctuating between the essentialist humanist subject and the decentered subject of poststructuralism. This solution seems, however, unsatisfactory, a kind of double talk.[3]

One alternative to Smith's doubling is to adopt a tactical and historical position, to use the term "feminist" in a strategic manner, as a designation for stances that women may endorse as valuable, without necessarily claiming for them an essential relationship to "the feminine." Perhaps there are some positions to which women have a historical if not an inherent connection, some aspects of human life that are distorted or depreciated in Western culture, some cases in which these distortions have been historically linked to a hatred of the feminine.[4] Clearly, one such area is our relationship to the body—to the female body, but also to the bodily in general: the concrete, the material, the empirical, the "brute fact," the "dumb object"—terms which register the fear, contempt, and hatred in Western culture of "mere matter."[5]

To take this course is to claim, not that the feminine is bodily, but that the bodily is feminist—not that a concern with the body is a guarantee of nonoppressive attitudes, but that a nonoppressive attitude would include a regard for the bodily. It is to claim that women can have a body without *being* the body.

How do these considerations apply to architecture? As an art which directly engages the body, architecture has the potential to be feminist in the sense I have just described. Architecture is involved in forming matter in conformance with ideas; thus it partakes of the rational, the nonmaterial, the ideal. But if the feminine is bodily, has body, this does not prevent it from encompassing reason as well. While architects cannot avoid the instrumentalization of the material, we can, within the limits of client preferences and budgets, choose the kinds of experience we create. A feminist architecture can attempt to create a "second nature," a "world" in Hannah Arendt's sense, which engenders particular perceptions and experiences.[6] Such an architecture can, by offering experiences that correspond to, provide modes for, the experience of the body, give validity to a sense of the self as bodily—a sense that may be shared by both sexes. The discipline of architecture can thus provide room to address Western culture's tendency toward abstraction, distortion, mistreatment, even banishment of the body. It can offer a counterexperience to our culture's indulgence in René Descartes's escape wish, one of the most compelling and persistent ever imagined—the desire to be only a mind.

In Western philosophy, the mind has been strongly connected with the organ of the eye and the sense of vision. Philosophers have employed vision as a metaphor for thought, and light for the faculty of reason. Sight has been opposed to the rest of the body as the least bodily sense (despite the fact that it consumes some twenty-five percent of our energy), and the eye has been conceived of as the most disembodied of the sense organs. In "The Nobility of Sight," Hans Jonas demonstrates that the concepts of time and eternity, form and matter, essence and existence, theory and practice, and even infinity can be derived from the characteristics of vision.[7] Although this imagery is as old as the Greeks, Martin Heidegger maintains that our emphasis on vision to the exclusion of the other senses occurs first, or most significantly, with Descartes. Heidegger's definition of representation [*Vorstellung*] as "to set out before oneself and to set forth in relation to oneself" and also as "standing over against" underlines the way that separating vision from the rest of the senses also separates the viewer from the material world.[8]

In the course of the thought experiment leading to the *cogito ergo sum*, Descartes posits a disembodied mind inhabiting a world without corporeality: "I nevertheless do not see that from this distinct idea of corporeal nature which I find in my imagination, I can derive any argument which necessarily proves the existence of any body. . . . [A]lthough perhaps, or rather certainly, as I will soon show, I have a body with which I am very closely united, nevertheless . . . it is certain that this "I"—that is to say, my soul, by virtue of which I am what I am—is entirely and truly distinct from my body and that it can be or exist without it."[9] In trying to construct a basis for certainty in thought, he maintains that "even bodies are not properly known by the senses nor by the faculty of imagination, but by the understanding alone."[10] He makes use of the metaphoric triad of light, sight, and knowledge to describe the purely mental entity which he presupposes. The organ that perceives these bodies he calls "the mind's eye." The ideas that the mind's eye knows are "images," similar to the representations in paintings. The *cogito*, the mental faculty given by God to human beings for direct comprehension of truth—that which exists even if the body does not—is envisioned as light—the light of reason, the light of nature: "Thus the light of nature makes me clearly recognize that ideas in me are like paintings or pictures."[11]

Heidegger observes that "through Descartes, realism is first put in the position of having to prove the reality of the outer world, of having to save that which is as such."[12] In "The Age of the World Picture," he contends that Descartes's "metaphysics of knowledge" constitutes a historical change in the relationship of the human being to the world. Descartes's separation of mental subject from physical object creates these two entities at the same time as it distinguishes between them. This separation also establishes the relationship of representation between subject and object. Thought is henceforth a process in which objects are represented to the mind: "Thinking is representing, setting-before, is a representing relation to what is represented (*idea* as *perceptio*)."[13] As Heidegger shows, Descartes's thought is emblematic of Western thought in this respect. The very name of the Enlightenment demonstrates the continuing connection between light and reason, the separation of sight from its bodily integument. In the twentieth century, our increasing technological capacity to make connections across space and time has intensified the traditional bodilessness of the sense of vision.[14]

Situated within this long-standing opposition between vision and the other senses, an architecture that required that it be experienced by senses other than vision in order to be understood could be claimed as a

FIGS. 1 AND 2 Maya Lin, Vietnam Veterans Memorial, Washington D.C.

strategically feminist architecture. It would merit this designation if it fostered an awareness of and posited a value to the experience of the concrete, the sensual, the bodily—if it used the body as a necessary instrument in absorbing the content of the experience.

It might be argued that modern architecture's emphasis on construction and materials would qualify it for inclusion in this category. For some late modernists, tangibility becomes both a value in itself and an index of the primitive or the timeless. Mario Botta's architecture—for example the house at Cadenazzo—possesses a materiality that asserts its own nature and "making." But for two reasons, I will pass over these examples. First, this tangibility is made to be perceptible by sight alone, to be obvious even in photographs. Second, for reasons that will become clear later, I am most interested in the use of the body to apprehend meanings beyond the self-referentiality of construction.

Le Corbusier's chapel at La Tourette, whose dark, high, oblong shape must be experienced more by the reverberation of sound and the movement of the body than by sight, comes to mind as an architecture that can be claimed as feminist in this way. Another is Maya Lin's

Vietnam Veterans Memorial in Washington D.C. Cut into the flat lawn of the capital, the memorial is invisible from a distance. The first sight of it comes as a visceral shock—a sudden opening in the earth, a gash in the green turf which ruptures the infinite extension and perfect rationality of the ground plane. The visitor's slow movement along the black wall becomes an imaginative descent into the tombs of the soldiers whose names are engraved on the reflective stone face (FIGS. 1 AND 2). A similar physical relationship to words and their enframing site occurs on the stair from Forty-third Street down to the United Nations Plaza in New York. Here one descends a gentle curve past carved

FIG. 3 United Nations, stairway down from Forty-third Street

words from the Old Testament prophesying peace. Moving down along the beautiful marble panel inscribed with a hope so often disappointed induces an experience of poignant sadness that makes actual the etymological connection between motion and emotion (FIG. 3).

Movement as a mode of apprehension is also inherent in the design of *Veiled Landscape*, an environmental sculpture by Mary Miss. The work consists of a series of highly articulated screens of wood and metal marking a narrow trail which descends into a New England forest. At the top, a wooden platform frames a view of the path dropping down into the distance (FIG. 4). From this vantage point, additional screens visible at various points along the path create a series of places in the uniform woods. These pull the viewer out in a forward projection, an anticipation of punctuation points to be experienced along the way (FIG. 5). As the sojourner moves down the trail towards these places, the screens frame, and thereby produce, a series of scenes, views made significant by these structures. The physical sensation of passing under these thresholds

FIGS. 4 AND 5 Mary Miss, viewing platforms, *Veiled Landscape*, Winter Olympics, Lake Placid, New York, 1980

draws the body progressively deeper, down and away into the depths of the woods, toward an imagined but unseen destination. Miss has written that the focus of her landscape constructions is "the direct experience" of "the physical or emotional content, the kind of physical connection that's taking place."[15] In this project, direct experience is invited and unveiled.

The body is also central to a visitor's experience of two Philadelphia parks by Venturi, Rauch and Scott Brown. Both Welcome Park and Franklin Court are found in the Center City area of Philadelphia.[16] Welcome Park (named after the ship that brought William Penn to Philadelphia) is located at the edge of the city near the Delaware River on the site of the Slate Roof House, Penn's residence and the seat of the government of Pennsylvania in the years 1700–1701. This park is one of several by Venturi, Rauch and Scott Brown—including Copley Square in Boston and Western Plaza in Washington D.C.—that employ the device of miniaturization. These designs have elicited a certain amount of incomprehension from critics, probably at least in part because the experience is not adequately represented by photographs—that is, it is not an entirely visual experience.[17]

At one level, Welcome Park is simply a miniature map of historic Philadelphia, its pavement pattern the replica of the original surveyor's plan (FIG. 6). The park is mostly open, a space meant to be traversed rather than meditated upon. The mural at the far end of the park, adapted from a seventeenth-century view from the site, pulls one across the map toward its bright colors, creating a heady feeling of power and freedom as one strides over several blocks at a time (FIG. 7). Small trees are located on the sites of Philadelphia's four squares. These and two miniature bronzes—the Slate Roof House, located in its proper square on the plan, and a statue of Penn in the center—intensify the sense of gigantic omnipotence. Not simply a picturesque experience of movement through an organized series of events, this translation through miniaturized space evokes a hyperawareness of the body.

The park's impact derives from relationships more complex than the scale differential of a Gulliver to Lilliputian city blocks, however. The effects of miniaturization are felt at several levels. First is the

FIG. 6 Venturi, Rauch and Scott Brown, Welcome Park, Philiadelphia, 1982, aerial view

FIG. 7 Welcome Park, view of mural and Slate Roof House

experiencing of the map. Seen in perspective, laid out on the ground, the subtle variations in the city grid are enhanced. The eye, accustomed to picking out differences in stereoscopic views, more readily comprehends the variations in block width and depth than in an orthographic drawing. Second is a curious undermining of identity. Stepping up to the bronze Slate Roof House at the far end of the park, conscious that one is actually standing on its site, one experiences a strange oscillation of identification between the house and one's own body. The ordinary unthinking connection of the mind with its physical home is momentarily disrupted by its tendency to project itself into places it is absorbed in. This produces an almost Cartesian doubt as to the relationship of mind and body—am "I" "in here" or "in there"? Perhaps this oscillation is also a part of the enjoyment of certain neoclassical buildings such as William Strickland's wonderful early-nineteenth-century Merchants Exchange located nearby (FIGS. 8 AND 9), whose cool blue-gray stones are so palpable in their own way. Its lions and gigantic arabesques, of about the same size and also about human-sized, induce their own form of oscillating identification in which the body equilibrates itself to another entity of similar size and configuration.

FIGS. 8 AND 9 William Strickland, Merchants Exchange, Philadelphia, 1835

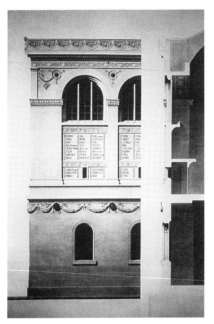

FIG. 10 Henri Labrouste, Bibliothèque Sante-
Geneviève, Paris, 1850, elevation detail
and wall section

This experience confers a heightened sense of physicality when the mind returns to its accustomed container. As one walks over the paving stones, the streets, blocks, and rivers, flat and graphic in photographs, take on depth and tangibility from the simultaneous sight and feel of the changing textures and colors of the stone underfoot—concrete, marble, red sandstone, and brick. The palpability of the surface is increased by the sharp incision of the letters of the street names and the stylized waves cut into the two rivers. Walking on them is eerie, like stepping on something one shouldn't—a dedication set into a wall, perhaps, or a commemorative inscription. The letters stretching along the marble stones of the streets are haphazardly chopped in two as they fall across the joints between stones. Like the jointed keystone of Venturi, Rauch, and Scott Brown's Wu Hall at Princeton University, these cloven letters confront the visitor with the materiality of the surface and the materiality of the word on that surface. Unlike Henri Labrouste's inscription of the library catalogue onto the façade of the Bibliothèque Sainte-Geneviève, which makes of the building a "book" whose words are to be read as abstract information (FIG. 10), this technique rematerializes letters into substance, prevents the unconscious taking in—consumption—of the street names as incorporeal information.[18] These words have emphatic presence—carved forms cut into rocks laid side by side, sharp Roman faces whose edges will someday be eroded and green from the wear of feet and the ravages of weather, thus to become themselves part of the history of the city.

A time line that runs along a side wall and falls as the site slopes down from the Delaware side to the "Skoolkill" side (as the old map spelled it) also requires a peripatetic reading. Not only lateral, but also descending movement is required—a movement "down through history." Even this most banal presentation of historical data engages the body in an action that adds to the sense of what might otherwise be ingested as pure sign, disembodied information.

My claim is not that this park is completely explained by its relationship to the body, but the more modest one that contemplation is not enough. The action of the body must be performed to complete the intellectual content of the park, to get the message. *Inter alia*, this places a higher value upon greater complexity and greater subtlety of experience, experience that includes both the body and the mind as opposed to developing one at the expense of the other. Preliterate Greeks knew that all of the senses and emotions must be engaged in order to remember; thus they inculcated important cultural knowledge with rhyme, rhythm, dance, song, and story. All knowledge was body knowledge.[19] In this postmodern park, history is incorporated—made a part of the individual—through a combination of visual, kinetic, and projective means involving the body in awareness and action.

Franklin Court is a few blocks away from Welcome Park on Market Street. Comprising a national landmark and museum as well as an urban park, it has a much more complicated program and design (FIG. 11). The site was owned by Benjamin Franklin, and the still extant Georgian row houses along Market Street, which provided him with rental income, are incorporated into the project. The majority of the exhibitions are contained in the brownstones and in an underground level housing a theater and various programmatic exhibits. Franklin's own mansion, once located at the back of the lot, disappeared many years ago, along with all record of its layout. Venturi, Rauch, and Scott Brown's design does not attempt to re-create it. Instead the Franklin mansion is embodied—or rather dis-embodied—by two ghost houses constructed of oversized smooth, gray-white metal members of square section. One of these struc-

FIG. 11 Venturi, Rauch and Scott Brown, Franklin Court, Philadelphia, 1972, aerial view

tures is the archetypal outline of a house, a child's drawing—a pitched roof, a chimney at each end, and one in the middle. It is located roughly over the foundations of the vanished house. A similar structure, an archway leading to an area of more private gardens, is set between Franklin's house and the brownstones lining Market Street. In photographs these gray ghost lines look too heavy, too cartoonlike; they seem a mockery of the "idea of history" in the old city. However, unlike the sharp skeletal wires of Giacometti's sculptures that served as their inspiration, the flat, broad, opaque smoothness of the members prevents them from being perceived as structural. Indeed, in some lights and from some angles, they seem to fade into the sky above the open park, appearing ghostly indeed.

It is the park itself, rather than the museum in its entirety, that interests me—the way in which it, like Welcome Park, employs the body as an essential organ of comprehension, and the way it uses narrative inscribed into the surfaces of the park to create a sense of history. Entering at the back from the little stone alley called Orianna Street, one is drawn immediately toward the first ghost house and the curious brown concrete hoods within its perimeter. These are somewhat hidden from view and of mysterious purpose. Walking down a few shallow steps, markers of a mythical descent into the past or the other world, one peers into these brown openings. The hoods envelope the head like shrouds, screening out the city and the immediate environment as one bends into them, enforcing contemplation. One looks down onto the few remaining stone foundations of the old house—foundations under glass, seen through periscopes onto a buried past. These "mute stones" are given a ventriloquist's voice by diagrams indicating what part of the house they supported.

As one straightens up, one's gaze, schooled in looking down, falls on the pavement below. The slate within the perimeter of the ghost house is inscribed with quotations from the seventeenth-century individuals who once lived here, telling stories of hardship and joy in the New World. To stand on these stones, which bear such a marked resemblance in their colors, textures, and letters to early American headstones, is to feel one-self in the place of the former inhabitants. If there was a slight feeling of transgression in walking over the city map in Welcome Park, here there is a strong sense of the sacrilege of walking over graves.

Stepping out of the depression of the house's domain, one moves up from the dream of the past, wandering toward a low wall made of worn brick and passing under the ghost arch into the garden precinct. This part of the park is provided with abundant seating covered by pergolas or set against walls (FIG. 12). Whereas the graveyard of quotations and the shrouded foundation stones are clearly marked as "past," these gardens are just as clearly in the present tense. Designed as a semblance of seven-teenth-century gardens, which were important sources of medicines and spices, their formal layout organizes an apothecary as well as an aesthetic

FIG. 12 Franklin Court, view of gardens and pergolas

experience. Seated under an oversized and simplified pergola positioned where Franklin might have placed it long ago, one understands oneself as a stand-in. The pergola as well as the walls, the gardens, and the trellises are representatives, not re-creations, of what might have been here, intellectually satisfying in their somewhat schematic forms.

By calling attention to what is (and is not) materially present, this park makes a clear distinction between old and new. Without fabricating a "living museum" or attempting to recreate an accurate, literal representation of previous times, it allows the history of the site to be experienced as simultaneously present to the imagination and past in actuality. It invites a subtle and precise understanding of the relationship of these fragmentary remains to the period which produced them. The elements of the site function both as presences and as signs.

In all four of these landscapes, imaginal projection, the psychic dimension of depth, is given architectural representation and concrete embodiment through the visitor's somatic experience. Depth takes on different meanings in each of the four projects—remembrance and grief, distance from civilization, historical span. But in each case, time and space attain an elastic dimension through the projective propensities of the body. In his villas, Le Corbusier used the body's movement along the *promenade architecturale* to tell the story of ascending through uniform, infinite space-time to the top of the world in order to contemplate, to theorize—to survey "the present situation" and to plan alternatives.[20] In contrast to this archetypal modern experience, these projects give being to alternatives to linear historical time and rational Cartesian space. Imaginative involvement produces, not a hegemonic narrative, but instead each person's individually constructed story. Cultural meanings given experiential presence by being embedded in the physical experience of places thus propose new relationships between form and content. The relaxation of Descartes's distinction between mind and body also allows for a relaxation in the distinction between sign and referent. Meaning escapes the strictures of semiotic theory to an enlarged dimension, in blithe disregard of the poststructuralist anxiety about presence. "Incorporation" of meaning, within both subject and object, gives it a reality not objective, but not illusory either.

Histories take the form of narratives, of readings. In literate cultures, in which recorded history has replaced an ever-present tradition, buildings need explanations to be understood as memories of the past. In the Vietnam Veterans Memorial and the two Philadelphia parks, these narratives are literally inscribed onto the architecture. By putting the body in an unfamiliar relationship to writing on man-made—or, I should say, humanly-created—surfaces, the architects have allowed history to become "part of" the individual. For a postliterate society, however, in which television and the computer are replacing the book which killed the building, this incorporated "body knowledge" cannot be a possibility in the same uncomplicated way that it was for the largely oral Greek society of Plato's time. Perhaps that is why body knowledge is used in these projects to establish a relationship with the distant—the dead, the past, the "natural."

These body experiences suggest possibilities for understanding the role of history in the postmodern, "posthistorical" present. Our period, when the modern idea of a unified and teleological history has dissolved into that of multiple, coexisting histories, has been called the "end of history." In this view, the simultaneous presence of objects and images from places far separated in location, and the contemporaneity of references to many historical periods, comprise a single, almost immaterial, postmodern place-time.[21] Theorists of postmodernism have ascribed this flattening of reference to problems in the structure of representation, to the lack of "a referential being or substance" engendered by commodity capitalism and the media.[22] Culture theorists such as Fredric Jameson have adduced postmodern architects' preoccupation with the surface as evidence for this assessment.[23] What these four landscapes provide, however, is an alternative model for the operation of history not dependent on this structure of representation—defined either as an object "standing over against" a subject or as "the presence of an absence." Rather, the flexible operation of imaginal projection into highly articulated substance couples literal surface with imaginal depth, creating physical presence without totalizing narrative, providing content without singular interpretation, replacing the separation of form and meaning with embodied meanings.

If these four projects point beyond the condition of disembodied subject "standing over against" corporeal object, then according to Heidegger they can only do so through a *Vervinding*, an overcoming, healing, acceptance, and deepening of the dichotomous definition of the person entailed by Descartes's epistemology. I would like to suggest that these four projects provide, through the knowledge of the body, glimpses of an alternate metaphysics of knowledge for the postmodern subject. The experiences they provide do not eliminate the subject, but the subject they do presume is neither the unified mental subject of humanism nor the fragmented subject of poststructuralism. Rather, through the knowledge of the body, a subject implicated in bodiliness is able to comprehend experiences that employ all of the senses. This implies the existence of a "nature" that even Descartes, towards the end of his *Meditations*, grudgingly admitted forms a "mixed whole" or "composite body."[24] Such a rapprochement of subject and object, ideal and material, mind and body, in a new, postliterate form of mixed whole could thus be said to "produce" a feminist subject whose strategy is the embodiment of knowledge.

NOTES

1. For a useful review of the extended debates on this vexed topic, see Paul Smith, *Discerning the Subject* (Minneapolis: University of Minnesota, 1988), who summarizes the arguments for and against defining a female subject in terms of essential bodily or psychic characteristics of women. Identifying women with the bodily or the imaginary (unconscious), domains that have been construed by patriarchal value systems as lower than that of conscious reason, runs the risk of equating women with the body or the unconscious, as they have been historically .

2. Smith summarizes Toril Moi's position in *Sexual/Textual Politics* as a representative of this point of view: "Women's experiences and identities are limited by dint of being forged in and by patriarchy: there can be no uncontaminated place from which a female 'subject' could speak or act her identity—'there is simply nowhere else to go'. . . . [W]omen's 'truths' and identities can currently be represented only within a symbolic field organized on a principle of difference which works to exclude and defend against them. Thus, the possibility of women as an identifiable set of 'subjects' mounting any kind of resistance to patriarchy is foreclosed upon immediately. According to such a perspective there can be no specifically female identity and therefore no specifically female agent except one committed to struggles which are in fact. . . not specifically feminist struggles." Smith, *Discerning the Subject*, 137. In the concluding chapter of *Sexual/Textual Politics*, Toril Moi, who is herself summarizing Julia Kristeva's work, puts it this way: "We have to accept our position as already inserted into an order that precedes us and from which there is no escape. There is no *other space* from which we can speak: if we are able to speak at all, it will have to be within the framework of symbolic language." But she continues, "In the end, Kristeva is unable to account for the relations between the subject and society." Thus Moi holds out for a subject that can act to change power relations, even as she praises Kristeva's subtle analysis of all subject positions. Toril Moi, *Sexual/Textual Politics: Feminist Literary Theory* (1985; reprint, London: Routledge, 1988), 170–71.

3. Smith, *Discerning the Subject*, 150. Jane Gallop's formulation in *The Daughter's Seduction* is more positive, but still flirts with the stasis of self-criticism: "Both psychoanalysis and feminism can be seen as efforts to call into question a rigid identity that cramps and binds. But both also tend to

want to produce a 'new identity,' one that will now be adequate and authentic. I hold the Lacanian view that any identity will necessarily be alien and constraining. But I do not seek some liberation from identity. That would lead to another form of paralysis—the oceanic passivity of undifferentiation. Identity must be continually assumed and immediately questioned." Jane Gallop, *The Daughter's Seduction: Feminism and Psychoanalysis* (Ithaca: Cornell University Press, 1982), xii. Later in her book, Gallop is more emphatic about the necessity for women to be "like men"—that is, to be able to represent themselves by taking on an identity (74).

4. This strategic approach avoids the problem articulated by the *Questions féministes* group: "It is legitimate to expose the oppression, the mutilation, the 'functionalization' and the 'objectivation' of the female body, but it is also dangerous to place the body at the center of a search for female identity. Furthermore, the themes of Otherness and of the Body merge together, because the most visible difference between men and women is . . . indeed the difference in body. This difference has been used as a pretext to 'justify' full power of one sex over the other. . . . In everything that is supposed to characterize women, oppression is always present." "Variations on common themes," trans. Yvonne Rochette-Ozzello, cited in *New French Feminisms: An Anthology*, eds. Elaine Marks and Isabelle de Courtivron (Amherst: University of Massachusetts Press, 1980), 218–22; originally published as "Variations sur des thèmes communs," *Questions féministes* 1 (1977). Compare Gayatri Chakravorty Spivak's complex defense of the necessity for being "against sexism and for feminism" in "French Feminism in an International Frame," *Yale French Studies* 62 (1981): 154–84, especially 179–84. Elsewhere, however, Spivak seems to endorse in a qualified way a strategic essentialism. See Gayatri Chakravorty Spivak, "Subaltern Studies: Deconstructing Historiography," in *In Other Worlds: Essays in Cultural Politics* (New York: Routledge, 1988), 206–7.

Since essentialism is often derogated as conservative, it is worth quoting Diana Fuss on its political mutability: "There is an important distinction to be made, I would submit, between 'deploying' or 'activating' essentialism and 'falling into' or 'lapsing into' essentialism. . . . [T]he radicality or conservatism of essentialism depends, to a significant degree, on *who* is utilizing it, *how* it is deployed, and *where* its effects are concentrated." Diana Fuss, *Essentially Speaking: Feminism, Nature & Difference* (New York: Routledge, 1989), 20.

5. The "body" of literature on the body in Western culture is enormous. For one history of the hatred of the female body as it is connected to the separation of mind and matter see James Hillman, "Part Three: On Psychological Femininity," in *The Myth of Analysis* (New York: Harper and Row, 1972). As Hillman notes, the etymological connection between *mater* and *matter* is an index of the close relationship of the female and the material in Western culture. This connection is at least as old as Plato's separation of Being into matter and form, with matter as the mother and form as the father of Being (*Timaeus* 50d).

To equate the bodily with the sexual is, I think, a phallocentric error, as if the body were only sexual, or the material only a metaphor for sexuality. Making a rigid separation between the sexual and non-sexual body is another phallocentric error, of course. But even when these terms are used metaphorically, I prefer "bodily" to "sexual" as the representative for this complex of experiences, since it is less reductive.

6. Arendt defines the world as that which relates and separates human beings and outlives individual existence. See Hannah Arendt, "The Human Condition" and "Work," in *The Human Condition* (Chicago: University of Chicago Press, 1958).

7. Hans Jonas's discussion of the role of vision in the development of philosophical concepts in "The Nobility of Sight: A Study in the Phenomenology of the Senses," in *The Phenomenon of Life: Toward a Philosophical Biology* (New York: Delta, 1966) is a classic in this field (originally published under the same title in *Philosophy and Phenomenological Research* 14, no. 4 [June 1954]: 507–19). He is careful to point out, however, that vision depends for comprehension on the body's dynamic involvement with its environment. For discussions of this constellation of meanings in Greek thought, see also Jean Pierre Vernant, *Myth and Thought among the Greeks* (London: Routledge and Kegan Paul, 1983) and Bruno Snell, *The Discovery of the Mind in Greek Philosophy and Literature* (New York: Dover, 1982). For a more recent history of attitudes toward vision, focusing on twentieth-century philosophers' attempts to dethrone vision as the sovereign sense, see Martin Jay, *Downcast Eyes: The Denigration of Vision in Twentieth-Century French Thought* (Berkeley: University of California Press, 1993). For a discussion of visual bias in psychoanalysis and Plato, and their devaluation of the feminine, see Luce Irigaray, *Speculum of the Other Woman*, especially "Plato's *Hystera*": "The feminine, the maternal are instantly frozen by the 'like,' the 'as if' of that masculine representation dominated by truth, light, resemblance, identity" (265). *Speculum of the Other Woman*, trans. Gillian C. Gill (Ithaca: Cornell University Press, 1985); originally published as *Speculum de l'autre femme* (Paris: Les Editions de Minuit, 1974).

8. See Martin Heidegger, "The Age of the World Picture," in *The Question Concerning Technology and Other Essays*, trans. William Lovitt (New York: Harper and Row, 1977), 127, 139–41.

9. René Descartes, "Sixth Meditation," in *The Meditations Concerning First Philosophy*, in *Philosophical Essays*, trans. Laurence J. Lafleur (Indianapolis: The Bobbs-Merrill Company, Inc., 1964), 128, 132. Having started by doubting the existence of the body, Descartes meditates on the evidence he has of its existence: "First, then, I felt that I had a head, hands, feet, and all the other members which compose this body which I thought of as a part, or possibly even as the whole, of myself. Furthermore, I felt that this body was one of a world of bodies, from which it was capable of receiving various advantages and disadvantages . . . [identified by] pleasure and pain. . . . I also experienced hunger, thirst, and other similar appetites, as well as certain bodily tendencies toward gaiety, sadness, anger, and other similar emotions. And externally, in addition to the extension, shapes, and movements of bodies, I observed in them hardness, warmth, and all the other qualities perceived by touch. Furthermore, I noticed in them light, colors, odors, tastes, and sounds, the variety of which enabled me to distinguish the sky, the earth, the sea, and, in general, all other bodies, one from another. . . . And because the ideas I received through the senses were much more vivid, more detailed, and even in their own way more distinct than any of those which I could picture to myself with conscious purpose while meditating, or even than those which I found impressed upon my memory, it seemed that they could not be derived from my own mind, and therefore they must have been produced in me by some other things. . . . It was also not without reason that I believed that this body, which by a certain particular privilege I called mine, belonged to me more properly and strictly than any other. For in fact I could never be separated

from it." Descartes, "Sixth Meditation," 128–30. How poignant this description of the joy of ordinary sense experience! Descartes describes it, however, only to subject it to a radical doubt as to
its reality. And although in the end he recuperates the reality of the sense-world, it is clear that the
separation of mind and body, employed perhaps for heuristic purposes, has been irrevocable.

10. Descartes, "Third Meditation," in *Meditations*, 90–91.

11. Descartes, Meditations, xvi, 95, 98.

12. Heidegger, "World Picture," 139.

13. Heidegger, "World Picture," 132, 149–50. In this essay and "The Question Concerning
Technology" in the same volume, Heidegger argues that with this shift in the relationship to the
world, the idea of a picture of the world also comes into being, an idea that also allows the
thought of control of that world through technology. The concept of the "world picture" sets a
subject who guarantees the reality of the world against the objects in that world and makes of
those objects a "standing reserve" available for exploitation.

14. In "Urban Ecology or the Space of Energy," Virilio emphasizes the need to restore the dimensions of time and gravity to the relationship of human beings with their world: "'Citizens of the
World,' inhabitants of nature, we too often omit that we also live in physical dimensions, in life-
size spatial scale and time lengths; so the obvious duration of the constituent elements of the sub-
stances (chemical or others) making up our natural environment is doubled with the unseen pol-
lution of the distances organizing our relationship with the other, but also with the world of
sensual experience. Therefore, it is urgent to affix to the ecology of nature, an ecology of the artifice of the techniques of transportation and transmission that literally *exploit* the field of the
dimensions of the geophysical milieu and degrade their scale." Paul Virilio, "Urban Ecology or
the Space of Energy" (paper translated and presented by Louis Martin at The New Urbanism
conference, Princeton University School of Architecture, October 1992). See also Paul Virilio,
The Lost Dimension (New York: Semiotext(e), 1991). I want to make clear that I am not suggesting that these technologies be rejected—rather, that they be "incorporated" consciously.

15. Mary Miss, "An Interview with Mary Miss," *Landscape: The Princeton Journal, Thematic
Studies in Architecture* 2 (1985): 96–104.

16. For basic information about the parks see *Stanislaus von Moos, Venturi, Rauch and Scott Brown:
Buildings and Projects* (New York: Rizzoli, 1987), 104–9, 138–40.

17. See for example Thomas Hine, "Welcome Park's Exposed Look Overshadows its Tribute to
Penn," *Philadelphia Inquirer*, 14 January 1983, sec. 1D, 8D; Paul Goldberger, "Western Plaza in
Washington Gets a Somewhat Flat Reception," *New York Times*, 18 December 1980, sec. A18;
Benjamin Forgey, "The Plaza that Might Have Been," *The Washington Star*, 28 December 1980,
sec. D11–D13. In what follows I will present the parks as the record of an experience—just as par-
tial a portrayal, of course, as photography, but one that allows for a description of the experience
of the body.

18. According to Neil Levine, Labrouste's purpose in decorating the library façade with words was
"to show that the content of architecture could no longer be the plastically qualified transformation of the word into stone but just its literal transcription—the descriptive naming on its surface
of the actual content of thought contained therein in books of printed words." As Levine notes,

Labrouste was closely connected with Victor Hugo, whose famous declaration in *The Hunchback of Notre Dame* that architecture had been replaced by the printed word—"This will kill that"—served as a motto for Néo-Grec architects. According to Emile Trélat, they desired to "make the stone speak as a book speaks, to borrow from the writer his ideas and his images, and to clothe our monuments in them." See Neil Levine, "The Romantic Idea of Architectural Legibility: Henri Labrouste and the Néo-Grec," in *The Architecture of the École des Beaux-Arts*, ed. Arthur Drexler (Cambridge: MIT Press, 1977), 350, 408.

19. Much has been written about the forms of knowledge and the means of transmission in nonliterate cultures. For an extensive discussion of the Greek case see Eric Havelock's history of mimesis in *Preface to Plato* (Cambridge: Belknap/Harvard University Press, 1963). Other sources include Vernant, *Myth and Thought*, and Snell, *Discovery of the Mind*. A more recent treatment of mimesis which also examines the Greek theories is Philippe Lacoue-Labarthe, *Typography: Mimesis, Philosophy, Politics* (Cambridge: Harvard University Press, 1989).

20. For descriptions of the promenade architecturale in Le Corbusier's work, see Beatriz Colomina, "Le Corbusier and Photography," *Assemblage* 4 (1987): 7–23; Stanford Anderson, "Architectural Research Programmes in the Work of Le Corbusier," *Design Studies* 5:3 (July 1984): 151–58; and Tim Benton, "Le Corbusier y la Promenade Architecturale," *Arquitectura* 264–5 (1987): 38–47.

21. For example, Marc Augé labels this phenomenon "non-place" (possibly referring to Melvin Webber's phrase "the non-place urban realm"). For Augé the non-place is characterized by an excess of history, an excess of place, and excess individuality. He claims that whereas modernity created a whole that included traditional organic places within it, supermodern non-place displays places as unintegrated nuggets without connection to the matrix within which they are set. *Non-Places: Introduction to an Anthropology of Supermodernity*, trans. John Howe (London: Verso, 1995). See also Gianni Vattimo, *The End of Modernity: Nihilism and Hermeneutics in Postmodern Culture*, trans. Jon R. Snyder (Baltimore: The Johns Hopkins Press, 1988). In his introduction, Vattimo seems to be describing a process of "retraditionalizing history." In a traditional society, the events of the past are simultaneously present because they are all equally available for use by living persons for their own purposes; thus a tradition is always being altered as it is being employed for new purposes by different persons and groups. The discipline of history, on the other hand, fixes the past—"as it was"— into one unalterable story. Both are concerned with the past—both have a sense of "pastness"—but the relationship to that past differs.

22. Jean Baudrillard, "The Precession of Simulacra," *Art and Text* 11 (September 1983): 3; Vattimo, End of Modernity, 10, 128.

23. Fredric Jameson, "Postmodernism, or The Cultural Logic of Late Capitalism," *New Left Review* 146 (1984): 33–92.

24. "Nature also teaches me by these feelings of pain, hunger, thirst, and so on that I am not only residing in my body, as a pilot in his ship, but furthermore, that I am intimately connected with it, and that the mixture is so blended, as it were, that something like a single whole is produced. . . . [These feelings] have their origin in and depend upon the union and apparent fusion of the mind with the body." Descartes, "Sixth Meditation," 134–35; see also 137.

a condensation, an illuminated manuscript: **see angel touch**

a collaboration: **LIQUID** incorporated

A collaboration is a condensation. It causes dreams to form.
It causes liquid to form. It moistens, lubricates our thoughts,
moistens our lips and loosens them . . . .

A MYOPIA

site

scan

cornea

cornice

A looking too close at

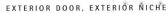

EXTERIOR DOOR, EXTERIOR NICHE

The locket door, an exterior door—you can lock it and it is a locket.
Enter the space of the door before you enter the space.
She is made of formed steel, has a footbrush threshold,
molded rubber gaskets and a ball-and-socket hinge.

VIEW THE PLAN

CLOSENESS DRAWING

site

see angel touch *is a project for an intervention in the cornice of angels of Louis Sullivan's Bayard Building, 65 Bleecker Street, New York, New York. She is the third angel from your right located by the dawning of light in our photograph of the elevation. The material site is the thickness of Sullivan's elevation, the seepage of its ornament. The Bayard's elevation exists as an apparently molten vertical mass—once literally molten terra-cotta— adhered to yet psychically distinct from the pure loft plan behind it. In the metaphoric gap between plan and elevation there is room for desire. The Bayard can be read as pure texture, and pure texture is the character of its site specificity. The range of the site is a sharing of closeness to Louie's angel—all the inches of its boundaries are equally near her. (The figure of the semicircle allows the sharing, but the angel has thickness so the boundary is a range, not an edge.) Square footage is determined by rumor and innuendo, not permit. Word of mouth tells us that one percent expansion of an existing building can slip by in New York City. The desire zone thus creates a thirteenth floor, a superstitious space . . . .*

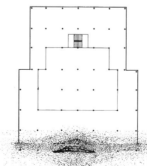

THICKNESS DRAWING

HORIZONTAL CUTS ARE IMAGINED THROUGH HOT SPOTS ON THE
ANGEL'S BODY:

EYES MOUTH BREASTS WINGS STOMACH SEX KNEES

TO CUT THROUGH AND TO REPRESENT ORNAMENT AS FROZEN IS AN
IMPOSSIBILITY. THE ORNAMENT CHANGES INFINITELY AS IF IN
MOTION.

THE CUTS ARE THEREFORE GIVEN IMAGE BY THE CAPTURE OF LIGHT,
BY PHOTOGRAPHING THE REFLECTED LIGHT OF MIRRORED MYLAR.
THE LIQUIDY IMAGE OF REFLECTED LIGHT UNDERSTANDS THE
IMPOSSIBILITY OF A CUT THROUGH LOUIE'S LAVISH TEXTURE.

THE SECTION CANNOT CONTAIN IN THIS CASE. AS SOON AS LIQUID
SPACE IS CUT, IT IS NO LONGER MERELY MATERIAL. IT LOSES ITS
DIMENSION AS THICKNESS, IT WIDENS AND BECOMES AN IMAGE.

THE BOUNDARIES BETWEEN INTERIOR AND EXTERIOR ARE
PROMISCUOUS.

ANGEL LOCATED BY THE DAWNING OF LIGHT ON LOUIE'S BAYARD BUILDING

FLORESCENCE
a motive of ornament

FLUORESCENT LIGHT
a leitmotif of architecture

Consider the qualities of this ubiquitous ornamentation of architecture's built space:

1. Radiation from fluorescent tubes weakens muscle strength (of test subjects and test administrators).

2. When full spectrum bulbs and radiation shields were used against fluorescent lights, hyperactive children quieted down, overcame learning disabilities, and developed one-third fewer cavities.

3. All AC lights have a flicker. This can't be seen with incandescents. Because of the "decay time" of fluorescents, they always cause a stroboscopic effect. Lead lags are introduced to prevent the recognition of the constant flicker, but it is nonetheless always there. The flicker can induce seizures in those who suffer from epilepsy.

4. Full spectrum fluorescent light counteracts bilirubinemia in infants. This means it is also affecting others' blood counts.

5. By manipulating the balance of color in fluorescent light the following conditions are affected:

The sex of pumpkin blossoms

The sex of guppies

The sex of chinchillas

Calcium deposits in heart tissue, and tumor development in humans

Irritability
Aggression
Cannibalism

SOURCES

Kuller, Rikard, *Non Visual Effects of Light and Color* (Swedish Council for Building Research, 1981).

Nuckolls, J. L., *Interior Lighting for Environmental Designers* (New York: John Wiley and Sons, Inc., 1983).

Ott, John, Light, *Radiation and You* (Greenwich, Ct.: The Devin-Adair Company, 1982).

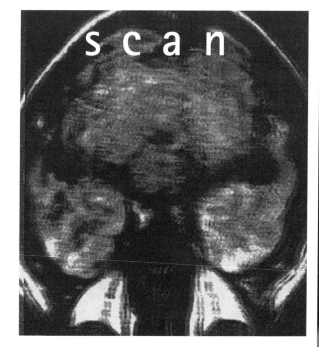

s c a n

CAT SCAN OF THE HUMAN BRAIN AT EYE LEVEL

The scan is a horizontal section cut through the brain at eye level. The cut is made by illuminating brain fluid. The scan cuts through matter and reveals the image of an angel. The figure of the angel appears to be female.

In see angel touch *details of material present themselves as image. Here the drawings are the primary objects having thicknesses no greater than the paper on which they are drawn. These drawings on translucent mylar are also reflective. They attempt to return the gaze and delay imagined passage to the passages we build.*

BODY BRUSH, INTERIOR DOOR
The brush is an interior door.
She is located at an entry
to an intimate space.
She brushes your
body as you enter.
She changes you.
MOLDED RUBBER,
SILICONE,
BOAR'S HAIR BRUSH
VIEW THE PLAN.

The details look too closely at architecture and prevent recognition of a whole. This operation refuses the strict and essential lines of schematic thought, which contain and limit, refuses the blind violence of parti, which presupposes all thought. Containment is an impossibility within the desire *zone where seepage is promiscuous. Our myopia gives priority to tactility and sensuality. Myopia is a looking too close at. It's biased, can't be objective; it's attached not detached, involved, emotional, intimate. Myopia's intimacy permits play, and the price we pay is merely the delay in the recognition of a plan. Without plan the architecture of* see angel touch *is insecure. Its details are therefore located at points of vulnerability and instability.*

EXPANSION JOINT, WINDOW/DOOR
She anticipates unequal and unstable
conditions and allows for visual passage.
MOLDED RUBBER, NEOPRENE SHEET,
CAST ALUMINUM
VIEW THE PLAN.

MANET'S OLYMPIA

The influence of photography has been seen here—less perhaps of photomontage (already frequent in the 1850's, with its awkward qualities and disconnected lighting effects) than of the semi-porn photo-"academics," "artistic poses"—which becomes widespread in these same years, and available to painters and collectors. Gerald Neddham considers the "pornographic" documents of the period (at which people peered in the stereoscope) as an important source for Olympia. He mentions a number of contemporaneous pictures that combine a setting borrowed from painting (that of the odalisque) and a less than ideal nude who stares boldly at the spectator. "By emphasizing the angularity of the human body," writes Neddham, "[Manet] knew that he could give Olympia that immediacy and reality that so startled the people who saw it." The bulge of the kneecap; (criticized by classical painters, as by Gerome and the eclectics), the silhouetting, the steady lighting, the haunting stare of the "bestial Vestal" (Valéry) can be said to have been transposed from photography. Victorine would appear to be all the more shocking in that she forms a blot on a background that rejects her, just as a reclining, unclothed model forms a strange

(The transparent membrane of the outer coat of the eyeball.) The elevation is tenuously located between an intimate interior and a public exterior. This political zone is complicated by our client. You know who she is. Jean Clay wonders if she is a painting of a

pornographic photograph. Her modesty is tongue-in-cheek. Olympia gazes from her bed. Is she gazing at a reflection of herself? Is she an image reflected? Olympia is an inhabitant of promiscous space, promiscous art.

She inhabits the cornice, a zone of privilege where excess is permissible. The cornice, a vertical seepage of the liquid-like elevation, may extend past the allowable building height and slip past those who enforce it. The cornice is a zone of elaborationand decoration.

cornea

UNDULATING WALL, WEEPING
SECTION. SECTION DRAWING

The section exposes its need to weep. It is sheathed outside with iridescent plastic shingles, inside with chamois to ripple with vibration.

Sighted next to the third angel from your right on the cornice of angels, under the angel's wing, is a window. The window provides a view out and a view of itself. She acts as an object and a frame, an eye that sees and an eye that is gazed at.

Because she is located in a fluctuating zone, the window is transformable and unstable. She is not passive. She presents herself as an object. Objectified, she allows light in, reflects images, allows the gaze out and in, and partitions the interior and exterior space. She is composed of multiple layers. She attempts to hold back the seepage of the ornamented wall. She acts as a baroque niche.

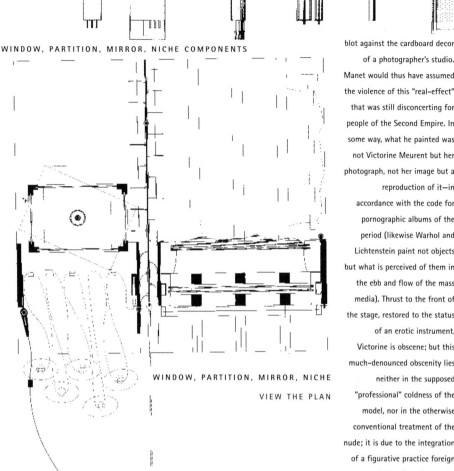

WINDOW, PARTITION, MIRROR, NICHE COMPONENTS

WINDOW, PARTITION, MIRROR, NICHE

VIEW THE PLAN

blot against the cardboard decor of a photographer's studio. Manet would thus have assumed the violence of this "real-effect" that was still disconcerting for people of the Second Empire. In some way, what he painted was not Victorine Meurent but her photograph, not her image but a reproduction of it—in accordance with the code for pornographic albums of the period (likewise Warhol and Lichtenstein paint not objects but what is perceived of them in the ebb and flow of the mass media). Thrust to the front of the stage, restored to the status of an erotic instrument, Victorine is obscene; but this much-denounced obscenity lies neither in the supposed "professional" coldness of the model, nor in the otherwise conventional treatment of the nude; it is due to the integration of a figurative practice foreign to painting. The photograph contaminates the painted image—accelerating here again what Walter Benjamin called the decline of the Aura. The condensation of various paintings would be completed by another synthesis: between two dissimilar modes of figurative representation. (Jean Clay, "Ointments, Makeup, Pollen," *October* no.27 (Winter 1983), 3–44 .

The window is the eye to the world in s e e a n g e l t o u c h . *Because the plan of the window is cut through the unstable terra-cotta wall, the window is complex, it's many things. Within a metal frame attached to a block is found a system of operating frame windows. In front of a casement sash, there is a double-hung sash. In front of the double-hung sash, there is a set screen. This system can be closed by a metal shutter, shown here in the open position. It is stored outside. Adjacent, there is a brass and glass box window, which can be draped by a curtain which when unfurled becomes a rolling partition. The components are inventoried in the illumination above.*

EXPANSION JOINT, WINDOW

The plan is designed for instability, and we build in its movement. The Undulating Wall is made as a light airplane framing structure attached to columns which allow play. The collar is bigger than the column.

SECTION CUT THROUGH
ANGEL'S MOUTH

cornice

Although the site of **see angel touch** is located literally in the cornice of angels, the nature of that place remains unfamiliar and unpredictable. What is behind the cornice? Where is the roof? The cornice prevents recognition of the plan condition behind it. That space is indeterminate and superstitious. Superstition inhibited Louis the Master; for the first time (the only time) Louie worked in New York City. He proposed a lean structure which, though tested in the Gage Group in Buffalo, failed to make the New York City engineers feel secure. Though the technology of the frame was feasible, Louie beefed up the structural system. In the cornice excess is permitted, in the structure excess is required. The steel frame thus secretly behaves as ornament. Ornament is not merely applied. Structural and ornamental properties become indistinguishable. The site and the project flicker between the two, presenting image and material superimposed. Function becomes most complex.

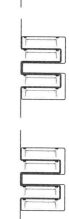

There is an incident of furnishing in the unstable space behind the third angel from your right in the cornice of angels in Louis Sullivan's Bayard Building. It is designed for the application of make-up and the making up of architecture. Program is superimposed throughout the desire zone. The space and the objects are complicated. The table is composed of one unit which is then repeated, bent, and flipped to make its "fraternal" twin. One unit supports a surface on which to draw, the other supports a surface that reveals what one has drawn, a reflective surface. Actually, two surfaces exist to draw upon: one vertical and one horizontal. The vertical surface is the face. The face aligns with the reflective surface. The horizontal surface is the table or the paper that lies upon the table's surface. The table exists in section only. Its section is its elevation, its image. (Section is an impossible view, it is always merely image, always something revealed.) This image holds storage drawers. The drawers are for the drawers who apply and produce at the table. The storage drawers are transparent, presenting their contents as image as well. The section is reflective of its occupation—literally (it is mirrored). The table is structurally dependent upon the wall to which it attaches and upon its monstrous legs, which are derived from the angel wing. The table is the sight of images created and images reflected.

MAKE-UP DRAFTING TABLE ELEMENT, FRATERNAL TWINS

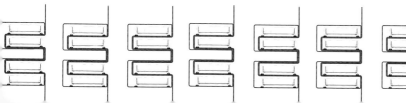

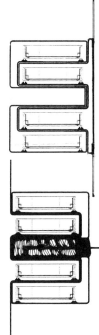

THE MAKE-UP DRAFTING TABLE:

Designed for the application of make-up and the making up of architecture. Bent aluminum, clear plastic drawers, rubber gasket, mirror, cast plastic legs.

CHAIR:

Clear molded plastic, hammered iron and stainless steel legs.

SECTION, ELEVATION

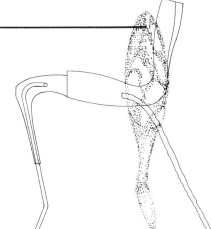

Mere

Mere is not a pejorative. It means famous, glorious, and beautiful. Mere tenuously borders see angel touch *without limiting it. Mere fluctuates and decorates along with the unstable facade and zone.*

La Mère

Mother. Not father. Not master.

Sea

La mer is also the sea. The sea has waves. The sea is liquid. The sea fluctuates and seeps. A liquid see.

See

site, scan, cornea, cornice

Angelfish

(Squatina squatina)

AMY LANDESBERG AND LISA QUATRALE, 1991 AND 1996

FOR MYRIAM BELLAZOUG

Project Manual for the Glass House

CHRISTINE S. E. MAGAR

WRITING SUPPLEMENTS BUILDING

One year after construction was completed on the Glass House, Philip Johnson wrote an article "House at New Canaan, Connecticut" for the British journal *Architecture Review* (September 1950). In this article Johnson discusses his conception of the house[BUILDING] as a "skin and bones" building whose typology originated with Mies van der Rohe, and describes the house as "frankly derivative," part of a succession of famous buildings.

The article is a ruse: an artifice produced by a man, a riddle giving clues about what the Glass House means, a stratagem of reinforcing the importance of the Glass House while disguising Johnson's own agenda of claiming the achievement of ideals at which others have failed. Seen in retrospect, what Johnson offered was a written substitute for his building.

The magazine article[WRITING] supplements the Glass House and exposes the building as a poor communicator. It operates alongside the Glass House, supplying it with facts, dates, anecdotes, and so forth about which the building is silent. While the Glass House appears to be autonomous, standing alone in New Canaan without addenda, the magazine article sits—simultaneously and independently—on innumerable book shelves. Most readers of this article have probably never visited New Canaan, and so, for them, the article is not only about the Glass House—Johnson's magazine article is the Glass House.

The article is organized in two parts, historical and autobiographical, and is composed of twenty-two footnotes, each comprised of an image and a commentary. The first part (footnotes 1-10) is intended to reveal sources from which the building is derived. Rather than arrange these consecutively ordered notes in chronological sequence, Johnson presents his examples in a spatial hierarchy. This hierarchy begins with the macroscale of site and ends with the microscale of detail. The second part of the article (footnotes 11-22) opens with two floor plans followed by a series of photo illustrations of the building—a kind of photo essay—pictorially describing the building with vignettes. The following five photographs (13-17) are views of the building precinct in the context of the site. The final five photographs (18-22) are views of the interior of the Glass House.

The historical sources, revealing the building as derivative, operate as apologetics and disclaimers. On one hand, Johnson[ARCHITECT] claims that Mies is the main source of inspiration for his house and repeatedly confesses his debt to Mies. Johnson includes in his article the following: "the arrangement . . . is influenced by Mies' theory of organizing buildings"; "the idea of the Glass house comes from Mies van der Rohe . . . My debt is therefore clear"; "details of the house are adapted from Mies' work"; "the plan of the house is Miesian"; "the guest house was derived from Mies' designs"; "a direct Miesian aim"; and "Mies van der Rohe has not only influenced the concept of the house. He has designed all of the furniture." On the other hand, Johnson points to historical figures such as Count Pückler of Muskau, Le Corbusier, Theo van Doesburg, Auguste Choisy, Karl Friedrich Schinkel, Emil Kaufmann, Claude Nicholas Ledoux, and Kasimir Malevich, from whose work he claims the house is also derived. A close look reveals that many of these sources appear to be at best incidental, implying that Johnson belongs to a succession of architects—Schinkel, then Mies, then Johnson. At worst, these sources are provisional, reinforcing Johnson's debt to Mies and exposing Johnson's guilty conscience.

This project manual is an addendum to Johnson's magazine article. It is part of the succession of references moving backward to Johnson's article to the Glass House to the Farnsworth House and so on, ad infinitum. From his twenty-two footnotes, I have interpreted ten of his wishes for the Glass House and received ten lessons on Mies's architecture. From these wishes and lessons, I have produced a series of corrections to the Glass House with the intention of satisfying Johnson's wish for a Miesian House.

I have also added to his article by constructing my own series of objects and images that modify his footnotes by inserting into the Glass House plan what is missing from or veiled by Johnson's writings. These additions were originally displayed as a large-scale installation at the Yale School of Architecture; the images scattered throughout this project were a part of this installation. My corrections not only "fix" Johnson's formal deviations from Mies's standards, but they also compensate for a symbolic lack of the fleshy female in the skin and bones building—a lack obscured by the presence fo an inert papier-mâche sculpture of two females. This lack is made more present in Johnson's own act of writing, shich is itself an attempt at compensation.

FOOTNOTE 1. SIMULATION OF A WISH: ASYMMETRICAL APPROACH

Describing the "approach to the house through meadow and copse," Johnson begins his series of twenty-two footnotes to the Glass House with the name of his "actual model" (but with the absence of its image). This is the only citation where Johnson's precedent is not illustrated. He compensates for this absence by citing four other precedents for building approach in his first five footnotes: Corbusier's off-axis foot path, Mies's asymmetrical grouping of buildings, the oblique approach to the Parthenon, and finally Schinkel's dead-level approach. However, Johnson's wish for the approach "through meadow and copse" is still not satisfied, even with these added precedents. Why is the image of his "actual model" absent?

Sigmund Freud, in the case of the Wolfman, offers a method of wish interpretation. He suggests that the method of symbolic substitution successfully diverts the Wolfman from his real concern. Similarly, Johnson's symbolic representation of the Glass House (the magazine article) is a diversion and a substitution for his real wish: that the Glass House were the Farnsworth House.

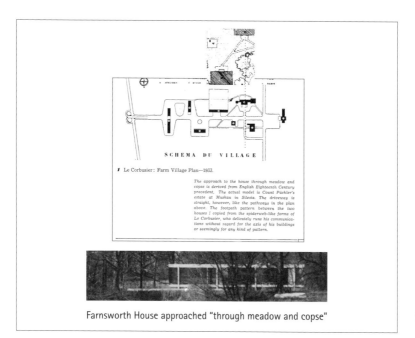

Farnsworth House approached "through meadow and copse"   1

WISH 1

The absence of the illustration of Count Pückler's estate, Muskau Park, implies an unsatisfied wish. Johnson wishes that the approach to the Glass House were like that of the Farnsworth House, "through meadow and copse."

FOOTNOTE 2. REPETITION OF THE SAME: ASYMMETRICAL ARRANGEMENT

In his monograph on Mies, Johnson includes two versions of his site plan for IIT (Philip Johnson, *Mies van der Rohe* [New York: Museum of Modern Art, 1947], 134, 137). Johnson calls one the "ideal" version (illustrated below). The other is the actual plan implemented on the IIT campus. In the monograph, he states that both versions exhibit "buildings . . . grouped around a central plaza in such a way that they created a continuous interchange of open and closed spaces. This interwoven effect is achieved by the simple but highly original device of sliding adjacent units past one another rather than placing them side by side" (n131). In his magazine article, Johnson only points to Mies's ideal site plan.

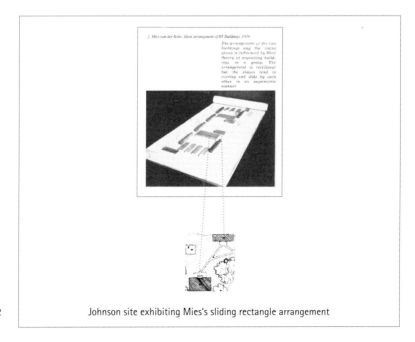

2   Johnson site exhibiting Mies's sliding rectangle arrangement

Why does he illustrate Mies's ideal, rather than built, scheme if both show the arrangement of sliding rectangles?

WISH 2

In the absence of a realized Miesian ideal is the presence of Johnson's wish to successfully execute Mies's ideal.

FOOTNOTE 3. DEFERRAL OF ORIGINS: PARTITIONS IN A BUILDING / BUILDINGS ON A SITE

The previous footnote sets the stage for footnote 3. Here, Johnson footnotes the previous reference to Mies's asymmetrical arrangement of sliding rectangles with Van Doesburg's drawing. Johnson's footnote of a footnote offers a succession of sources starting with the Glass House and working backwards from Mies to Van Doesburg and finally to Piet Mondrian. This succession of references exposes a deferral of origins and suggests that Johnson's theory of building arrangement was not inspired by Mies, nor by Van Doesburg, but by Mondrian. Thus, Johnson succeeds in deflecting his own guilt for being derivative by the logic that everyone is derivative, including Mies.

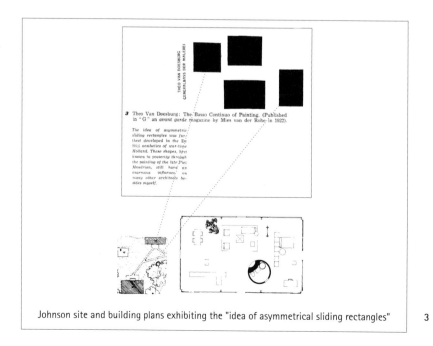

Johnson site and building plans exhibiting the "idea of asymmetrical sliding rectangles"   3

WISH 3

In the absence of an actual origin is the presence of Johnson's wish to deflect his own guilt for deriving the Glass House from the Farnsworth House.

FOOTNOTE 4. FIRST SUBSTITUTION: AMERICAN ACROPOLIS

In this fourth footnote, Johnson continues his discussion about building approach by citing the French historian Auguste Choisy. According to Choisy, buildings at the Acropolis are as a rule approached and viewed off-axis. This oblique angle arrests the visitor's gaze. The exception to this rule is given to the prominent buildings: the Propylaea and the Parthenon. Contradicting Choisy's analysis, Johnson suggests that all buildings at the Acropolis are approached obliquely. He then proceeds to carry out a guided tour through his own site, referring in parenthesis to the Propylaea when the brick house is encountered and the Athene Promachos when the statue group is encountered. These additions are substitutions. However, when the reader encounters the Glass House on the guided tour, Johnson leaves out the obvious substitution: the Parthenon. Following Johnson's previous substitutions, the Glass House

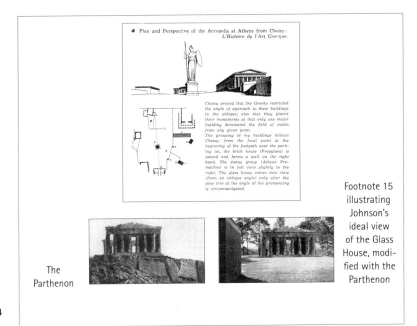

4 Plan and Perspective of the Acropolis at Athens from Choisy: *L'Histoire de l'Art Grecque.*

Choisy proved that the Greeks restricted the angle of approach to their buildings to the oblique; also that they placed their monuments so that only one major building dominated the field of vision from any given point. The grouping of my buildings follows Choisy: from the focal point at the beginning of the footpath near the parking lot, the brick house (Propylaea) is passed and forms a wall on the right hand. The statue group (Athene Promachos) is in full view slightly to the right. The glass house comes into view (from an oblique angle) only after the pine tree at the angle of the promontory is circumnavigated.

The Parthenon

Footnote 15 illustrating Johnson's ideal view of the Glass House, modified with the Parthenon

should, by analogy, be replaced by the Parthenon. The message is obvious: Johnson's House at New Canaan, Connecticut, is the American Acropolis.

WISH 4

In Johnson's confusion over Choisy's rules of approach and in the absence of the parenthetical Parthenon, Johnson makes present a wished-for substitution: The Glass House is the American Parthenon.

FOOTNOTE 5. THE POWER OF RHETORIC: WORD AND IMAGE

This footnote and the next are references to a clubhouse and site composition designed by Schinkel. In footnote 5, Johnson observes an analogy between his own site composition and Schinkel's: "Like his [Schinkel's] Casino [clubhouse] my house is approached on dead-level and, like his, faces its principal (rear) facade toward a sharp bluff." He illustrates this with a photograph of an axial approach to the clubhouse similar to the approach to the Parthenon. By analogy, Johnson suggests that the Glass House should also be approached on axis. However, as discussed in footnote 1, one approaches the Glass House from an oblique angle, on

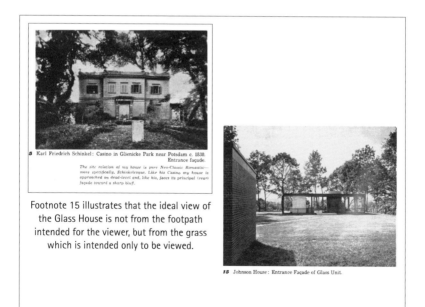

5 Karl Friedrich Schinkel: Casino in Glienicke Park near Potsdam c. 1830. Entrance façade.
The site relation of my house is pure Neo-Classic Romantic—more specifically, Schinkelesque. Like his Casino my house is approached on dead-level and, like his, faces its principal (rear) façade toward a sharp bluff.

Footnote 15 illustrates that the ideal view of the Glass House is not from the footpath intended for the viewer, but from the grass which is intended only to be viewed.

15 Johnson House: Entrance Façade of Glass Unit.

5

a footpath "though meadow and copse." Johnson conceals this oblique view by denying the reader a photograph of the Glass House from the point of view that the footpath offers. What he does offer is an ideal on-axis view (see my discussion on footnote 15).

WISH 5

The presence of the contradiction between what is written and what is illustrated exposes Johnson's own confusion about what he wants, and demonstrates the power of rhetoric.

FOOTNOTE 6. SECOND SUBSTITUTION: CLUBHOUSE PROGRAM

Johnson's site does not resemble any of the descriptions in this footnote. It is not a regular site. There is no "sharp bluff" or "cliff edge" or "shelves" or "hill top" on his site. Most importantly, it does not match the site of Schinkel's Casino, which does sit on a sharp bluff or cliff edge which descends abruptly into a body of water. The site of the Glass House starts with a gentle slope that begins at the crest of a hill and descends with an increasingly steep slope into a small valley where Johnson later dug a pond. The Glass House is situated with the Guest

16 Johnson House: Entrance Façade of Brick Unit.
The guest house with central door and severely axial plan is jointly descended from the Baroque and from designs by Mies. (See 12.)

Schinkel's drawing of his Casino showing the "sharp bluff"
or "cliff edge" with a body of water below

House and the Sculpture Group midway between the crest and valley on a level plateau. The question is: Why did Johnson include the Schinkel Casino as part of his repertoire of precedents?

WISH 6

In the absence of an actual site relation to Schinkel's Casino, with its principle facade and its on-axis approach, is the presence of a program substitution: The Glass House is a clubhouse.

FOOTNOTE 7. VOLUME VERSUS MASS

Johnson suggests in this footnote that, like the forms and compositions of Ledoux, the Glass House is comprised of "absolute forms" whose shapes and distinction are motivated by function. Elsewhere, however, Johnson states that "architecture is surely not the design of space, certainly not the massing or organizing of volumes. These are ancillary to the main point which is the organization of procession. Architecture exists only in time" (Philip Johnson, "Whence and Whither: The Processional Element in Architecture," *Perspecta* 9/10 [1965]). Even though Johnson wishes to follow Ledoux, he favors the processional over the play of mass

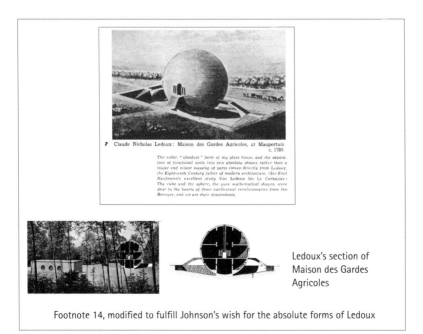

7   Claude Nicholas Ledoux: Maison des Gardes Agricoles, at Maupertuis
c. 1780.

The cubic, "absolute" form of my glass house, and the separation of functional units into two absolute shapes rather than a major and minor massing of parts comes directly from Ledoux, the Eighteenth Century father of modern architecture. (See Emil Kaufmann's excellent study Von Ledoux bis Le Corbusier.) The cube and the sphere, the pure mathematical shapes, were dear to the hearts of those intellectual revolutionaries from the Baroque, and we are their descendants.

Ledoux's section of Maison des Gardes Agricoles

Footnote 14, modified to fulfill Johnson's wish for the absolute forms of Ledoux   7

and volume. Emil Kaufmann, writing about Ledoux's meditations of mass and volume exemplified by his sphere house and cube garden, sees Ledoux's aspirations carried out in America (Emil Kaufmann, *Three Visionary Architects: Boullée, Ledoux, Lequeu* [New York: Princeton Press, 1951], 492). Unlike Johnson, Mies draws distinction between mass and volume. In the Farnsworth House he defines the volume by opaque horizontal planes and the mass by vertical transparent planes. (See my discussion on footnote 8.)

WISH 7
The absence of both absolute forms and the distinction between form and mass exposes Johnson's confusion over these formal characteristics, which Mies successfully employs in the Farnsworth House.

FOOTNOTE 8. REPETITION OF THE SAME: MIESIAN DEVIATIONS
In this footnote, Johnson cites the Farnsworth House as his true precedent. However, the following list points out the differences between the Glass and Farnsworth Houses:

- APPROACH: Where Mies's approach to the Farnsworth House is through copse and meadow, Johnson's is a confused assemblage of asymmetrical and axial approaches.
- MASS & VOLUME: Where Mies's volume is described by the Farnsworth roof and floor planes and his mass is described by its glass walls, Johnson blurs the distinction between mass and volume, and between horizontal and vertical planes, by his confused use of materials. For example, both his floor and cylinder core are brick, collapsing their formal distinction as separate programmed elements.
- COLUMNS: Where Mies's columns are clearly distinguished from other elements, Johnson's columns cut into both the vertical and horizontal planes.
- DETAILS: Where Mies's details reinforce the distinction between the elements, Johnson's reinforce their interdependency. Consider the roof details of both houses. In the Glass House, the outside face of the fascia is

lined up with the outside faces of the floor and the columns. The glass skin is outside of the primary zone of the building, while everything else is within this zone. Johnson's fascia sits on the column as if to stop the column from rising, confusing its function of completing the roof. The distinction between elements is blurred. In the Farnsworth, the outside of the fascia lines up with the outside face of the floor and the inside face of the columns. The columns are outside and the glass is inside.

The manner in which Mies connects the elements reinforces both their completeness as units and their independence from the other elements. His roof sits on top of the fascia but it goes horizontally beyond it into the zone of the column. At the same time, the column is also aligned with the glass and fascia. Its indifference to the roof is expressed by its termination well beneath the roof at some arbitrary position on the fascia.

WISH 8

The presence of Johnson's debt to Mies for the idea of glass exposes his wish to be part of Mies's lineage, despite innumerable deviations from it.

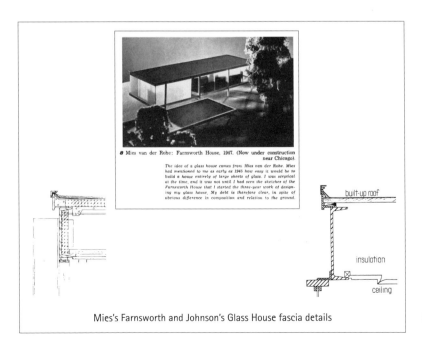

8 Mies van der Rohe: Farnsworth House, 1947. (Now under construction near Chicago).

The idea of a glass house comes from Mies van der Rohe. Mies had mentioned to me as early as 1945 how easy it would be to build a house entirely of large sheets of glass. I was sceptical at the time, and it was not until I had seen the sketches of the Farnsworth House that I started the three-year work of designing my glass house. My debt is therefore clear, in spite of obvious difference in composition and relation to the ground.

built-up roof

insulation

ceiling

Mies's Farnsworth and Johnson's Glass House fascia details   8

FOOTNOTE 9. REPETITION OF THE SAME: MIESIAN PERVERSIONS

This footnote is presented as if it refers to Johnson's corner detail. In fact, the detail is derived from an unrealized building designed by Mies. The title to this footnote should read: "Mies Van der Rohe, Administration and Library Building, IIT, section at corner perverted." Although this building was never executed, it was considered by Mies the ideal in the art of building (*baukunst*) because it was like Gothic construction, revealing structure from both the interior and exterior. The I-beam section exhibits the axial (directional) diagram for his directional buildings such as the Farnsworth House. A biaxial or nondirectional diagram appears in Mies's cruciform column, Ledoux's House, or in the Parthenon. Johnson borrowed the axial detail even though it was unsuited for his corner condition. According to the Mies historian Ludwig Hilberseimer, Mies always connected his walls to I-beam columns symmetrically. Johnson connected his Glass House walls to his I-beam columns asymmetrically and consequently perverted Mies's detail. Johnson used a column and detail intended for a directional building when he wished for a nondirectional building like the Parthenon or Ledoux's Maison des Gardes Agricoles. Interestingly, in an interview, Mies commented on Johnson's misuse of his details, stating, "He did come around here from time to

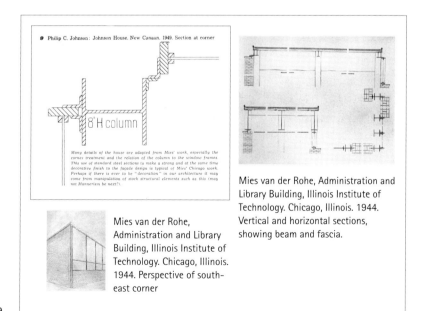

9 Philip C. Johnson: Johnson House. New Canaan. 1949. Section at corner

8"H column

Many details of the house are adapted from Mies' work, especially the corner treatment and the relation of the column to the window frames. This use of standard steel sections to make a strong and at the same time decorative finish to the façade design is typical of Mies' Chicago work. Perhaps if there is ever to be "decoration" in our architecture it may come from manipulation of stock structural elements such as this (may not Mannerism be next?).

Mies van der Rohe, Administration and Library Building, Illinois Institute of Technology. Chicago, Illinois. 1944. Perspective of southeast corner

Mies van der Rohe, Administration and Library Building, Illinois Institute of Technology. Chicago, Illinois. 1944. Vertical and horizontal sections, showing beam and fascia.

time. He would snoop through all the details and copy them. The mistakes he made in the details occurred because he hadn't worked them through, but just sniffed around them" (Franz Schulze, *Mies van der Rohe: A Critical Biography* [Chicago: University of Chicago Press, 1985], 283).

WISH 9

Johnson wishes to execute simultaneously an ideal Miesian building (based on the directional I-beam section) and a symmetrical Miesian detail (based on the non-directional cruciform section), an awkward union that Mies never intended to produce. Johnson's building is biaxial, and therefore is unsuited for details intended for a directional building.

FOOTNOTE 10. THE POWER OF WRITING IS IN ITS REWRITING

This footnote closes Johnson's historical survey with a reference to Kasimir Malevich. It is a drawing by Malevich that looks like a diagram for Johnson's Glass House floor plan. Johnson implies here that the Malevich drawing is of a filled-in circle asymmetrically placed in a rectangular field, when in fact the field is square. In his reproduction he

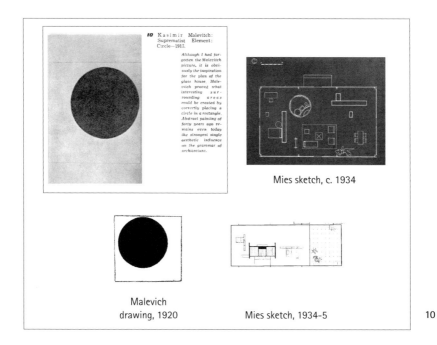

Mies sketch, c. 1934

Malevich
drawing, 1920   Mies sketch, 1934–5   10

obscures the actual boundary of the drawing to make it look more like the Glass House. This reframing reinforces Malevich as another precedent and perhaps deflates Mies as the "actual model" for the Glass House.

WISH 10

In the absence of an accurate reproduction of Malevich's drawing is the presence of Johnson's revision. In a similar way, Johnson presents a revised, reframed reproduction of the Glass House in the form of his magazine article.

The first ten footnotes in Johnson's article expose a number of Johnson's wishes which I have addressed in terms of substitutions and supplements.

JOHNSON:	I INTEND TO:
1. Wishes for an approach "through copse and meadow" like the Farnsworth House, but offers one on a footpath.	Substitute grass for footpath.
2. Wishes to execute Mies's unrealized ideal site plan, but produces its deviant.	Supplement the Glass House with the Miesian ideal.
3. Wishes to deflect his own guilt for his assumed debt to Mies.	Supplement Johnson's magazine article with the wishes and lessons offered in this project manual as absolution of his guilt.
4. Wishes the Glass House were the American Parthenon but produces a confused modern icon.	Substitute Johnson's oblique approach to the Glass House for an axial approach on grass.

5. Wishes for many meanings in written form in his article, suggesting that his building does not stand on its own.

Supplement Glass House with this project manual.

6. Wishes that his domestic program were a clubhouse, but has a glass house for a home.

Substitute club program for existing domestic program.

7. Wishes that, like the Farnsworth House, the Glass House would satisfy the mass and volume distinction, but instead confuses form and function.

Substitute private function for public function.

8. Wishes that the Glass House were the Farnsworth House but produces countless deviations from it.

Substitute Mies's design standards for Johnson's design standards. These will be offered in the next section of the project manual in the form of lessons.

9. Wishes to execute Mies's unrealized ideal building, but produces its deviant.

Supplement Johnson's detailing with Mies's detailing in the Administration and Library Building, IIT.

10. Wishes that his published article could reformat the Glass House as the executed Miesian ideal site and building.

Supplement Glass House with magazine article. Substitute this project manual for magazine article.

In the first part of the article Johnson reveals that, at best, he is in debt to a number of architects, and at worst, his Glass House aspires to be a Miesian temple. The second part of Johnson's article is very different in character from the first. Where the first part presents the Glass House in the context of historical precedents, the second part exhibits the Glass House in a format of exterior and interior photographs.

Johnson avoids autobiographical information with two exceptions. First, he includes a self-portrait in footnote 13 that shows him sitting at the writing table in his bedroom. Here he is present and yet concealed, since he only exposes his back. (In footnote 22, Johnson illustrates the same space, but he is altogether absent.) Second, he offers a personal anecdote in his reference to the brick cylinder and platform in the caption of footnote 17, clouding his own design process. In the other footnotes he diverts attention from himself onto Baroque and Miesian influences. He cites Mies's experiments on the play of reflections in glass, Mies's use of a sculpture as a necessary architectural foil, and Mies's furniture. He also suggests that his guest house, the placement of the Glass House entry, and the framed view of the landscape are derived from the Baroque and from Mies. Where in the first part Johnson supplements the Glass House with a series of preferred buildings, in the second section Johnson offers a series of diversions that form the real act of substitution. Johnson substitutes his own furniture for Mies's, his own quotations for Mies's, his own ideas about art and nature for Mies's. In the absence of a Miesian building, the presence of the perpetual deflection from himself and onto Mies amounts to a substitution.

In the following passages, I will point out how Johnson substitutes Mies for his own subjectivity by providing a series of lessons about Mies's architecture. Meanwhile, deficiencies in the Glass House are made apparent by means of Johnson's continual reflection of the Baroque. These deficiencies are compensated for by a series of corrections that I develop and intend to etch onto the glass of the house. These corrections are offered in this project manual with the intention of satisfying Johnson's wishes and putting into practice the lessons I learned about Mies's standards in architecture.

FOOTNOTE 11. TEN LESSONS ON MIES: ARCHITECTURAL PUNS:
CABINET/PARTITION THAT BINDS/DIVIDES SPACE

In 1947, before the designs for either house were finalized, the plans for the Farnsworth House and the Glass House looked strikingly similar. Below are reproductions of their early plans. Each shows a steel-and-glass rectangular volume, within which a rectangular mass is asymmetrically placed. In addition, two long, thin, rectangular bars—programmed as cabinet/partitions—are located around the mass. (Johnson provides the precedent for these "sliding rectangular bars" in footnotes 2 and 3.) One bar is placed parallel to one end of the mass, and the second bar is perpendicular to its other end. The form and composition of mass and bars separate the volume into more-or-less distinct rooms while maintaining a continuous flow of space. In the built version of the Farnsworth House, Mies achieves the quality of binding and dividing space with only the rectangular mass. The mass is carefully formed with extended planes that secure the kitchen/bath programs that they hold, and mark separate spaces for the living, sleeping, eating, and writing areas. Like Mies, Johnson marks separate spaces while maintaining a continuity. He keeps the bars that Mies discards and deviates from Mies's rectilinear mass with

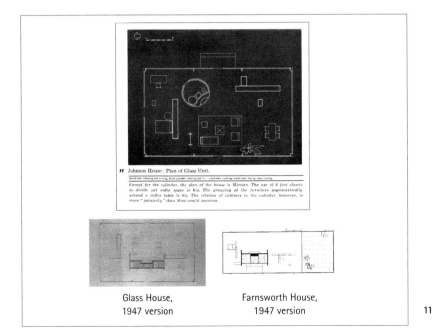

11 Johnson House: Plan of Glass Unit.

Glass House,	Farnsworth House,
1947 version	1947 version

a cylinder. His composition is clumsy and breaks the Miesian continuous flow.

LESSON 1

Mies uses an assembly of mass and planes as a means to bind heterogeneous spaces of difference and divide homogenous spaces of sameness, similar to a sewing seam that can bind two disparate pieces of fabric or divide homogenous pieces. Mies stitches space to bind heterogeneity and to divide homogeneity.

FOOTNOTE 12. TEN LESSONS ON MIES: ROUND WINDOW ADDS TO THE CONTINUOUS BRICK WALL

The difficulty in commenting on the next five footnotes is a result of Johnson's insistence on linking himself and Mies to the Baroque. In footnote 12, Johnson makes this link by describing the round window form in the brick unit (guest house) as both Miesian and Baroque. Verifying Johnson's link to Mies, the front facade of Mies's courtyard house at Ulrich does indeed utilize the circular aperture for the passage of views and light. Mies achieves a continuity that might be characterized as

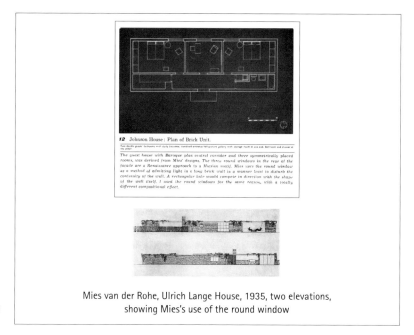

Mies van der Rohe, Ulrich Lange House, 1935, two elevations, showing Mies's use of the round window

Baroque with the circular window in the brick wall in two ways. First, the round shape does not compete with the rectilinear plane, but allows the brick to flow continuously around the window. In contrast, the square corners of a glass plane would abruptly stop the flow of brick. Second, the boundary between inside and out is maintained because the circle reads like a foreign object added through the wall plane (unlike a square window, which would read like a transparent plane competing with the opaque wall plane, diminishing the strength of the wall as boundary between inside and out). The architectural elements, rectilinear wall and round window, coexist by means of a connection that is similar to the way that a patch is added to the elbow of a sleeve.

LESSON 2

If Baroque demonstrates continuous flow reinforced by additions, then Mies's window is Baroque. Mies uses the round shape for windows, achieving the continuous flow of the wall plane and maintaining the boundary between interior and exterior. Like the round window that adds an additional view within a continuous membrane, appliqué stitched on cloth adds to a continuous piece of fabric.

FOOTNOTE 13. TEN LESSONS ON MIES: SURFACE
REFLECTIVITY CONFUSES ELEMENTS

In this footnote, Johnson refers to Mies's interest in the reflective characteristics of glass. In 1922, Mies published two skyscraper entries for a competition. He wrote a brief summary about his design process including his discovery of the inherent quality of reflectivity in glass: "My experiments with a glass model helped me along the way and I soon recognized that by employing glass, it is not an effect of light and shadow one wants to achieve but a rich interplay of light reflections," (Fritz Neumeyer, *The Artless Word*, trans. Mark Jarzombek [Cambridge: MIT Press, 1991], 240) Mies not only intended for glass walls to appear to be solid by means of reflection, obscuring the view of the interior; he also intended that the walls would appear to be moving. According to Heinrich Wölfflin, Baroque architects had similar intentions, wanting to produce the "impression of movement, attained when visual appearance supplants concrete reality." He writes, "The rococo liked wall-mirrors . . . [and] wished to discount the wall as concrete surface by what is apparently impalpable not-surface—the reflecting of glass" (Heinrich Wölfflin, *Principles of Art History* [New York: Dover, 1950], 66).

LESSON 3

Mies segregates architectural elements such as columns and horizontal and vertical planes, which Wölfflin characterizes as "definite, solid, and enduring." However, his surfaces are like Baroque wall-mirrors which create a visual appearance of "constant movement and change."

FOOTNOTE 14. TEN LESSONS ON MIES: BIAXIAL ENTRIES
PRODUCE STASIS WHERE MOVEMENT IS FORCED
BY A SEQUENCE OF AXIAL PLAY

In the written part of this footnote, Johnson continues to compare his building to Ledoux's (see my discussion on footnote 7) by mentioning

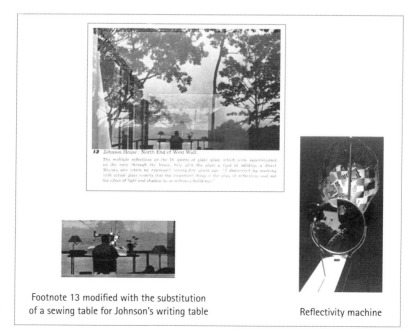

Footnote 13 modified with the substitution of a sewing table for Johnson's writing table

Reflectivity machine

the biaxial nature of the Glass House, and points again to the Baroque. Where Ledoux's two axes are identical, Johnson's differ in length. Johnson refers to them as major and minor axes and suggests that this deviation from Ledoux is Baroque. If the classical is symmetrical and the Baroque deviates from that in the pursuit of movement, then Johnson's distinction of axes follows in the Baroque tradition. However, the two axes are developed to confuse their difference in terms of their program. Johnson provides four entries with equal doors framed with similar steel and glass compositions. The Farnsworth House is also biaxial. However, its two axes are developed to distinguish them as different. There is only one entry to the Farnsworth House, and it forces movement around the house in a way that the Glass House never does. One approaches the Farnsworth from a long side where a few steps lead to the entry porch attached to one of its short sides. This procession forces the visitor to turn around a corner of the house and experience it in movement.

LESSON 4

Mies provides a play of oblique and axial sequences that produces the entry and experience of a space in movement.

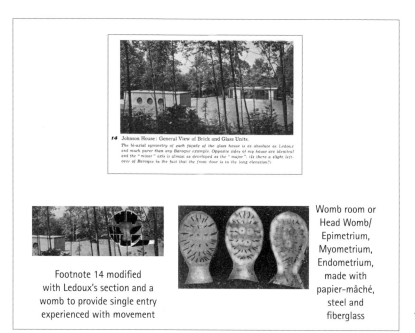

14 Johnson House: General View of Brick and Glass Units.
The bi-axial symmetry of each façade of the glass house is as absolute as Ledoux and much purer than any Baroque example. Opposite sides of my house are identical and the "minor" axis is almost as developed as the "major". (Is there a slight left-over of Baroque in the fact that the front door is in the long elevation?)

Footnote 14 modified with Ledoux's section and a womb to provide single entry experienced with movement

Womb room or Head Womb/ Epimetrium, Myometrium, Endometrium, made with papier-mâché, steel and fiberglass

14

FOOTNOTE 15. TEN LESSONS ON MIES: A FEMALE ABSENCE IS SUPPLEMENTED WITH A SCULPTURE

This footnote illustrates the ideal approach to the Glass House, the view indicated by Johnson in his discussion of the Acropolis in footnote 4, which, as discussed, is never seen from Johnson's footpath. While this footnote does not support the analogy, there is one way that the two structures are alike: Both the Parthenon and the Glass House contain the representation of a female. For Johnson, the Elie Nadelman sculpture is a figure intended to set off his building. (This is addressed in my discussion on footnote 19.) The Parthenon, on the other hand, houses the goddess Athena, represented by a sculpture that is no longer present. Similarly, the Farnsworth House was designed to house a woman. A new analogy can be made after presenting some of the history of the migration of the female presences at the Acropolis, which reveals a substitution of a representation of a goddess by the representation of a more abstract meaning of change and flux as structural support. In 451 B.C., the Erechtheum was executed as a substitute for the old temple of Athena. It housed the original statue and was located on the original site. In 500 B.C., the Parthenon was executed as a kind of addition to the old temple of Athena. Today, the porch of the Erechtheum, supported by caryatids,

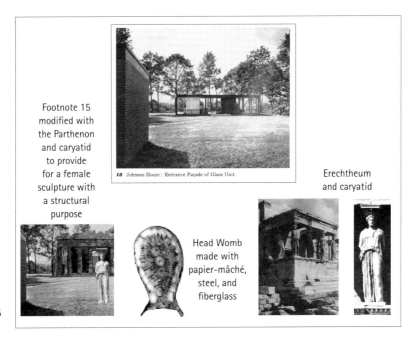

Footnote 15 modified with the Parthenon and caryatid to provide for a female sculpture with a structural purpose

15 Johnson House : Entrance Façade of Glass Unit.

Erechtheum and caryatid

Head Womb made with papier-mâché, steel, and fiberglass

is the only portion of this structure that remains on the original site and exhibits the only female presence in sculpture form at the Acropolis. In addition, the caryatid was originally a priestess of Artemis Caryatis, modeled on the moon priestess of Caryae who represented the cycle of life, death, and regeneration. Therefore, the sculpture of Athena was substituted by the column for regeneration at the Acropolis. By analogy, Johnson substitutes Mies's building for a woman with a building that houses a papier-mâché representation of the female.

LESSON 5

Mies's Farnsworth House has many similarities to the Parthenon in terms of color, its separation of columns from walls, its relationship to the ground, and its oblique approach with an axial entry. A difference is that the Farnsworth House was built for a woman and not a goddess.

FOOTNOTE 16. TEN LESSONS ON MIES: BAROQUE IN
THE FORM OF ORNAMENT

In this footnote, Johnson reiterates the guest house's connection to Mies and Baroque architecture. (Please see my discussion on footnote 12.)

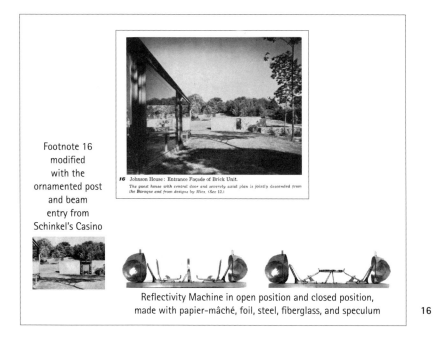

Footnote 16 modified with the ornamented post and beam entry from Schinkel's Casino

16 Johnson House: Entrance Façade of Brick Unit.
The guest house with central door and severely axial plan is jointly descended from the Baroque and from designs by Mies. (See 12.)

Reflectivity Machine in open position and closed position, made with papier-mâché, foil, steel, fiberglass, and speculum

16

Thus far, Johnson defines Miesian Baroque as having one or more of the following characteristics: "a severely axial plan," "a central door," "a central corridor with three symmetrically placed rooms," and a "round window." (These I have retermed as continuous flow, moving surfaces, and play of axis.) Interestingly, Johnson neglects to directly characterize the Baroque by its traditional association with ornamentation. Although he calls the metal pieces in a detail in Mies's Administration and Library Building decoration, he fails to link this to the Baroque. (Please see my discussion on footnote 9.) In this detail, Mies uses brick veneer as a device to conceal the differences in fascia and beam depths while still maintaining their distinct relationships of form and function.

LESSON 6
Mies's Baroque use of bound/divided space, continuous flow, constant movement and change, and play of obliqueness and axiality is complemented by his detailing, where he hides differences while exaggerating similarities.

17
Footnote 17 modified with the Farnsworth House and animated with the female sculptures Mies uses in his buildings

FOOTNOTE 17. TEN LESSONS ON MIES: PROCESS-DIRECTED
ARCHITECTURE

In this footnote, Johnson provides an insight into his own process for the generation of form that is contrary to Mies and confuses his earlier footnotes. He writes that his own memory "formed the main motif of the house," which is the brick cylinder and platform. However, in footnotes 7 and 10, he cites both Ledoux's and Malevich's work as the cylinder's precedents. Here, Johnson's form is determined by a preconceived image which is later justified with personal memories. In an article called "Regarding the New Volume" in *Die Form*, Mies offers an alternative view of process: "I am not addressing myself against form, only against form as goal. . . . We value not the result but the starting point of the form-giving process. This in particular reveals whether form was derived from life or for its own sake. This is why the form-giving process appears to me so important. Life is what matters. In its entire fullness, in its spiritual and concrete interconnection." Mies advocates a process-directed architecture whose origin is life, manifested in material and spiritual terms, as opposed to an art for art's sake.

LESSON 7

Where Mies understands form as process-directed, Johnson's goal-oriented process is encumbered by preconceptions that lead to deviations and perversions.

FOOTNOTE 18. TEN LESSONS ON MIES: A SKIN-AND-BONES
BUILDING IS DEFICIENT

This footnote not only exhibits Miesian furniture, it also exhibits two sculptures produced with papier-mâché—one by Elie Nadelman and the other by Alberto Giacometti. The small Giacometti represents a skinny, frail, bent nude man that blends in with the Miesian glass-and-leather "skin" and stainless-steel "bones" furniture. In contrast, the larger-than-life Nadelman sculpture of two clothed and heavyset women stand on a special pedestal in the Glass House and cannot be missed. Mies represents a similar distinction in his drawings. Below, in Mies's illustration of the Administration and Library Building, the figures look like the Giacometti sculpture; they are bent, thin, male silhouettes scratched in the paper. They almost disappear within the lines that represent the architecture. On the other hand, the second illustration of a museum for a small city presents figures that look like the Nadelman sculpture. They are bronzes of female nudes in full photographic color, montaged onto anemic, abstract, ink-lined perspectives. Their contrasting presence cannot be missed.

LESSON 8
Mies clothes his skin-and-bones paper architecture (drawings) with disappearing scratches of male figures and with shimmering, living photographs of bronze sculptures representing the female.

18   Mies's Administration and Library Building, IIT   Mies's Museum for a Small City

FOOTNOTE 19. TEN LESSONS ON MIES: A SUPPLEMENT COMPENSATES FOR THE DEFICIENCY AND PROVIDES A PLETHORA

In this footnote, Johnson identifies the nude female sculpture in the Barcelona Pavilion as a "foil"; in his monograph on Mies, he identifies the sculpture as a "decorative element." *Foil* is defined by Webster as "anything that serves by contrast of color or quality to adorn another thing or set it off to advantage." *Decoration*, as I discussed earlier, is ornament that reveals and conceals. We are instructed in the introduction of this article that the Glass House is a "skin and bones" building. In the monograph, Johnson writes about the Barcelona Pavilion that "the only decorative elements besides the richness of materials are two rectangular pools and a statue by Georg Kolbe, and these are inseparable components of the composition" (Philip Johnson, *Mies van der Rohe*, 58). The female sculpture not only serves and reinforces the building, it is necessary. It compensates for something that the building lacks.

LESSON 9

For Mies, the female sculpture is an inseparable contrasting component which serves to adorn the skin-and-bones building.

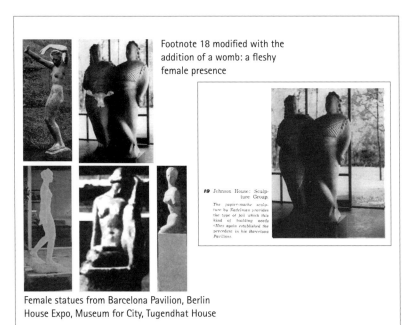

Footnote 18 modified with the addition of a womb: a fleshy female presence

Female statues from Barcelona Pavilion, Berlin House Expo, Museum for City, Tugendhat House

FOOTNOTE 20. TEN LESSONS ON MIES: BLURRY BOUNDARIES

In an interview, Mies addressed the relationship between the building and the landscape, as well as the frame that frames the view. He told Christian Norberg-Schulz that "nature, too, shall live its own life. We must beware not to disrupt it with the color of our houses and interior fittings. Yet we should attempt to bring home nature, houses, and human beings together into a higher unity. If you view nature through the glass walls of the Farnsworth House, it gains a more profound significance than if viewed from outside. This way more is said about nature—it becomes a part of a larger whole." (Christian Norberg-Schulz, "Ein Gespräch mit Mies van der Rohe," *Baukunst und Werkform* 11 [1958]: 615) Mies blurs the boundary between inside and outside, between dwelling and nature, in a variety of ways. He encloses nature by confusing building walls with site walls, such as in the courtyard houses. He blurs the boundary between inside and outside by extending roof planes and floor planes into the landscape beyond the enclosing wall, such as in the Barcelona Pavilion. He creates the appearance of having no enclosing walls by using full sheets of glass in place of walls in the Farnsworth House, where the columns become part of the grid of trees. The Tugendhat House is an extreme case where the glass walls drop from

20 Johnson House: Interior looking west.
The view of the valley, with its repoussoir of giant trees, is contrived with the aid of many Baroque landscapes. A view without a frame seems impossible after the Seventeenth Century.

Footnote 20 modified with a skeleton to reinforce
the skeleton nature of Mies's furniture and architecture

view into the basement leaving the interior entirely open to the exterior. Johnson describes it as having "a classic modern interior. . . . The feeling of endless, flowing space is increased by the two outer walls, composed entirely of glass, which command a view of the sloping garden and the city beyond. At the press of a button alternating panes of glass slide into the floor, further uniting interior and exterior. With window walls, the house became a frame for the landscape and the landscape entered the dwelling." (Philip Johnson, *Mies Van der Rohe*)

LESSON 10

The Miesian extension of wall planes, of roof planes, and of floor planes widens the boundary between inside and outside. The transparency of glass makes the view of the landscape perpetually present from the interior of a building. The boundary between dwelling and nature is either widened or transparent.

FOOTNOTE 21. TEN LESSONS ON MIES: A SKIN-AND-BONES PROGRAM

In the caption of footnote 21, Johnson writes, "The kitchen I reduced to a simple bar so that it would not close off space. I have no idea what prece-

21 Johnson House: Cooking Unit.
The kitchen I reduced to a simple bar so that it would not close off any space, I have no idea what precedent I followed on that.

21

dent I followed on that." Although Johnson claims not to be aware of the precedent for the kitchen/cabinet, the original floor plan of the Farnsworth House from 1947, illustrated and addressed in my discussion on Footnote 11, shows a precedent. More interesting is the inclusion of this view of the interior. Here he introduces us to the domestic program of the kitchen, and yet it looks like a bar. The person behind the counter appears ready to serve a cocktail and not a meal. This view is a reminder that Johnson's house appears to have a domestic program, but in actuality is more suited to the bachelor pad or clubhouse. (See my discussion on footnotes 5 and 6.)

FOOTNOTE 22. TEN LESSONS ON MIES: THE FINAL MASK

The photograph in footnote 22 is the same space viewed from the same direction as in the photo in footnote 13. In footnote 13, Johnson is visible from behind, seated at his writing desk, reading. However, in that view, Johnson is obscured by the reflections of nature on the glass that is between the camera and its subject. He also quotes a statement Mies made about the play of reflections. Johnson is not only obscured by the images of nature; he is also obscured by the words and authority of Mies

22

van der Rohe. In footnote 22, there is no Johnson, there is no quote, there is no glass with reflections. A book is on the nightstand next to the telephone and there are pandana screens pulled to shield the writing desk from the sun or from spectators. Similar props are present in the photograph of Johnson's apartment in New York—designed by Mies van der Rohe—included in the book *The International Style* (Henry-Russell Hitchcock, Jr. and Philip Johnson, *The International Style: Architecture Since 1922*, rev. and enl. [New York: W. W. Norton, 1966]). The writing desk and chair are present in all three photographs. These are Johnson's props that bear witness to Johnson's play of presence and/or absence. Where footnote 13 is symbolic of a connection between Mies's act of writing and Johnson's act of reading, footnote 22 is an allegory of Johnson's act of substitution. Instead of Mies's words, Johnson uses the pandana screens to obscure his own absence.

CORRECTIONS

Two design features in Johnson's Glass House motivate my research and analysis of his magazine article: the presence of the perverted corner detail and the larger-than-life papier-mâché sculpture of two females. These offer me the opportunity to correct the Glass House in terms of formal and meaningful (symbolic) architecture. Thus, the corrections not only "fix" Johnson's formal deviations from Mies's standards (by etching the "actual," "ideal" detail on the glass), but they also compensate for a symbolic lack that has been implied by the presence of the inert papier-mâché sculpture (by etching and foiling on the glass shimmering, living photographs of bronze sculptures representing the female). As a kind of thought experiment, I have produced the following list of corrections modifying the Glass House plans and elevations, to satisfy Johnson's wishes and to test my own understanding of Mies's standards for architecture. Although theoretical, they are feasible and could be applied in practice to Johnson's building, since they are sited within the steel frame, they are formed as ornament, they are executed by etching and foiling on the glass, and they are programmed by Johnson's own magazine article.

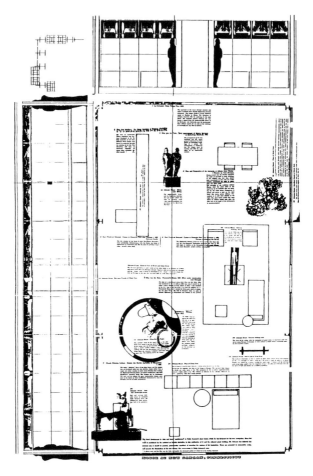

Christine S.E. Magar, corrections to the Glass House plan, elevations and plan

To start with, the actual function of the house is acknowledged as clubhouse (his wished-for *program*) not domestic. Next, lesson 11, where Mies *stitches space to bind heterogeneity and to divide homogeneity*, suggests that I sew the corrections to achieve the desired Miesian spatial relations. My translation of this is to etch Johnson's glass with a sewing needle, which reinforces his desire for the use of glass and steel as his *material and method of construction*. I then proceed step by step to correct Johnson's Glass House with the suggested wishes and Miesian lessons from his own magazine article.

Johnson's *approach and entry* sequence to the Glass House is corrected to provide *a play of oblique and axial sequences that produces the entry and experience of a space in movement*, like that of the Farnsworth House. The visitor walks toward the house, viewed as illustrated in footnote 15, on the grass (through copse and meadow). Because I have closed three of the four existing entries (including the one on view upon approach) and have thereby defined a new entry, the visitor must move to the left around the house, then right toward the short end of the house, reinforcing *constant movement and change*. Here the Nadelman sculpture of two papier-mâché women is in oblique view (like the Athene Promachos in the Acropolis where she is in oblique view from the Propylaea). This new entry is framed (symmetrically like the Propylaea) and supported by the caryatids formed by the Nadelman sculpture. In addition, on each of the four elevations, I have placed a small scratching machine that etches the glass with a needle. I have situated them by projecting the location of the sculpture's wombs onto the elevations, to clothe Johnson's skin-and-bones architecture with disappearing scratches like Mies's, and to animate the inert sculpture with movement, as Mies would.

The *volume/mass proportioning* and the biaxial elevations are corrected with a well-proportioned grid like that of the Farnsworth House. I have laid an even silvered grid in both vertical and horizontal directions over all four elevations to reinforce *reflectivity* and the *continuous flow* between inside and out, which I think the existing low mullions defeat. This gives me the opportunity to reinforce the difference between elevations (entry versus no entry) while acknowledging their similarities (continuous grid of silver lines) as in the Farnsworth House.

The *detailing* is corrected to give the Glass House the ideal structure which can be observed from both interior and exterior, like a Mies building. I have emulated the roof structure and corner brick veneer of the Administration and Library Building, discussed in footnote 9, by etching a band of ornament just beneath the roof and caryatids at the corners of the Glass House. The ornament etched on the short ends of the Glass House is deep, reflecting the deeper beam size. The ornament etched on the long ends is shallow, reflecting the shallower fascia depth. The difference in depth is concealed by the caryatids etched on the corners of the building (like Mies's use of brick veneer in the Administration and Library Building). These are intended to assist Johnson in having Mies's ideal building, which expresses the structure from both the interior and exterior as well as conceals the difference in beam and fascia depths.

Finally, although these corrections are framed by the formal wishes that Johnson has suggested in the magazine article, their symbolic content comes from the implied absence of a regenerating, continuously moving and changing female. The reflectivity machines that configure the image of the ornament, illustrated in footnotes 13, 14, 15, and 16, are, like a womb, programmed to be regenerating and formed of three layers of continuously fluctuating wall. These three layers are the epimetrium (skin-womb), the myometrium (muscle-womb), and the endometrium (fluctuating womb). The ornament is placed within the boundaries of the silvered grid, the entry, and the new fascia and beam depths.

Although my initial instinct in this project was to argue against Johnson's architecture for its impurity, I found it increasingly difficult to make that judgment because my standard for purity changed as I learned more about Mies's architecture. My preconception of his architecture and pure architecture was by definition a skin-and-bones—steel-and-glass—architecture devoid of ornament or the feminine. If this definition of a pure architecture is true, then it was undermined by the lessons I discovered in Johnson's magazine article. For Mies's pure, ideal architecture expressed structure from the interior and exterior. However, in a steel-and-glass building where the roof beams are deeper than the fascia due to different structural loading, the transparent corner exposes the difference in depths and appears formally unresolved. Mies uses non-structural brick veneer in the Administration and Library Building to conceal this depth difference. Consequently, the intention to maintain purity of form undermines the represented purity of structural function. (Please see the illustrations in my discussion on footnote 9.) In addition, after reviewing drawings and photographs of Mies's buildings, I discovered that many of his buildings house sculptures gendered as feminine. I interpreted this as Mies gendering the pure skin-and-bones buildings as male, and compensating for their inadequacy by adding female sculpture. His exclusion of the female gender from architectural form and his inclusion of her through sculpture, reflectivity, binding/dividing partitions, et cetera, reinforced for me the impurity of Mies's architecture. These unexpected discoveries—Mies's use of ornamentation and gendered form—made my mission to distinguish the pure form or pure meaning from the impure impossible. The impure is inextricably bound up with the pure.

This project comes from my research at Yale, 1989-90. I would like to thank Karsten Harries, Tom Beeby, and Alan Plattus for their support.

NOTES

BUILDING Two generations of critics/historians offer two different interpretations on the relationship of the Glass House to Miesian architecture. The first generation stressed similarities and the second stressed differences. The first interpretation, determined by Henry-Russell Hitchcock, Jr. and Vincent Scully, Jr., was formed by taking Johnson's magazine article at face value. Hitchcock, who gave the title "The Glass House" its debut, acknowledged that the Glass House was derivative of the Farnsworth House and also suggested that the Mies monograph Johnson authored in 1947 may have had a detrimental effect on his legacy as an original designer (Henry-Russell Hitchcock, Jr. "Philip Johnson," *Architectural Review* [April 1955]: 236-47). In his book *Modern Architecture*, Scully divided architecture into two movements: Romantic-Classicism and Romantic-Naturalism (or English Picturesque) and argued that Johnson succeeded Mies in the Romantic-Classical tradition, which favors "continuity and permanence" (Vincent Scully, Jr., *Modern Architecture, The Architecture of Democracy* [New York: George Braziller, 1961]). In the same year, Hitchcock claimed that although Johnson's Glass House resembles Farnsworth, it also recalls the Palladian with its "axially placed" doors, "Wrightian sort of flow," and "De-Stijl-like asymmetry," and the "Romantic villas by Schinkel at Potsdam" (Henry-Russell Hitchcock, Jr. "Current Work of Philip Johnson," *Zodiac* 7 [1961]: 66). In the introduction to a later publication, Hitchcock refined his Glass House discussion further. This time he moved from a previous discussion on space to that of procession (Philip Johnson, *Philip Johnson: Architecture 1949-1965* [New York: Holt, Rinehart and Winston, 1966]). Other publications from this generation that discuss the Glass House appropriate Scully's and Hitchcock's texts. See, for example, Bryan Robertson, introduction to *Philip Johnson. Global Architecture*, ed. Yukio Futagawa (Tokyo: ADA Edita, 1972).

WRITING The second generation—determined by Manfredo Tafuri, Kenneth Frampton, Craig Owens, and Charles Jencks—observed the differences between the Glass House and the Farnsworth and recognized the significance of Johnson's 1950 magazine article. Kenneth Frampton called the article a collection of "cultural sources," Craig Owens called it a "miscellany of historical sources," Peter Eisenman simply called it a "1950 presentation" of the Glass House, and Charles Jencks called it among other things an "explication de texte" and "historical programme notes." This project manual continues this discourse. See Kenneth Frampton, "The Glass House Revisited," *Catalog* 9 (September/October 1978); Peter Eisenman, ed., *Philip Johnson, Processes* (New York: Institute for Architecture and Urban Studies, 1978), 39; Craig Owens, "Philip Johnson: History, Genealogy, Historicism," in *Philip Johnson: Processes*, 3; Peter Eisenman, introduction to *Writings*, by Philip Johnson (New York: Oxford University Press, 1979), 20; and Charles Jenks, *Modern Movements in Architecture* (New York: Anchor Press/Doubleday, 1973), 206.

ARCHITECT A series of monographs on Philip Johnson have appeared since 1962, all titled *Philip Johnson*. Coincidentally, each appeared soon after a major addition to the Glass House site was executed. See John M. Jacobus, Jr., *Philip Johnson* (New York: George Braziller, 1962), which published the enlargement of the site at the southeast corner of the 1949 site; Philip Johnson, *Philip Johnson: Architecture 1949-1965* (New York: Holt, Rinehart and Winston, 1966), which published the underground Painting Gallery of 1965; and Charles Noble, *Philip Johnson* (New York: Simon and Schuster, 1972), which published the Sculpture Gallery of 1970.

The Walled-up Bride: An Architecture of Eternal Return

MANUELA ANTONIU

DOWN THE ARGESH LEA,
BEAUTIFUL TO SEE,
PRINCE NEGRU HE WENDED
BY TEN MATES ATTENDED:
NINE WORTHY CRAFTSMEN,
MASONS, JOURNEYMEN,
WITH MANOLE TEN,
THE HIGHEST IN FAME.
FORTH THEY STRODE APACE
THERE TO FIND A PLACE
WHERE TO BUILD A SHRINE,
A CLOISTER DIVINE.

The adjacent *Legend of Master Manole and the Monastery of Argeş*,[1] finding itself inscribed within the larger circle of distribution of a mythical theme that has been termed "the builder's sacrifice," filters universal motifs through the specifics of a given time and place.[2] Throughout cultural history, sacrificial rites have been integral to construction, yet in spite of their ubiquity it is only in the countries of southeastern Europe that constructional sacrifices found expression in a remarkable corpus of folk literary creation.[3] Over this geographical area, different regional sensibilities produced numerous variants of the master builder's legend, yet in all of them the central theme is disseminated through the same narrative sequence:

1. an incipient construction collapses unaccountably every night;
2. the builders involved enter a covenant by agreeing to sacrifice a woman kin;
3. the wife of the master mason (or of the only builder who keeps the oath) is immured, in most cases, alive;

AND, LO, DOWN THE LEA
A SHEPHERD THEY SEE,
IN YEARS SO UNRIPE,
PLAYING ON HIS PIPE.
TO HIM THE PRINCE SPED
AND THUS SPOKE AND SAID,
"HANDSOME LITTLE SWAIN
ON THY SWEET PIPE PLAYING!
UP THE ARGESH STREAM
THY FLOCK THOU HAST TA'EN;
DOWN THE ARGESH GREEN
WITH THY FLOCK THOU'ST BEN;
DIDST THOU HAP TO SEE
SOMEWHERE DOWN THE LEA
AN OLD WALL ALL ROTTEN,
UNFINISHED, FORGOTTEN,
ON A GREEN SLOPE LUSH,
NEAR A HAZEL BRUSH?"
"THAT, GOOD SIRE, I DID;
IN HAZEL BRUSH HID,
THERE'S A WALL ALL ROTTEN,
UNFINISHED, FORGOTTEN.
MY DOGS WHEN THEY SPY IT
MAKE A RUSH TO BITE IT,
AND HOWL HOLLOWLY,
AND GROWL GHOULISHLY."

4. a child is orphaned or dies as a result of the woman's immolation.

However, implicit among the legend's predominantly male exegetes have been certain underlying assumptions, ones that the present examination of the text of *Master Manole* will attempt to restructure.[4] Commentators have defined the woman as the sacrificial victim, and the master mason as "the builder," the architecton (etymologically the one who is ἀρχι—in the sense of surpassing the others). Yet when builder and victim are brought together in the frequently utilized appellation "builder's sacrifice," the contextual implication is not that the master mason is the one performing the woman's sacrifice, but that *he* is the one actually suffering it, the ultimate recipient of a tragic absence of choice. Therefore, he is the builder, and even though she is the victim, "builder's sacrifice" attributes both construction and sacrifice to him alone.[5]

Such established assumptions seem to limit the scope of the legend's true modernity by not allowing fundamental questions to remain alive. Since the woman is undeniably crucial to the construction's morphosis, how could her building role be overlooked or considered as peripheral, one that is secondary to the masons'? Who *is* the builder? *Whose* sacrifice is being performed? Whose immortality is secured through the woman's immurement?

An additional problem posed by denoting the legend as the "builder's sacrifice" is that doing so moves with disquieting ease into sanctioning sacrifice by substitution within the broader consideration of personal sacrifice as the sine qua non of creation. Once the notion is inoculated—that it is the male builder who experiences the sacrifice by inbuilding his wife—a projective distance of architectural significance is introduced. For what seems to emerge from the *Legend of Master Manole* as defining personal sacrifice is precisely that porous space in which duality is dissolved through one's level of involvement, where the distance of difference between being and doing is collapsing, where one's work and one's life become indistinguishable from one another.

The interest of this study is to gain entry into the generic space of opposition: the seeming disparity between the naturalistic specificity of the *Legend*'s settings, characters, and actions and the abstraction of the lyrical line; the distance between the physical and the metaphoric; the span between the instrumental (woman as building material) and the mythical (woman as generative principle). What is being proposed here is that potentially this is also the space in which a realignment of woman's fundamental participation in building culture can be realized. The *Legend*'s text is thus probed for its contemporary relevance to entrenched dichotomies of architectural making.

AS THE PRINCE DID HEAR
GREATLY DID HE CHEER,
AND WALKED TO THAT WALL,
WITH NINE MASONS ALL,
NINE WORTHY CRAFTSMEN,
WITH MANOLE TEN,
THE HIGHEST IN FAME.
"HERE'S MY WALL!" QUOTH HE.
"HERE I CHOOSE THAT YE
BUILD FOR ME A SHRINE,
A CLOISTER DIVINE.
THEREFORE, GREAT CRAFTSMEN,
MASONS, JOURNEYMEN,
START YE BUSILY
TO BUILD ON THIS LEA
A TALL MONASTERY;
MAKE IT WITH YOUR WORTH
PEERLESS ON THIS EARTH;
THEN YE SHALL HAVE GOLD,
EACH SHALL BE A LORD.
OH, BUT SHOULD YOU FAIL,
THEN YOU'LL MOAN AND WAIL,
FOR I'LL HAVE YOU ALL
BUILT UP IN THE WALL;
I WILL~SO I THRIVE~
BUILD YOU UP ALIVE!"

In order to arrive at a better appreciation of this position, it would be useful to place the *Legend of Master Manole and the Monastery of Argeş* in its broader geographical context by an overview of noteworthy local variants.

It is generally accepted that, due to the archaism and thematic simplicity of its versions of the legend, Greece was the locus of transition from construction ritual to literary folk expression.[6] In the neo-Greek variants, the construction that collapses overnight is almost invariably a bridge (or else it is placed by a body of water).

The legend of the bridge of Arta has three regional versions. In one of them, the masons and journeymen toil fruitlessly for three years to counteract the collapse of the bridge, until a *stoicheion* (ghost, spirit)

‖

THOSE CRAFTSMEN AMAIN
STRETCHED OUT ROPE AND CHAIN,
MEASURED OUT THE PLACE,
DUG OUT THE DEEP BASE,
TOILED DAY IN, DAY OUT,
RAISING WALLS ABOUT.
BUT WHATE'ER THEY WROUGHT,
AT NIGHT CAME TO NOUGHT,
CRUMBLED DOWN LIKE ROT!
THE NEXT DAY AGAIN,
THE THIRD DAY AGAIN,
THE FOURTH DAY AGAIN,
ALL THEIR TOIL IN VAIN!
SORE AMAZED THE LORD
HIS MEN HE DID SCOLD,
AND HE COWED THEM DOWN
WITH MANY A FROWN
AND MANY A THREAT;
AND HIS MIND HE SET
TO HAVE ONE AND ALL
BUILT UP IN THE WALL;
WE WOULD~SO HE THRIVE~
BUILD THEM UP ALIVE!
THOSE NINE GREAT CRAFTSMEN,

reveals to them the price of its completion: a human sacrifice not of the common kind (orphan, passer-by, beggar), but rather of the beautiful wife of the chief mason himself. Grief-stricken, he sends her a letter to come to the site unhurriedly, but the carrier bird reverses the message and urges her to join the builders at once. Seeing him downcast, she offers to descend into the foundation and look for his wedding ring, which he claims to have just lost. Realizing the trap, she laments her fate while being hastily built in; her two older sisters had ended in similar manner under bridges, one over the Danube, the other over Avlon. She finishes with imprecations, but is advised by the *stoicheion* to soften them lest they befall her brother, should he happen to be the first to cross the finished bridge.[7]

In another version, the price of completion is revealed in the architect's dream. The following day, as his wife is being sacrificed, she bemoans the fate of the three sisters built into foundations: one under a church; the other under a monastery; and now she, the youngest, under the bridge of Arta.[8]

In the final bridge-building variant, an impressive number of masons (1,400) receive the revelation from a bird endowed with human voice. Again, the sacrifice must go outside of the common practice (child, stranger, invalid) and claim none other than the chief mason's wife. As she dies, she laments that, with her sacrifice, she and her two sisters who have already been built under bridges will have all turned into *stoicheia*. This is an interesting turn, since it echoes a belief from Greek popular tradition that immured beings continue to live as tutelary spirits of the place where they were sacrificed.[9]

In the Macedo-Romanian version of the legend, the masons are three brothers who struggle in vain for seven years to build a bridge over Narta. Having lost his patience, the king threatens to put them to death. But a bird reveals to the eldest that in order for the construction to stand, they must immure the wife of the youngest brother. She too, as in the Greek versions, is credulous to look for the supposedly lost wedding ring. But while she is being built in, she implores her sacrificers to leave an opening for her bosom so that she can continue to suckle her infant (but they refuse).[10] This is a notable narrative detail since, as will be seen further on, it develops and acquires symbolic significance in other national variants. The theme of continuity through breast-feeding beyond the mother's death can be traced to Greek mythology. As the historian Pausanias recounts, Aerope, daughter of Cepheus, was seduced by Ares and died during childbirth. Yet she continued to provide the infant, who refused to detach himself from her, with abundant and nourishing milk.[11]

MASONS, JOURNEYMEN,
SHOOK WITH FEAR WALLS MAKING,
WALLS THEY RAISED WHILE SHAKING,
A LONG SUMMER'S DAY
TILL THE SKIES TURNED GREY.
BUT MANOLE SHIRKED,
HE NO LONGER WORKED,
TO HIS BED HE WENT
AND A DREAM HE DREAMT.
ERE THE NIGHT WAS SPENT,
FOR HIS MEN HE SENT,
TOLD THEM HIS INTENT:
"YE NINE GREAT CRAFTSMEN,
MASONS, JOURNEYMEN,
WHAT A DREAM I DREAMED:
IN MY SLEEP MESEEMED
A WHISPER FROM HIGH,
A VOICE FROM THE SKY,
TOLD ME VERILY
THAT WHATEVER WE
IN DAYTIME HAVE WROUGHT
SHALL NIGHTS COME TO NOUGHT,
CRUMBLE DOWN LIKE ROT;
TILL WE, ONE AND ALL,
MAKE AN OATH TO WALL
WHOSE BONNY WIFE ERST,

In the Serbo-Croatian version, the mythical king Vukasin and his two younger brothers, along with three hundred workmen, are building the fortified city of Skadar (the actual city of Scutari in Albania), but their "attempt to fix the wall's foundation" is in vain, since a sprite (*Vila*) destroys all their day's work during the night. After three years, the *Vila* reveals to Vukasin that unless they are able to find and immure the twins Stojan and Stojana, the city can not be built. An envoy searches the world over, but the brother and sister cannot be found.[12]

Finally the *Vila* suggests the immurement of she among the brothers' wives who will be the first to come to the site with food. They enter a covenant, but the two older brothers break it by alerting their wives to what is in store for them. Seeing his own wife approach, the youngest brother uses the familiar pretext of the lost wedding ring. Only here, instead of offering to find it, the woman suggests that her brother, a goldsmith, could replace it. She gives the same reply when her husband feigns having lost a golden apple, but in the end she is seized. While she is being

WHOSE DEAR SISTER FIRST,
HAPS TO COME THIS WAY
AT THE BREAK OF DAY,
BRINGING MEAT AND DRINK
TO HUSBAND OR KIN.
THEREFORE IF WE WILL
OUR HIGH TASK FULFIL
AND BUILD HERE A SHRINE,
A CLOISTER DIVINE,
LET'S SWEAR AND BE BOUND
BY DREAD OATHS AND SOUND
NOT A WORD TO SPEAK,
OUR COUNSEL TO KEEP:
WHOSE BONNY WIFE ERST,
WHOSE DEAR SISTER FIRST,
HAPS TO COME THIS WAY
AT THE BREAK OF DAY,
HER WE'LL OFFER UP,
HER WE SHALL BUILD UP!"

III

WHEN DAY FROM NIGHT PARTED
UP MANOLE STARTED,
CLIMBED A TRELLIS FENCE,
CLIMBED THE PLANKS, AND THENCE
THE FIELD HE LOOKED OVER,

immured, she begs to be substituted by a slave her mother could afford to procure. Resigned, she asks for, and is granted, two openings in the wall: one for her bosom, the other for her eyes so that she can continue to see their home. The infant is suckled through the wall for a full year (this recalls the model of Aerope), after which the stream of milk proves a miraculous cure for mothers whose own milk has ceased. It is worth noting here the concepts of replacement and substitution, as they carry significant architectural implications.

The city of Scutari is also the object of construction in the Albanian variant of the legend. Here the fairy tells the three brothers to go and wed, then return to build the city. When their attempts to secure its foundation are fruitless, the fairy asks that one of the wives be immured therein. The story follows the familiar pattern of immolation of the wife-mother, whose infant is, in this version, fed through the wall for two years after her death. Here, too, the stream, after having changed from milk to clear water, is everlasting and has curative properties.

City founding epitomized in boundary wall construction is present also in the Bulgarian versions of the legend. One variant about the building of the city Tirousa follows the usual narrative development in which only Manoil, the master mason, does not break the oath and, when faced with inbuilding his wife, invokes the fictitious loss of the wedding ring.[13]

Another variant is actually a folk wedding song. In it, three brothers try to overcome the nightly collapse of their day's attempts to build the fortified city of Smilen on the Strumdja. Each one of them dreams that they must immure the first of the three wives to reach the construction site. The brothers take an oath to abide by what was revealed to them, but only the youngest keeps it and thus must help build in his wife. The loss of the ring is invoked, the victim is lowered into the foundation to look for it, and the wall rises around her. She, too, asks for the opening through which she could continue nursing the infant; the stream of milk eventually turns into a spring.

In another version, Manoil's wife is marked as the victim who would secure the construction, but God, taking pity on her, blocks her approach to the site by sending first a wind storm, then a rain storm in her path, to no avail. Not being able to find her husband's supposedly lost wedding ring, she asks to be hoisted up from the cellar but is instead built in with the words "if only you knew what you don't know" and "you'll be the sacrifice to hold up the walls." She beseeches the masons to let her go home and part with her twin sons, after which she would come back as a willing victim the following day. She is, however, summarily walled up.

The last Bulgarian variant deals with a peculiar form of victim substitution, whereby a person's shadow is surreptitiously measured on the ground with either a rope or a stick, which is then built into the foundation as a perfect simulacrum of the living being. However, a shadow obtained and used in this manner portends the person's impending death. Whatever Manoil the master mason and his companions build by day collapses at night, and what they build at night collapses during the day. For the bridge construction to rise without crumbling, Manoil asks for a covenant: "Let us brethren make a blood sacrifice, a blood sacrifice for propitiation." They consent to immure the first wife to come to the site bringing food. Full of sorrow, Manoil is faced with sacrificing his own wife by building her shadow's measure into the foundation. The construction finally rises, but Manoil's wife dies soon after returning home. However, when her crying infant is brought to the bridge, milk trickles

THE PATH THROUGH WILD CLOVER.
AND WHAT DID HE SEE?
ALAS! WOE IS ME!
WHO CAME UP THE LEA?
HIS YOUNG BRIDE SO SWEET,
FLOWER OF THE MEAD!
HOW HE LOOKED AGHAST
AS HIS ANN CAME FAST,
BRINGING HIS DAY'S FOOD
AND WINE SWEET AND GOOD.
WHEN HE SAW HER YONDER
HIS HEART BURST ASUNDER;
HE KNELT DOWN LIKE DEAD
AND WEEPING HE PRAYED,
"SEND, O LORD, THE RAIN,
LET IT FALL AMAIN,
MAKE IT DROWN BENEATH
STREAM AND BANK AND HEATH,
MAKE IT SWELL IN TIDE
AND ARREST MY BRIDE,
FLOOD ALL PATH AND TRACK
AND MAKE HER TURN BACK!"
THE LORD HEARD HIS SIGH,
HEARKENED TO HIS CRY,
CLOUDS HE SPREAD ON HIGH
AND DARKENED THE SKY;

ꓯND HE 5ENT ꓯ RꓯIN,
MꓯDE IT FꓯLL ꓯMꓯIN,
MꓯDE IT DROWN BENEꓯTH
5TREꓯM ꓯND BꓯNK ꓯND HEꓯTH.
YET, FꓯLL ꓯ5 IT MꓯY,
HER IT COULD NOT 5TꓯY.
ONWꓯRD 5HE DID HIE,
NIGH 5HE DREW ꓯND NIGH.
ꓯ5 HE WꓯTCHED FROM HIGH,
5ORELY DID HE CRY,
ꓯND ꓯGꓯIN HE WꓯILED,
ꓯND ꓯGꓯIN HE PRꓯYED,
"BLOW, O LORD, ꓯ GꓯLE
OUER HILL ꓯND DꓯLE,
THE FIR-TREE5 TO REND,
THE MꓯPLE5 TO BEND,
THE HILL5 TO O'ERTURN,
MꓯKE MY BRIDE RETURN,
5TOP HER PꓯTH ꓯND TRꓯCK,
MꓯKE HER, LORD, TURN BꓯCK!"
THE LORD HEꓯRD HI5 5IGH,
HEꓯRKENED TO HI5 CRY,
ꓯND HE BLEW ꓯ GꓯLE
OUER HILL ꓯND DꓯLE
THꓯT THE FIR5 DID REND,
THE MꓯPLE5 DID BEND,

out of the place where her shadow was immured as though she were physically there, pointing to the complete ritualistic equivalence between victim and substitute.

All the Hungarian variants deal with the building of the fortified city of Deva.[14] In most of them the victim is not immured alive; rather she is killed and either her blood or her ashes are mixed with the lime for construction. One notable exception is the variant in which "the woman was with child, and far gone, and when they were walling her up, her little son was born. *For they didn't kill her, they walled her up alive.*"[15]

The most common version is that in which twelve masons are promised gold and silver for building the city. Because of the systematic collapse, the masons take an oath to burn alive the first of their wives to arrive at the site. The master mason's wife has a foreboding but misinterprets it and, fearing for her husband's life, hurries to him in spite of obstacles (a sudden storm, the coach's unwillingness to drive her). Seeing her approach, the husband prays to God to make her turn away, but his prayer remains unanswered. Upon hearing what is in store for her, she asks to go home to part with her child, and when she returns she is burned and her ashes are mixed into the mortar. The completion of the city thus secured, the masons take their promised reward. At home, the master mason's child asks for his mother and is finally told the truth. Talking to her through the city wall, the child is overcome with grief and longing; the earth parts and he falls into its abyss.

In the last variant, it is the master mason himself who suggests the sacrifice of his wife to counteract the wall's collapse. As she approaches unsuspectingly, carrying food and her little child, the husband has a change of heart and prays to God to divert her. While being sacrificed, she consoles her child that he will be well cared for as an orphan, washed by the rains, sung to sleep by birds and rocked by the winds; in other words, she will continue to be present in the form of natural elements.

The legend's variants visited here share a number of narrative themes, such as the absence of the wedding ring, the sublimation of the immured victim into tutelary spirit (*stoicheion*) of the construction, the curative properties conferred on the building by the (nursing) woman's immolation, the shadow measure as simulacrum of the living victim, and the continuity of the victim (a woman of confirmed fertility) in the form of natural elements. These themes, when brought to bear on the text of the *Legend of Master Manole*, help uncover other avenues of interpretation; but an articulation of their architectural relevance needs to be preceded by a brief discussion based on building type.

THE HILLS DID O'ERTURN,
NOR WOULD SHE RETURN.
ANN CAME UP THE DALE
STRUGGLING 'GAINST THE GALE,
REELING ON HER WAY;
NOTHING COULD HER STAY.
POOR SOUL! THROUGH THE BLAST,
THERE SHE WAS AT LAST!

IV

THOSE WORTHY CRAFTSMEN,
MASONS, JOURNEYMEN,
GREATLY DID THEY CHEER
TO SEE HER APPEAR.
WHILE MANOLE SMARTED,
WITH ALL HOPE HE PARTED,
HIS SWEET BRIDE HE KISSED,
SAW HER THROUGH A MIST,
IN HIS ARMS HE CLASPED HER,
UP THE STEPS HE HELPED HER,
PRESSED HER TO HIS CHEST,
AND THUS SPOKE IN JEST,
"NOW, MY OWN SWEET BRIDE,
HAVE NO FEAR, ABIDE;
WE'LL MAKE THEE A NEST,
BUILD THEE UP IN JEST!"

In the literary examples surveyed, the object of construction could vary regionally from bridge to tower, castle, or city wall.[16] Yet, in all Romanian versions of the legend (as in the one whose text is being examined here), the construction is invariably a monastery. Although the structures named in all national variants relate to actual architectural works,[17] to approach them strictly on historical grounds would be to limit the legend's signification. For as Eliade points out, a legend or "any other creation on the imaginary plane, no longer deals with 'real objects' but with images, archetypes, symbols."[18] In other words, the architectural objects described in the legend's variations no longer belong in a concrete context, but recover a primordial symbolism freed from spatio-temporal specificity. However, in order to confirm the universality of their message, they need to be re-placed, re-inscribed in a contemporary realm of architectural possibility. While the architectonic and cosmological symbolism of Bridge, Tower, or City Wall is virtually inexhaustible, they do not possess the religious explicitness of a monastery. This is why the ritual killing

ANN LAUGHED MERRILY,
SHE LAUGHED TRUSTFULLY,
AND MANOLE SIGHED,
HIS TROWEL HE PLIED,
RAISED THE WALL AS DUE,
MADE THE DREAM COME TRUE.
UP HE RAISED THE WALL
TO GIRD HER WITHAL;
UP THE WALL DID RISE
TO HER ANKLES NICE,
TO HER BONNY THIGHS.
WHILE SHE, WELLAWAY,
CEASED HER LAUGH SO GAY,
AND WOULD PRAY AND SAY,
"MANOLE, MANOLE,
GOOD MASTER MANOLE!
HAVE DONE WITH YOUR JEST,
'TIS NOT FOR THE BEST.
MANOLE, MANOLE,
GOOD MASTER MANOLE,
THE WALL SQUEEZES HARD,
MY FRAIL FLESH IS MARRED."
NOT A WORD SPOKE HE,
BUT WORKED BUSILY;
UP HE RAISED THE WALL
TO GIRD HER WITHAL;

of a woman within a monastery's wall brings notions of constructional sacrifice and historical verisimilitude to their highest tension.

For it seems that the magico-religious behavior revealed in the customs and beliefs of the Balkano-Danubian region comes from a spiritual universe of extreme archaism. Its survival both in practice[19] and in the form of folk poetry has weathered numerous religious re-evaluations "of which the last, Christianity, was also the most radical."[20] Some of the less esoteric Romanian variants of the *Legend* reflect precisely the difficult reconciliation of the belief in the necessity of the sacrifice with moral accountability for the "sin" of immolating an innocent victim.[21]

Across cultures practicing this form of sacrifice, it was axiomatic that in order for a construction to last, it had to be "animated" by means of a transference of life and soul.[22] At the same time, the necessity of the sacrifice was inextricably linked with religious beliefs in local divinities of earth and water. Any human intervention in the natural order of things was assumed to be a disturbance and violation of the divinities' particular space of influence. Therefore, the sacrifice was offered in propitiation for the imposition as well as for securing a protective spirit for the new construction.[23] This will recall the *stoicheion*, the guardian spirit of the construction, who is a transfiguration of the immolated victim.[24]

A curious dialogue is thus set up between the spirit of the site and the spirit of the building, since the latter exists in order to arrest the former's retaliation. But this dialogue is mute, not unlike a tension that is never fully resolved, since the two forces are locked into the bellicose stance of holding each other in check. Here the ambivalence of the sacrificial offering becomes manifest: is the propitiatory gesture a genuine apologia for the necessity of building, or does it actually trace the extent to which humanity is prepared to go in order to create *its* place in the order of things?

The ambiguity is perhaps most poignant in the building of a monastery, where the symbolic and the telluric exist in synergism. Sacrificial killing within a monastery's wall concretizes a point of intersection between the line of Seth (pious builders of prayer temples) and the line of Cain (bloodstained tillers of the Earth, who dug their plows into its skin and erected dwellings, all as a recalcitrant reaction to their forebears' expulsion from Eden). It is perhaps at this confluence of the two most primeval building impulses, between the need to build and the will to build, that the operational space of architecture is perpetually being redefined.

Through the sacrifice, the spirit of the place (as distillation of a natural order), and the spirit of the building (*stoicheion*) are being silenced by the emerging presence of an edifice. Such presencing betrays the necessity of an absence. Before proposing that the resultant silencing finds an anagogical echo in the immolation of the woman, an inquiry into what the absence might be, and what architectural repercussions are embedded therein, will have to be made.

AND THE WALL DID RISE
TO HER ANKLES NICE,
TO HER BONNY THIGHS,
TO HER SHAPELY WAIST,
TO HER FAIR,YOUNG BREASTS.
WHILE SHE, WELLAWAY,
SHE WOULD CRY AND SAY,
SHE WOULD WEEP AND PRAY,
"MANOLE,MANOLE!
THE WALL WEIGHS LIKE LEAD,
TEARS MY TEATS NOW SHED,
MY BABE IS CRUSHED DEAD."
MANOLE DID SMART,
SICK HE WAS AT HEART;
AND THE WALL DID RISE,
PRESSED HER IN IT VICE,
PRESSED HER SHAPELY WAIST,
GUSHED HER FAIR,YOUNG BREASTS,
REACHED HER LIPS NOW WHITE,
REACHED HER EYES SO BRIGHT,
TILL SHE SANK IN NIGHT
AND WAS LOST TO SIGHT!
HER SWEET VOICE ALONE
CAME THROUGH IN A MOAN,
"MANOLE,MANOLE,
GOOD MASTER MANOLE!

Once "the object of sacrifice is to give strength and stability to the building,"[25] a profound shift in architectural intentionality has taken place. Indeed the practice has become divorced from any spiritual tension and is now relegated to a plane of practical considerations only. This is reflected in the sacrificial *subject*, which in this realm assumes a substitutive character.

Out of the multitude of subjects used as substitutes for the human victim (ranging from personae non gratae such as prisoners, derelicts, or fatherless children to animals and even inanimate objects), one in particular carries important conceptual ramifications for architecture. It is the practice of shadow building, mentioned earlier in connection with a

THE WALL SQUEEZES HARD,
CRUSHED IS NOW MY HEART,
WITH MY LIFE I PART!"

V

DOWN THE ARGESH LEA,
BEAUTIFUL TO SEE,
PRINCE NEGRU IN STATE
CAME TO CONSECRATE
AND TO KNEEL IN PRAYER
TO THAT SHRINE SO FAIR,
THAT CLOISTER OF WORTH,
PEERLESS ON THIS EARTH.
THERE IT STOOD SO BRIGHT
TO HIS EYES' DELIGHT.
AND THE PRINCE SPOKE THEN,
"YE GOOD TEAM OF TEN,
YE WORTHY CRAFTSMEN,
TELL ME NOW IN SOOTH,
CROSS YOUR HEARTS IN TRUTH,
CAN YOU BUILD FOR ME,
WITH YOUR MASTERY,
YET ANOTHER SHRINE,
A CLOISTER DIVINE,
EVER FAR MORE BRIGHT,
OF GREATER DELIGHT?"

Bulgarian version of the legend. The shadow presents the disquieting ambiguity of not being entirely a substitute (since it depends on the human who casts it to exist), yet not being a physical object either (since it is immaterial); therefore its presence is simulated in the ritual of construction by one of its attributes: its measured length, which is an abstraction, and in its turn a substitute (of the shadow proper). The resultant twine or reed measure that gets built in is inanimate, yet it re-presents a human being; it is not a blood sacrifice, yet it heralds death, as previously described.

The ambiguity of this practice also accounts for the difficulty in ascertaining its place in the history of constructional sacrifice. Does it predate live immurement or does it replace it? Paradoxically, proponents of both theories start from the same premise: the shadow stands for the life or soul of the person who casts it. Before scientific knowledge explained it as an optical phenomenon, the synchronism of movement between shadow and body was understood, not unlike breath, to be the spiritual projection of 'soul' or 'second I'. In ancient Semitic languages, notions of 'soul' and 'shadow' were expressed by the same word.[26] In the mythology of ancient Egypt, the shadow was a protective 'second I', since it constantly accompanied one in front, beside, or behind. Among Asian cultures, a diminishing shadow was considered a sign of illness, and its disappearance impending death. An old Turkish greeting was to wish one: "may your shadow never decrease or distance itself from you." And, of course, in the *Divine Comedy*, Dante's shadow gave him away as a living being among the dwellers in Purgatory.

But however ancient and universal the animistic beliefs about shadows, the practice of burying them as ritualistic simulacra in construction is limited only to southeastern Europe.[27] Bulgarian masons were reputed shadow-takers; in Greece the practice was connected with the laying of the foundation stone; and in Romania the custom was in use as late as the middle of the last century. In fact, one of the variants of the *Legend of Master Manole* was recorded (in 1856) from a professional shadow trader, whose occupation was to supply architects with shadow measures for ensuring secure foundations.[28]

As illustrated earlier in one of the Bulgarian versions of the legend, the double simulacrum of victim substituted by shadow substituted by measurement underscores the equivalence between the victim and her simulated presence. However, this equivalence is established only by a projection at the end of which the woman is entirely disembodied by, and into, her *image*. This projective operation gives rise to a structure of replacements of which Manole's sacrifice of Ana in the legend of the Monastery of Argeş is perhaps the most enigmatic.

THEN THOSE GREAT CRAFTSMEN,
MASONS, JOURNEYMEN,
BOASTING CHEERFULLY,
CHEERING BOASTFULLY,
FROM THE ROOF ON HIGH,
UP AGAINST THE SKY,
THUS THEY MADE REPLY,
"LIKE US GREAT CRAFTSMEN,
MASONS, JOURNEYMEN,
IN SKILL AND IN WORTH
THERE ARE NONE ON EARTH!
MARRY, IF THOU WILT,
WE CAN ALWAYS BUILD
YET ANOTHER SHRINE,
A CLOISTER DIVINE,
EVER FAR MORE BRIGHT,
OF GREATER DELIGHT!"
THIS THE PRINCE DID HARK,
AND HIS FACE GREW DARK;
LONG, LONG THERE HE STOOD
TO PONDER AND BROOD.
THEN THE PRINCE ANON
ORDERED WITH A FROWN
ALL SCAFFOLDS PULLED DOWN,
TO LEAVE THOSE TEN MEN,
THOSE WORTHY CRAFTSMEN,

It has been argued that, by inbuilding his wife, Manole is in fact offering himself up (that is, the best part of himself), and that the substitution unites sacrificer and victim in both the human and the divine realms.[29] This perspective, if espoused, calls to mind other mythical sacrifices of self through an other, notably that of Iphigenia by her father Agamemnon and of Isaac by Abraham. But there is a fundamental difference. Both Agamemnon and Abraham were offering flesh of their flesh, a unique connection with their innermost being that could not be re-created. The relationship between Manole and Ana is of a different order.

In one of the legend's variants, the master builder, asked by a celestial voice what he is prepared to sacrifice in order for the construction to stand up, answers, "If I give you my daughter, I will have no daughter; if I give you my mother, I will have a mother no longer; but if I give you my wife, I will have a chance to find a better one."[30] Lest this be considered

ON THE ROOF ON HIGH,
THERE TO ROT AND DIE.
LONG THEY STAYED THERE THINKING,
THEN THEY STARTED LINKING
SHINGLES THIN AND LIGHT
INTO WINGS FOR FLIGHT.
AND THOSE WINGS THEY SPREAD,
AND JUMPED FAR AHEAD,
AND DROPPED DOWN LIKE LEAD.
WHERE THE GROUND THEY HIT,
THERE THEIR BODIES SPLIT.
THEN POOR, POOR MANOLE,
GOOD MASTER MANOLE,
AS HE BROUGHT HIMSELF
TO JUMP FROM A SHELF,
HARK, A VOICE CAME LOW
FROM THE WALL BELOW,
A VOICE DEAR AND LIEF,
MUFFLED, SUNK IN GRIEF,
MOURNFUL, WOEBEGONE,
MOANING ON AND ON,
"MANOLE, MANOLE,
GOOD MASTER MANOLE,
THE WALL WEIGHS LIKE LEAD,
TEARS MY TEATS STILL SHED,
MY BABE IS CRUSHED DEAD,

an isolated case, perhaps it is necessary to reiterate that in all versions of the legend, the interchangeableness of wife and sister as potential victims (first woman kin to approach the site) is present only in the masons' resolve, but the actual sacrifice is never other than that of the master mason's *wife*. This will recall the numerous versions in which the loss of the wedding ring serves not only as a trap for the wife, the victim-to-be, but is also symbolic of the husband's distancing from the marriage, since in order to sound convincing, he would have to have taken the ring off his finger, thus signaling the end of his marriage to that particular woman. A wife is indispensable for the life of the construction, yet is also matrimonially replaceable.

Any discussion of substitution and replacement invariably brings into play notions of uniqueness and its antonyms. The Prince's desideratum is an architectural work "peerless on this Earth." It could be argued that, faced with the prospect of its replication (hence its devaluation), he condemns the masons to perish when, from the rooftop of the completed building, they give his insidious question an affirmative unanimous answer. But to subscribe to this canonic interpretation would be to overlook the very premise of the *Legend*: despite their superior skill ("highest in fame") the masons *could not* build unless and until Ana became part of the construction. Thus it becomes plausible that the masons are sentenced not as much to prevent them from transporting their craft and reproducing their accomplished work elsewhere, as to ensure that Manole does not wed again. Manole's answer in particular betrays a presumptuous reliance on future marital repetitions which would render his work possible. By anticipating that his potential next bride (if she again be the one to outdistance the other women to the site) will have the same capacity to confer upon the building that ineffable quality that would arrest its collapse, he implies that Ana is replaceable and thus divests her of uniqueness.[31]

But who is Ana? Is she a projection of Manole's "dream come true," his ideal self, his sacrificeable double whom she incarnates because of her explicit generative power (her confirmed fecundity)? Or is she physically distinct, a real woman (as Manole is a real man), with real tears of real suffering? Or is she an existence of a different order? Her remarkable braving of the natural elements that were meant to divert her suggests a consubstantiality; to be able to emerge unscathed, Ana cannot be nature's opposite, but its double. The storms separate nothing but the same from itself.[32] This will recall the posthumous presence of the mother in the form of natural elements, as described in one of the Hungarian versions of the legend. If, as was seen earlier, the sacrifice is for appeasing the chthonian spirits of the place, and if Ana is a force of nature, then the ritual amounts to the sacrifice of nature in order to propitiate a violation of nature. This profoundly paradoxical condition subsumes an architectural conditionality: the construction can only beget a presence while Ana is actively absent within it, while her "muffled voice" is being perpetually silenced.

AWAY MY LIFE'S FLED!" AS MANOLE HEARD HIS LIFE-BLOOD DID CURD, AND HIS EYESIGHT BLURRED, AND THE HIGH CLOUDS WHIRLED, AND THE WHOLE EARTH SWIRLED; AND FROM NEAR THE SKY, FROM THE ROOF ON HIGH, DOWN HE FELL TO DIE! AND, LO, WHERE HE FELL THERE SPRANG UP A WELL, A FOUNTAIN SO TINY OF SCANT WATER, BRINY, SO GENTLE TO HEAR, WET WITH MANY A TEAR!

When the building is completed, Ana's transfiguration is countenanced in the fountain, which is Manole's own transfiguration once he reaches the phreatic folds of the earth. The ensuing relationship of building to reflection, thus of object to image, offers the possibility of entering an architectural discourse on re-presentation. Ana's transmuted presence (her architectonic body), infinitely repeated in its aqueous reflection, is the presence in a representation made possible only through an absence (her physical body). Although dematerialized as a reflection, Ana's new body is fully contained by, yet remains insoluble in, Manole's new body, thus retaining a material integrity only at the level of the image. (An analogy to traditional means of communicating an architectural design is obvious.)

While he helped immure Ana, Manole "saw her through a mist." As a literary device, the mist is the fountain's prefiguration, a metaphor for the way in which Manole will *see* his wife, namely through the depth of projective distance. His seeing either occurs in a mediated way ("through a mist," with "his eyesight blurred") or away from the site when, with his eyes closed, he dreams; he images an occult trade secret, a specialized form of knowledge equipped with which he subsequently "made the dream come true."[33]

Seen from this perspective, Manole emerges as a maker of images. He could not build—not until that for which Ana stands was subsumed.

Is Ana a maker of buildings? The monastery exists to this day, and so does the fountain. Their historical survival would be unimportant were it not for the wealth of allegorical readings they invite. One in particular may be of pertinence here. As themes of ingravidation, immortality, and transmutation suffuse the *Legend*, they echo the dream of the alchemical project.

For it is in pursuit of immortality that alchemists sought the Philosopher's Stone, the *elixir vitae* of a final, transcendental transmutation of matter, a process that had as its mineral analog the quickening and obtention of gold from baser metals. It was believed that all ores would, in the course of time, become gold and that the alchemist's task was to contribute to Nature's work by accelerating this gestational process.[34] The crux of the alchemical operation, the *opus alchymicum*, lay precisely in the discovery that, through intervention in Nature's own process of growth, the alchemist could "take upon himself the work of Time" by eliminating the temporal gap between the initial and final conditions.[35]

The desire for thaumaturgical works has stirred the human imagination across many cultures and epochs, but nowhere does its element of time compression appear more dramatic than when the work is the emergence of an edifice.[36] In the *Legend of Master Manole* Ana's sacrifice in the foundation wall is the pivotal point of such thaumaturgy, while the wall itself (in both forward and reversed chronology[37]) stands as a concentrator of key alchemical tenets. First encountered as a marker for the site, the wall is "rotten," decayed, fully subject to the passing of time, but it is also "unfinished," which in the alchemical lexicon would be called *in potentia*, in embryonic form.[38] These two superpositions on the wall construe it as an old embryo whose delivery must be quickened by a new wall through the alchemical operations of *homo constructivus*. This endows architecture, already chthonic, with an obstetric dimension; it implies that only through germination of all previous building efforts could the essence of the architectural dream be extracted. "The alchemical preparation of the embryo of immortality" is thus made possible.[39]

The wall also becomes "a nest" into which, once on the site, Ana is asked to accept being built. Thus Ana, who is with child, is in turn contained as the embryo of the masons' alchemical operation, by being assimilated into a cavity of the foundation wall, the womb of the whole construction. An architectonic equivalence is established: the carnal wall of a pregnant life renders the structural masonry wall of the monastery impregnable to the ravages of time, by arresting its collapse and procuring its everlastingness. As long as the wall is *in potentia*, pregnant with Ana, it offers the promise of the highest distillation into the "gold" of an architectural nonpareil.

The womb received her "till she sank in night." Therefore Ana's day is now finished. She had started "at the break of day" and stopped at "night," but this charts a complete day within a day that is still unfolding for the others. Such passage through time encapsulates both the means and the goal of the *opus alchymicum*: the acceleration of the rhythm of time toward the final sublimation, which is an irreversible movement outside of time. For Ana has now entered an existence of a different order, one that escapes time in the outer day.

By quickening the delivery of the construction, Ana's insertion into the wall is as obstetric as it is therapeutic: she is the medicine that restores the living integrity of a building menaced by the sickness of time. The alchemical pharmacopoeia ascribes therapeutic properties to the Stone, thus engendering the notion of an *elixir vitae* capable of dispensing its dosage of immortality if assimilated orally.[40] Since the *elixir* was a hypothetical substance, "a Stone which is not a stone," it had many appellations, of which one was "the Virgin's milk."[41] This will recall the curative properties of the immured mothers' milk, as described in the Macedo-Romanian variants of the legend. A bit of lime rubbed off (or stone chipped) from the place on the wall where the stream of milk had trickled served as a *pharmakon* to living mothers by restoring their own lactation.[42] One of the Romanian variants of the legend explicitly calls the immurement therapeutic for the construction:

> This was the *healing remedy* [in Romanian, *lecuirea*] to keep the wall standing; And henceforth the monastery ceased to crumble. Wind, earthquake, don't shake it *for she holds it up from within the wall.*[43]

Within the wall Ana serves as a *pharmakon* and dies as a *pharmakos.*[44] Only if she is the sui generis builder, with a unique, direct connection to both site and construction, can the latter no longer be rejected by the former, once the ingested cure takes effect.

But what kind of builder?

In one of the Bulgarian variations cited at the beginning of this study the last words that the condemned woman hears from the masons are the haunting "If only you knew what you do not know." These words are less rhetorical than perhaps intended, since they seem to rely on substituting know-how (the trade secret transmitted to the men) for knowledge. Yet at the same time, on one level, the woman both knows and does not know; what is more, she knows that which she does not know. For she embodies the capacity to encompass paradox, not in order to overcome it, but rather to sustain it fully, viscerally, unwaveringly. And it is with this capacity that knowledge begins.

In a contemporary context saturated with know-how substituting knowledge and images substituting experience, to interrogate notions of projection, presence, simulation, absence, or indeed thaumaturgy seems transhistorically apposite. For it may be that a building culture of fast-tracking and planned obsolescence (both based on physical absence and eludible time) is being maintained by a discontinuity of tectonic presence in building imagination. Were that to desist, the figure of Ana could be constantly emptied of death by withstanding being subdued into image, while allowing a latent material memory to body forth in architectural re-presentation.

NOTES

1. The text is the English translation of the most commonly known version of the legend in Romania. Dan Duțescu, trans., *Master Manole*, in *Meşterul Manole*, (Bucharest: Editura Albatros, 1976), 23–39; calligraphy and graphics by Emil Chendea. Unless otherwise stated, quotations from the *Legend* cited in the essay are from this source.

2. See, for instance, Mircea Eliade's essay "Master Manole and the Monastery of Argeş," in *Zalmoxis: The Vanishing God*, trans. Willard R. Trask (Chicago: University of Chicago Press, 1972), 164–90.

3. According to Lazar Sainean, "the practice of immuring a live being in the foundations of a city, a bridge, a tower, any edifice, is one of the most widespread in the world." "Les rites de la construction d'après la poésie populaire de l'Europe Orientale," *Revue de l'histoire des religions* 45 (1902): 359. See also Eliade, "Master Manole," 179, 188.

4. One (and perhaps the only) exception to the preponderance of male critics is Zoe Dumitrescu-Buşulenga, but she espouses the same point of view with respect to the attribution of sacrifice to the male builder. See the canonic interpretation she presents in her preface to the polyglot volume *Meşterul Manole* (specifically the English translation of her preface).

5. A separate discussion and indeed a separate study is warranted here with respect to the number of commentators who concur in viewing the immolated women as willing victims, in spite of strong textual evidence to the contrary.

6. Eliade, "Master Manole," 179, 188.

7. See Eliade, "Master Manole"; Sainean, "Les rites"; Giuseppe Cocchiara, "Il Ponte di Arta e i sacrifici di costruzione," in *Annali del Museo Pitrè* 1 (Palermo, 1950): 38–81; Lajos Vargyas, *Researches into the medieval history of folk ballad* (Budapest: Akadémiai Kiado, 1967), 173–233.

8. See Eliade, "Master Manole"; and Sainean, "Les rites."

9. Sainean, "Les rites," 367.

10. See Eliade, "Master Manole"; Sainean, "Les rites"; and Cocchiara, "Il Ponte."

11. Born in Magnesia, in Asia Minor, around A.D. 170, Pausanias traveled extensively and recorded his observations on customs, ethnography, and folklore in his ten-volume work, the *Periagesis*. The passage about Aerope (VIII, 44) is cited in Sainean, "Les rites," 383, and in Cocchiara, "Il Ponte," 43.

12. See Eliade, "Master Manole"; Sainean, "Les rites"; Cocchiara, "Il Ponte"; and Vargyas, *Researches*. See also Ovidiu Papadima, "Neagoe Basarab și vînzătorii de umbre," *Revista de folclor* 7, nos. 3–4 (1962), 68–77. In this example of the legend, there is an interesting semantic metaphor at play: in Serbian, *stàjati* means "that which lasts, that which stands upright." Thus the elusiveness of the children underscores the construction's elusive stability.

13. See Sainean, "Les rites"; and Vargyas, *Researches*.

14. See Eliade, "Master Manole"; Sainean, "Les rites"; and Vargyas, *Researches*.

15. Vargyas, *Researches*, 205 (emphasis added).

16. For building types not discussed in the text, see Sainean, "Les rites," 359; Vargyas, *Researches*, 196; and Papadima, "Neagoe Basarab," 68.

17. See, for instance, the bridge over Agraida in Greece, the city of Scutari in Albania, and the castle of Deva in Transylvania. The present *Legend of Master Manole and the Monastery of Argeș* is associated with the existing monastery of Curtea de Argeș in central Romania, built between 1512 and 1517.

18. Eliade, "Master Manole," 178.

19. See, for instance, Lewis Dayton Burdick, *Foundation Rites with some kindred ceremonies* (New York: Abbey Press, 1901); Nigel Davies, *Human Sacrifice in History and Today* (New York: W. Morrow, 1981); Richard Allen Drake, "Construction Sacrifice and Kidnapping Rumor in Borneo," *Oceania* 59 (June 1989): 269–79; Nicole Loraux, *Tragic Ways of Killing a Woman* (Cambridge: Harvard University Press, 1987); Ralph Merrifield, *The Archaeology of Ritual and Magic* (London: B.T. Batsford, 1987); Giuseppe Morici "La vittima dell'edifizio," *Annali del R. Instituto Superiore Orientale di Napoli* IX (1937): 177–216; Paul Sartori, "Ueber das Bauopfer," *Zietschrift für Ethnologie* 30 (1898): 1–54; and Patrick Tierney, *The Highest Altar: the story of human sacrifice* (New York: Viking, 1989).

20. Eliade, "Master Manole," 188–9.

21. See Sainean, "Les rites," 378; and Lorenzo Renzi, *Canti narrativi tradizionali romeni. Studio e testi*, Biblioteca dell' Archivum Romanicum, vol. 96 (Florence: Leo S. Olschki , 1969), 75–86. Both Sainean and Renzi maintain that the tragic fate of the builders is thus explained in terms of divine punishment veiled as human punishment.

22. Eliade, "Master Manole," 182; Sainean, "Les rites," 359.

23. Papadima, "Neagoe Basarab," 70; Cocchiara, "Il Ponte," 71.

24. See the preceding discussion of the three neo-Greek variants.

25. Sir James George Frazer, *The Golden Bough; A Study in magic and religion*, 3d ed. (London: Macmillan and Co., 1911), 89-90.

26. This and subsequent references to shadows in ancient cultures are found in Papadima, "Neagoe Basarab," 74–75, and in Burdick, *Foundation Rites*, 104–16.

27. Frazer, *Golden Bough*, 89; Papadima, "Neagoe Basarab," 75.

28. See Papadima, "Neagoe Basarab"; and Burdick, *Foundation Rites*, 104-16.

29. Cocchiara, "Il Ponte," 74; Renzi, *Canti narrativi*, 76.

30. Eliade, "Master Manole," 170; Sainean, "Les rites," 363–4.

31. Throughout the *Legend*, Ana is never referred to as Manole's wife, but as his "bride." Among many other levels of signification, this acts as a repeated reminder of a perpetual wedding, a hierogamy.

32. As illustration of this point, see the alchemical engraving "Nature Teaches Nature How To Conquer Fire," Michael Maier, *Atalanta Fugiens*, 1618 (Kassel: Bärenreiter-Verlag, 1964), 89, emblema XX .

33. "He who *makes* real things is he who *knows* the secrets of making them." Eliade, *Forgerons et Alchimistes* (Paris: Flammarion, 1956), 105. See also the discussions about trade secrets of shadows in Frazer, *Golden Bough*, 89, and strengthening mortar with blood in Burdick, *Foundation Rites*, 50.

34. Eliade, *Forgerons et Alchimistes*, 53–54. Further on Eliade writes, "To hasten the growth of metals by the operation of alchemy is tantamount to absolving them from the laws of Time" (118).

35. Eliade, *The Forge and the Crucible* (New York: Harper Torchbooks, 1971), 80, 175.

36. For instance, Lewis Spence describes how, in Teutonic lore, the rapid construction of certain cathedrals occurs thanks to demonic assistance. *Germany*, Myths and Legends Series (London: Senate, 1994), 106-8, 110-11. A similar theme is encountered in the folklore of Québec where the devil is deceived into building the parish church *in one day*. Marie-Françoise Guédon, conversation with author, November 1990.

37. Throughout the *Legend* there are numerous pointers to an inverted chronology of the narrative line, and the wall is their favored locus.

38. Eliade, *Forgerons et Alchimistes*, 55.

39. Ibid., 122.

40. Ibid., 122*ff*. Eliade cites Roger Bacon's allusion, in *Opus Majus*, to a "medicine which gets rid of impurities and all blemishes from the most base metal, can wash unclean things from the body and prevents decay of the body to such an extent that it prolongs life by several centuries" (173).

41. Eliade, *The Forge and the Crucible*, 164.

42. Vargyas, *Researches*, 202.

43. From the Cezar Bolliac version of the *Legend*, quoted in Papadima, "Neagoe Basarab," 72 (author's translation and emphasis).

44. The ritual expiator sacrificed on the city boundary by the early Greeks offers another instance of curative absence; it is necessary for the *pharmakos* to perish, to become manifestly absent, in order for the city to be preconized as cured.

Edith Wharton, The Decoration of Houses, and Gender in Turn-of-the-Century America

VANESSA CHASE

A woman's nature is like a great house full of rooms: there is the hall, through which everyone passes in going in and coming out; the drawing room, where one receives formal visits; the sitting room, where the members of the family come and go as they list; but beyond that, far beyond, are other rooms, the handles of whose doors are perhaps never turned; no one knows the way to them, no one knows whither they lead; and in the innermost room, holy of holies, the soul sits alone and waits for a footstep that never comes.   —EDITH WHARTON, "THE FULLNESS OF LIFE"[1]

I believe I know the only cure [for nervous disorders] which is to make one's center of life inside one's self, not selfishly or excludingly, but with a kind of unassailable serenity—to decorate one's inner house so richly that one is content there, glad to welcome anyone who wants to come and stay, but happy all the same in the hours when one is inevitably alone.

—EDITH WHARTON TO MARY BERENSON (1918)[2]

FIG. 1 The Mount, c. 1904

Edith Wharton is known primarily for her fictional portraits of affluent New York Society in the late-nineteenth and early-twentieth centuries; one of the foremost features of these fictional portraits is their piercing observations regarding women's place in that society. Yet Wharton also contributed extensively to architectural thought, practice, and knowledge during the period. She wrote several books about architecture, decoration, and gardening, most notably *The Decoration of Houses* (1897), designed her own home, The Mount, in Lenox, Massachusetts (FIG. 1), and decorated her other homes in Newport, New York City, and France. Perhaps it should not be surprising that these two interests—women in society and architecture—informed one another. In fact, they were very much linked. This essay will examine the houses described in such novels as *The House of Mirth* (1905), *The Custom of the Country* (1913), and *The Age of Innocence* (1920), the formulations for decorating, arranging spaces, and living found in *The Decoration of Houses*, and Wharton's own house in Massachusetts, with respect to the way gender resonates in spatial constructions and decorative details; it will propose that gender played a significant role in Wharton's conception of architectural design and society.[3]

At the end of the nineteenth century, decoration and gardening were seen as "feminine" pursuits; they were lighter, less challenging, and more appropriate activities for women than the "masculine" profession of architecture. Wharton believed that decoration and gardening were part of the practice of architecture; her work served to elevate the status of these feminine arts by integrating them with the masculine art of architecture. In her novels, houses are the space of women: where they live and where they have power. The decoration of the house becomes a metaphor for the woman who creates and inhabits it, a symbol of her power and self-expression. Yet the house was, in Wharton's period, only allowed to women by men; the actual order—social, economic, and architectural—was that of men. In her own houses, however, Wharton was the dominant figure socially, economically, and intellectually. The spatial arrangement and decoration follow a distinctly different agenda: one mandated by a woman who is truly in control. In *The Decoration of Houses*, one can see both a traditional gendering of space and an opening for a new equality between men and women; this provides a transition between what Wharton saw in American society and what she envisioned for herself. Wharton's architectural books and homes are prescriptions for how she envisioned architecture *ought* to be, while her novels are critical descriptions of how architecture and society *are*. Taken together, they offer a valuable insight into the way in which gender and architecture functioned together in elite circles of turn-of-the-century America.

Examination of the status of women, architecture, and women in architecture during Wharton's period provides important background for understanding the significance of gender in her architectural formulations. Architecture and women both carried great symbolic weight in American culture at the turn of the century; architecture was the leading art of the American Renaissance and women too functioned as symbols of Gilded Age prosperity.[4] With the World's Columbian Exposition of

1893 in Chicago, the language of Beaux-Arts European classicism was established as the dominant architectural mode in the United States. Wharton believed that interior decoration and gardening ought similarly to follow principles of harmony, proportion, and decorum.[5] In her architectural writings, *The Decoration of Houses* and *Italian Villas and Their Gardens* (1904), Wharton reintegrated the neglected arts of decoration and gardening into the discipline of architecture.[6] Part of the reason behind this neglect was that while architecture was a masculine profession, decoration and gardening were viewed as not only mere diversions, but women's diversions.

Women writing about architecture were not rare in the period; Mariana van Rensselaer, certainly Wharton's social peer, wrote extensively for the newly-emerging trade journals such as *American Architect and Building News* and *Century* and published several books of architectural criticism. Yet women were discouraged from entering the actual practice of the profession. In 1900, there were only 100 women architects registered in America, as opposed to 10,500 men.[7] The very same trade journals that allowed female writers suggested that instead of pursuing architecture, women should pursue "various forms of decorative art" and gardening.[8] Women who did practice architecture were often limited to buildings for women: the campuses of new women's colleges, women's clubs and hotels, YWCAs, and women's centers at fairs and expositions.[9] When women architects were acknowledged by the press, it was in condescending terms. For example, Sophia Hayden, the first female graduate of M.I.T.'s school of architecture and the architect of the Women's Building at the World's Columbian Exposition, received praise for the "graceful timidity" and "feminine character" of her building.[10] Yet when Hayden suffered a nervous breakdown soon after the completion of the building, she received as much public condemnation for not being able to handle the pressures of her profession, revealing the animosity and disapproval a woman might experience in the field.[11]

Not only was architecture seen to be strictly the pursuit of men, but the standards of the time seem to have favored so-called "masculine" traits in architecture. Louis Sullivan attacked what he termed "feminine" qualities as inappropriate to public buildings as well as public life; true architecture was to be virile, forceful, and straightforward.[12] Ogden Codman, Wharton's own architect and collaborator, was even censured for his interior designs, which "gained variety at the expense of virility."[13] By the second decade of the twentieth century, interior decoration had been secured as a true profession and one dominated by women, in a great part due to Wharton's influence.[14] Gardening, too, became a profession available to women, as the acclaimed career of Wharton's niece Beatrix Jones Ferrand proves. The professional goals of Wharton's book—the integration of traditionally female and male professions and the new empowerment of women as professionals—are nicely balanced by its social goals—the integration of female and male spaces and the new empowerment of female spaces. For it was these very places, the interior and the garden, that were understood as feminine and as containing, or restricting, women.

Just as decoration was a feminine pursuit in the late nineteenth century, women themselves were seen as decorative. In 1899, Thorstein Veblen in *The Theory of the Leisure Class* defined the American woman as the embodiment of his newly-coined phrase "conspicuous consumption." Her purpose was ornamental: to display the wealth and power of her husband, father, and family. The American woman was idealized by art and culture, yet she was an ideal with no power, in a public sense, but the decorative. According to Henry Adams, the American woman of 1900 was caught temporally between the animating forces of the Virgin Mary and the twentieth-century Dynamo. She was not a cultural force, but was instead the image of one: Columbia, America, Freedom. Moreover, she had no power but that assigned to her by men. "An American Virgin would never dare command," Adams insisted, "An American Venus would never dare exist."[15] Henry James noted that "the most salient and peculiar point in our social life . . . [is] the situation of our women."[16] He found that the American woman lived in an "abyss of inequality, the like of which has never before been seen under the sun," which he attributed to "the growing divorce between the American woman (with her comparative leisure, culture, grace, social instincts, artistic ambitions) and the male American immersed in the ferocity of business, with no time for any but the most sordid interests, purely commercial, professional, democratic and political."[17] There was thus a real and perceived difference between the status of men and women which placed the woman as a signifying object within the home.

To a great extent, Edith Wharton lived within and wrote about these definitions of women and American culture. In works with titles such as *The Age of Innocence* and *Old New York*, Wharton revisited the New York of the 1870s, when women did have a role in society: they were the keepers of the moral fabric. Matriarchs in their homes, women dictated the actions of sons and husbands as well as daughters. By the first decade of the twentieth century, however, this status had disappeared. The vast fortunes amassed by the newly rich during America's Gilded Age asserted a more powerful social arbiter than women: money. And money was a realm reserved for men. Women were merely signifiers of men's hard-earned wealth and could only flex power through the signs of this affluence: fashion and the decoration of houses. Thus, even though the house was seen as expressive of a woman, she only inhabited it as an inscribed figure: the real body displayed through the house, and woman, was the man's.[18]

At the same time, the social fluidity and urban growth caused by the financial boom of the late nineteenth century also allowed women new freedoms, including the possibility of independence. Feminist reformers began to develop new social institutions to help the independent urban woman.[19] However, the alternatives of career, boarding house, or private flat were not open to women of Wharton's social world without some disgrace. These elite women were inextricably caught: they had to marry to assume a position within society, yet as soon as they did so they became society's pawns, immured to an even greater extent. Independence was not attainable without a fall; an American Venus was impossible. It is just this tension that is played out in the architecture of Wharton's novels. Architecture, specifically the home, becomes the vessel of a woman's position; she is locked into the house but thereby gains a power within it—the power of social position.

FIG. 2 Edith Wharton, 1907

Despite her criticism of women's place in society, Wharton was emphatically not a feminist, and called herself "just an old fashioned man's woman."[20] Her self-image, however, was very much caught up in conflicts of gender. On account of her literary pursuits, she was often described as having masculine traits,[21] yet she presented herself publicly and privately as the picture of the American feminine woman (FIG. 2). Her interests were masculine, her person feminine; society could not "place" her. Like many of her female characters, Wharton desired to flout some of her society's conventions of masculine and feminine propriety, yet at the same time wanted complete acceptance by that society.

Wharton seems to have found the condition of women in Europe far better. In Europe, women could cultivate their minds "by contact with the stronger masculine individuality"; in the figures of George Sand and Hortense Allart, she saw a certain liberation of women as well as a support for their literary activities, which corresponded to a certain sense of partnership between men and women in marriage.[22] In *The Custom of the Country*, Bowen remarks that in Europe a woman "is not a parenthesis, as she is here—she's in the very middle of the picture." (*CC*, 119) The Europe from which *The Age of Innocence*'s Ellen Olenska fled in the 1870s is her haven by 1900. Wharton, too, found Paris a haven; after her divorce, she lived in a neighborhood not dissimilar from Ellen Olenska's.[23] Like Lily Bart or Ellen Olenska, Wharton felt trapped by the society that produced her. Wharton's architectural formulations can thus be seen as a strategy to circumvent the gender confinements of her society. In *The Decoration of Houses* and at The Mount, she advocated the creation of a domestic interior that allowed, or even enabled, men and women to interact on equal grounds. She sought to transform the situation of inequality that she saw in society and described in her fiction.

The House of Mirth is a particularly rich example of the interplay between architecture and gender in Wharton's fictional works. Not only does the book vividly and tragically recount the difficulties with which the American woman was faced at the turn of the century, but it continually describes this dilemma within architecturally telling spaces; its very title conjures ideas of architectural space and emotional experience.[24] The sad story of Lily Bart's social decline is a history of her descent through architectural settings. For Wharton, architecture and its decoration both define and are defined by the inhabitants; the house one builds or the room one decorates is an expression of one's character, and the house or room in which one is obliged to live creates that character.

Lily begins the book living at the apex of social and moral correctness, her Aunt Peniston's house on Fifth Avenue. However, the social and architectural limitations of this house make it as "dreary as a prison." (*HM*, 110) The house belongs to the New York of the 1870s, secure in its moral support but limiting in what it will allow Lily, or any woman, to do. She contrasts her bedroom, with its flocked magenta wallpaper, to the country estate of the Trenors, Bellomont; it is the latter which seems to Lily to be her most natural setting. Yet even at Bellomont, she looks at the people gathered for dinner and thinks, "How dreary and trivial these people are!" (*HM*, 55) Moreover, it is within its grounds that she contemplates and envies Selden's "republic of the spirit."

From the time Lily leaves Bellomont, we see her in increasingly less-pleasing architectural spaces. At the nouveaux-riches Brys' upper Fifth Avenue house, Lily exposes herself like an object "at auction" in a tableau vivant. While the effect is mesmerizing on all her suitors, the setting is less than complementary. Old New Yorker Ned Van Alstyne comments to Selden that

> [the Architect] has put the whole of Mrs. Bry in his use of the composite order. Now for the Trenors, you remember, he used the Corinthian, exuberant, but based on the best precedent. (*HM*, 160)

And Selden notes that on the interior,

> the air of improvisation was in fact strikingly present: so recent, so rapidly-evoked was the whole *mis-en-scène* that one had to touch the marble columns to learn they were not of cardboard, to set one's self in one of the

damask gold arm-chairs to be sure it was not painted against the wall.
(*HM*, 132)

Wharton invokes classical architectural considerations of the orders
as classed taste indices to place the Brys socially below the Trenors.[25] The
interior, rapidly evoked and seemingly false, also shows that the Brys are
new arrivals to Society, and still subject to scrutinizing tests for deceit.
Class status and a woman's measure are both inscribed into her house.[26]

Lily's trip to Europe with the Dorsets on the boat *Sabrina* is disas-
trous; she returns to New York less secure than ever. Disinherited by her
aunt, she moves to a small private hotel. When even that becomes too
expensive, she takes a position with Mrs. Hatch, a vulgar Midwestern
divorcée, and lives with her at the Emporium Hotel, thereby crossing all
manner of social distinctions. The grand hotel was a new architectural
and social type of the period, created for the enormously wealthy who
did not have the time, patience, or taste to bother with a house and servants of their own; it was, however, very much against the mores of established New York and bespoke a new level of social crudity.[27] Although
sumptuous and fulfilling all Lily's physical needs, Lily can not stay; the
space lacks any differentiation between public and private rooms or classes and genders, and provokes in her the feeling of "being Venus." (*HM*,
273) Rather than take the charity of Gerty Farish and live in a flat, an alternative that, from the very beginning of the book, she could not imagine
for herself, Lily chooses to live in a boarding house. Here the only privacy
to her small, dark room is a visual one; the smells and sounds of her
neighbors continually drift in and remind her where she is.

Lily's last day takes her to the very lowest of the conceivable low:
she is entertained by a working woman in her kitchen. The word *kitchen*,
let alone the space, had never before entered Lily's vocabulary. As she
drifts into her final drug-induced sleep, she understands herself as "root-
less, something ephemeral."

> She herself had grown up without any one spot of earth being dearer to her
> than any other: there was no center of her early pieties, of grave endearing

traditions, to which her heart could revert and from which it could draw strength for itself and tenderness for others. In whatever form a slowly-accumulated past lives in the blood—whether in the concrete image of the old house stored with visual memories or in the conception of the house not built with the hands, but made up of inherited passions and loyalties—it has the same power of broadening and deepening the individual existence of attaching it by mysterious links of kinship to all the mighty sum of human striving. (*HM*, 319)

The house, for Lily as well as Wharton, describes more than social level and taste; it describes mental state, moral associations, and tradition. Before a woman's marriage, it is her childhood home that gives her a place in society; it is in the house of her parents that a woman acquires her sense of morals and tradition. Lily is an orphan without a home, a flower with no ground in which to put her roots; her lack of place is the cause of her demise. Similarly, Ellen Olenska yearns for a home of her own, believing it will give her both freedom and security in society. (*AI*, 72–76) Undine Spragg, on the other hand, is censured for having "forgotten the very house she was born in" and thus having no moral roots. (*CC*, 307) For women especially, who are uprooted objects in a world of commercial exchange, the house is their center. It defines a woman socially and spiritually and it gives order to her life.

Specific rooms in the house also functioned as spaces of empowerment for women. Throughout *The House of Mirth* (as well as many of Wharton's other works of fiction) the drawing room assumes a singular importance as both an indicator of character and as a site for the decisive action of women. In turn-of-the-century America, the drawing room was the room where guests were entertained on social visits and where pre- and post-dinner conversation took place. It was the prime space of social interaction between the sexes and seems to have been particularly affiliated with the woman who entertained within it.

In Wharton's fiction, the drawing room seems to express the character of the woman who presides over it. Mrs. Peniston's "imagination is shrouded, like the drawing room furniture," (*HM*, 123) while Lily thinks

Rosedale lacks a "drawing room manner." (*HM*, 115) In the story "New Year's Day," the narrator notes that "the most perilous coquetry may not be in a woman's way of arranging her dress, but in her way of arranging her drawing room."[28] In *The Age of Innocence*, the Europeanized Ellen Olenska's drawing room is "unlike one [Newland Archer] had ever known."

> [It had] small slender tables of dark wood, a delicate little Greek bronze on the chimney-piece, and a stretch of red damask nailed on the discolored wallpaper behind a couple of Italian-looking pictures in old frames . . . . [T]hese pictures bewildered him, for they were like nothing that he was accustomed to look at (and therefore able to see). . . . The atmosphere of the room was so different from any he had ever known that self-consciousness vanished in the sense of adventure. . . . What struck him was the way . . . the shabby hired house, with its blighted background of pampas grass and Rogers statuettes, had, by a turn of hand, and the skillful use of a few properties, been transformed into something intimate, "foreign," subtly suggestive of old romantic scenes and sentiments. (*AI*, 69–70)

Newland attempts to compare Ellen's drawing room to the one that he imagines his fiancée, May, will create—but he can not. It is too painful for him to realize that, like his wife and the life he will lead with her, his wife's drawing room will lack all imagination. The drawing room is its woman, and articulates her more directly than she can. Wharton's characters, who are so tragically limited in their words and actions by their society, can see truth in the drawing room, even when they are unable to speak it.

Indeed, Lily seems to be aware that decorating the drawing room is a powerful tool of a woman's self-expression. Her inability to redecorate the room causes her problems; she says to Selden, "If only I could do over my aunt's drawing room, I know I should be a better person." (*HM*, 8) At the same time, the threat that she might do so is one of her most dangerous aspects. One suitor is swayed against her by her refusal to swear to his mother that she will not "do over the drawing room," which is "the very thing [she] was marrying for."(*HM*, 10) She wounds her aunt most when she suggests that the drawing room be done over. (*HM*, 101) Decoration of the drawing room is like a woman's weapon. Having a room of one's own to decorate is for Lily "delicious" and "pure bliss," (*HM*, 7–8) yet she sees that she is not entitled to that privilege, as independent men like Selden, women like Gerty Farish, or married women are. "What a miserable thing it is to be a woman!" she cries in frustration. (*HM*, 7) To decorate a room, especially the drawing room, is to announce and flex power in architectural and social space.

Despite her lack of a drawing room of her own, this room type still functions as Lily's source of strength and authority. Indeed, when picturing herself, Lily "could not figure herself anywhere but in a drawing room." (*HM*, 100) She is in control of situations with both male and female characters as long as they take place in the drawing room; yet, in a library, on the street, at a threshold, on a boat, or even in a garden, she is unable to cope. Thus, the drawing room not only expresses a woman's character, it is the seat of her power in society. Similarly, in *The Age of Innocence*, the major decisions of the story are made by women in Mrs. Mingott's drawing room.[29] Yet, by the time of *The Custom of the Country* (c. 1910), power has moved from the woman's drawing room to the offices of Wall Street. Bowen asks, "Where does the real life of most American men lie? In some woman's drawing-room or in their offices?" (*CC*, 119) The answer is clear—real life exists in the business place. The drawing room has become a symbol of the husband's wealth and the social cachet it awards rather than a place with its own distinct power; likewise the woman who inhabits the drawing room no longer controls it for herself, but instead ornaments it for her husband.

An emphasis on the drawing room as a locus of female character and power is found in *The Decoration of Houses* as well. The book predates Wharton's novels and was written with Ogden Codman, the architect who decorated her homes in Newport and New York and drew up designs for The Mount. It is an index to her beliefs as well as a guide to her architecture. While its major thrust is to educate in good—classical,

European—taste in interior decoration, gender considerations play a large role. According to Wharton and Codman, the drawing room is historically a female space. It derives from

> the 'with-drawing-room' of medieval England, to which the lady and her maidens retired from the boisterous festivities of the hall, [and] seems at first to have been merely a part of the bed chamber in which the lord and lady slept. In time it came to be screened off from the sleeping room; then, in the king's palaces, it became a separate room for the use of the queen and her damsels; and so, in due course, reached the nobleman's castle, and established itself as a permanent part of English house-planning. (*DH*, 122)

This idea was widely accepted. Elsie deWolfe's enormously popular 1911 book on interior decoration *The House in Good Taste* elaborates further on the idea of the drawing room as historically female and suggests that modern house planning itself has its origins in women's designs.[30] Although deWolfe's book was written after women's suffrage and more than a decade later than Wharton's, it shows continued support for the drawing room and its decoration as a locus of women's authority in society.

To underscore the idea of the drawing room as a woman's space, it is helpful to consider Wharton's treatment of the library and den. In *The Decoration of Houses*, the den (or smoking room) is the only room that is presented as a male space; Wharton doesn't even address the man's bedroom. The "master's den" is furthermore directly opposed to the "lady's drawing room." (*DH*, 124) This "male lounging room" is to have "common sense, comfortable, office-like furniture"; "freed from the superfluous, it is often the most comfortable in the house." (*DH*, 152) The library, on the other hand, is a semipublic room where Wharton recommends floor-to-ceiling built-in bookcases filled by visible book bindings. (*DH*, 147)

In her novels, however, Wharton rarely mentions the den; rather, she presents the man's space as his library. Selden's library is "small, dark but cheerful, with its wall of books, a pleasantly faded Turkey rug, a littered desk." (*HM*, 6–7) Newland Archer reflects that "his only comfort was that [his wife] would probably let him arrange his library as he wished—which would be, of course, in 'sincere' Eastlake furniture and the plain new book cases without doors." (*AI*, 71) Ralph Marvell, Undine Spragg's first husband in *The Custom of the Country*, has a similar book-filled library within his grandfather and mother's house. For all three of these characters, the library is a retreat from the outer world where they can be themselves. But these libraries still are not idyllic spaces: Selden retires into his library with the desire for a "republic of the spirit" and is thus unable to forgive Lily; Ralph Marvell, who wants to write, goes insane and commits suicide in his library; and Newland Archer spends his time in his library dreaming of Ellen Olenska. Only the library at Bellomont, which "was in fact never used for reading" but was instead used for smoking and flirtation, seems to function positively.[31] The library, for Wharton, was thus not to be exclusive to men, but to be shared by both sexes and could even be sexually charged.

The tradition of gender distinctions in domestic interiors may derive from nineteenth-century English architectural planning, which was quite influential in America.[32] Robert Kerr's *The Gentleman's House; or, How To Plan English Residences* (1864) suggests no less than twenty-seven necessary rooms, each one carefully described by site, furnishings, and the sexes that could have access to and use of them.[33] Kerr defines three rooms as particularly feminine: the drawing room, boudoir, and morning room, and six as specifically masculine: the library, billiards room, gentleman's room, study, smoking room, and "gentleman's odd room." The men's rooms are to form a suite with their own bathroom, access to the outside, and service entrances, and thereby constitute an exclusively male territory within the house. There is no female counterpart to this area. Although the drawing room is "the Lady's apartment essentially" and is to be furnished in an "entirely ladylike" fashion, both drawing room and the similarly decorated morning room are to be used by both sexes; even the boudoir could be accessed by men.[34] Although the drawing room is the woman's space and reflects her character, it is still one of interaction between the sexes. The restricted male sanctuary signifies that it is the men of the house who hold the real power; it is they who have access to all architectural space and knowledge.

While the rigidity of Kerr's houses was much tempered in America, especially by 1900, such gender demarcations are still recognizable in Wharton's writings. She advocates women having power within their homes and supports the identification of drawing room and decoration as signs of that power; she also tends to depreciate the role of male spaces within the home. At the same time, she contends that restricting women to their homes, and thereby limiting their roles, is suffocating. There is, then, a tension between what she describes and what she promotes. As we shall see, Wharton attempted to resolve this tension in her own home by creating a house that truly signified its female resident.

Other issues important to Wharton's architectural ideas, but perhaps not so evident in her novels, are privacy and comfort. According to Wharton, home and room must conform to the living requirements of the inhabitants. (*DH*, 17) She sought to reform the living patterns inherited from the previous generation, abhorring them as testaments and regulators of social intolerance. Although she aims her argument primarily at women—"men in these matters are less exacting than women, because their demands, besides being simpler, are uncomplicated by the feminine tendency to want things because other people have them, rather than to have things because they are wanted" (*DH*, 17)—she levels this criticism specifically at nouveaux-riches American women in *The Custom of the Country*. (*CC*, 307) Her criticism is not of women *per se* but of women as symptomatic of a general lack of taste in newly-wealthy America.

"Privacy," she argues, "is one of the first requisites of civilized life," and a room should thus be a "small world on its own." (*DH*, 22) In opposition to the open, passage-like rooms of the previous generation, which allowed for constant surveillance and little privacy, she advocates single-utility rooms with many doors. Her greatest quarrel with the American house is that the door has disappeared. (*DH*, 49) She calls for its reinstatement with ample architectural treatment to give the door, and the privacy it occasions, added weight. The first thing the reader is told about the individual components of the house is that "while the main purpose of a[n entrance] door is to admit, its secondary purpose is to exclude" and that the "outer door should clearly proclaim itself as an exterior barrier" to give a sense of security. (*DH*, 103) Several examples of locks are even included in the illustration of the book. The house is a woman's shelter, her barrier against anything or anyone that she does not choose to allow into her life.

Wharton's ferocity about privacy is related to both class and gender distinctions. Closed rooms keep the servants out of the served spaces. Passage spaces are unequivocally reserved for passage. The hall is never to be used as a living-room; it is instead like a public square where all manner of people pass but never stop. (*DH*, 115) It should be adorned monumentally but plainly, the kind of space that both welcomes and arrests, but is never beheld for long. (*DH*, 117) While the presence of servants in the hall increases its public nature even more, this is the only space she mentions that servants use. This underscores her refusal even to discuss the mundane service-oriented aspects of the house. There is no chapter on kitchen, pantry, or servants quarters; such issues do not concern ladies of her class. She presents all the rooms in relation to their degree of publicity or privacy, and says that their decoration should be in accordance to that quality.

Such closed, inflexible, controlled spaces hardly seem to correspond to what many might consider to be "female" principles of architecture—such as openness of form and social interaction, fluidity, and flexibility.[35] Yet, they are understandable within a world where a woman's intimacy, whether with another or oneself, had to be in private. Just as rooms communicated what was unsayable about a woman, they also offered spaces for communications that went unsaid in public. For instance, the hearth, which some of Wharton's contemporary architectural thinkers saw as the heart of the house on account of its associations with the motherly nurturer, is for Wharton an intimate and private place for men and women to converse—the place of the heart rather than the heart of the place. It is by the fireplace in the little-used library at Bellomont that Lily pretends to surprise Selden and Mrs. Dorset while she herself is on a mission for such an intimate tête-à-tête. (*HM*, 59)

If these semipublic rooms are reserved as "quiet retreat[s] for flirtation" and smoking, the bedroom is for more personal intimacy. The bedroom is the most private room in the house, according to *The Decoration of Houses*, (*DH*, 169–70) and seems to be equated in Wharton's novels with self-reflection. Lily dreads the "self-communication" that awaits her in her bedroom at Bellomont, so she lingers in the gallery-hall. (*HM*, 24)[36] Later, she suspects that Mrs. Bry is "not even herself in her bed-room." (*HM*, 189) Finally, Lily faces herself and her life in her bedroom at the boarding house. (*HM*, 317–23) The bedroom, frequently not shared with her husband, is where a woman contemplates herself and her actions. Undressed, free of the social obligations of her sex, she can think of and by herself.[37] Thus, only in the most private and inaccessible spaces of the house is a woman her real self; in the public areas of the house, such as the drawing room and dining room, she plays a representational role. However much the house is equated with its woman, it is always actually the sign of the man who "owns" both wife and home. The power of the woman within the house is thus a power inscribed within and restricted by an overarching system of male spatial and social control.

Gender distinctions take on a very different form in Wharton's own homes. Her activity as a writer and intellectual, and her independent wealth, meant that the signification of power—social and economic—was inverted from the norm that she described in her novels. While her husband, Edward (Teddy) Wharton, had a small personal income and no occupation, Edith had quite a substantial inheritance and even made money from her writing. In 1883, when her father died, she received $20,000 outright and a portion of his estate generating $8,000–$9,000 *per annum* income. In 1888, her grandfather's cousin, Joshua Jones, the sole stockholder of the family's bank, Chemical Bank of New York, passed away, leaving her close to $120,000—nearly two million dollars in today's terms. At her mother's death in 1901, she received an additional $90,000 in trust (only a sixth of the family estate), the rest going to her two brothers and their children. Her annual income must have been about $22,000, a very respectable sum for the period.[38] The Joshua Jones legacy established the Whartons' financial security, and it was at this time that Edith became interested in decorating to her own tastes.

The first house she was involved in decorating was Land's End, her summer cottage in Newport (1892–97). It was during the interior remodeling of this standard "stick style" 1870s resort house that she first met and collaborated with Ogden Codman. They "drifted into" writing *The Decoration of Houses* while working on the house; the interior corresponds, as much as a remodeled house can, to the ideas expressed in the book.[39] In 1900, tired of the "trivialities and frivolities" of Newport in the summer and New York the rest of the year, Wharton purchased land in Lenox, Massachusetts, which was fast becoming a more artistic inland counterpart to Newport.[40] She asked Codman to help her design the new house, but he proved too expensive for their friendship. Instead, she employed an up-and-coming young architect, Francis Hoppin, to draw up her ideas.[41] The similarity between Codman's sketches and Hoppin's final plans shows a continuity of planning ideas that must be due to Wharton's very active involvement (FIGS. 3–4).

The Mount, finished and decorated by 1905, follows the prescriptions of *The Decoration of Houses* to a great extent. However, because the house functioned as signifier of her intellectual and economic independence—not as a sign of her husband's wealth and power—gender is inscribed differently here than in the houses described in her novels and in *The Decoration of Houses*. As a woman's house, the signification of public, social power is displaced from the feminine rooms of the man's house into the masculine rooms of a woman's house. Likewise, the woman's private space becomes empowered as a place of artistic and intellectual creativity.

One enters at the basement level to a grotto-like hall. The staircase is in a separate hall; thus, direct access and visibility are denied to the unwanted visitor. The hall is suitably decorated in a monumental, severe way; the sobering effect of cold, white stone prompts the visitor to move on or leave. At the top of the stairs is a gallery that affords views to the outdoors and access to all of the public rooms of the floor, each of which are discrete entities with closable doors for privacy. The main body of the

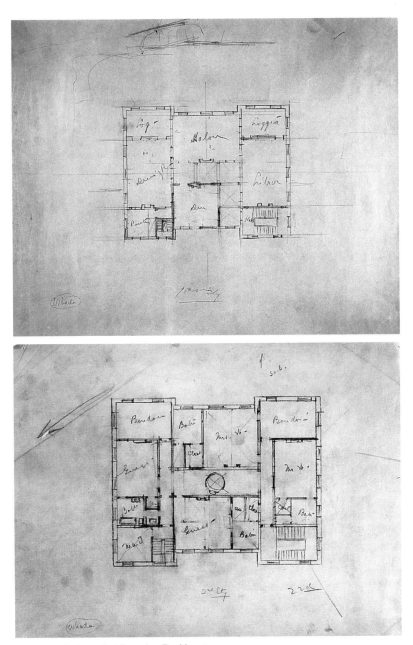

TOP: FIG. 3A Codman, first floor plan, The Mount
BOTTOM: FIG. 3B Codman, second floor plan, The Mount

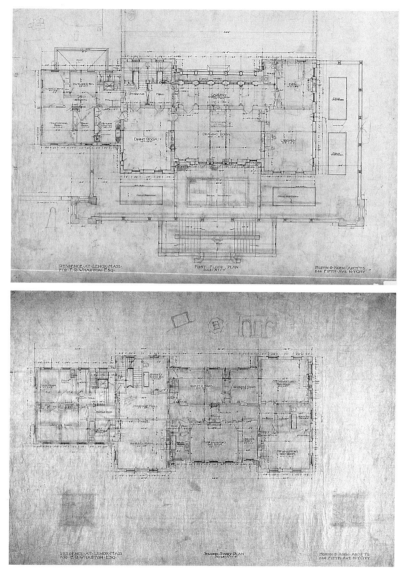

TOP: FIG. 4A Hoppin, first floor plan, The Mount
BOTTOM: FIG. 4B Hoppin, second floor plan, The Mount

house is symmetrical; false and concealed doors obscure any discrepancies in this symmetry. The drawing room is at the center of the plan; dining room and library flank it on either side. The den is pushed far into a corner.

Although only a few photographs record the original arrangements of The Mount's rooms, we can tell that Wharton considered decoration to be part of the architectural plan because furniture is sketched, in her hand, onto Hoppin's first floor plan (FIG. 4A). Only one faint photograph remains to testify to Wharton's own drawing room (FIG. 5). It appears to have been a place of "gay first impression," comfort, leisure,

FIG. 5 Drawing room, The Mount, c. 1904

and easy circulation, as she recommended in *The Decoration of Houses*. (*DH*, 125–29) White paneled and carved walls were covered, in part, by tapestries; *objets* were judiciously placed about the room and the decor seems to have been light, airy, and entertaining. The dining room, according to Wharton a feminine space historically (*DH*, 155), was more officious, although it too was white. Architectural details such as the paneling play a much greater role, and Grinling Gibbons-style carving adds to its historical quality. Both rooms were furnished with French pieces, as she had favored in *The Decoration of Houses*, although the carvings add an English touch. While these rooms certainly accord with *The Decoration of Houses*, their femininity is in no way emphasized or exaggerated. Rather than increase the importance of the feminine public spaces of the house and thus further ingrain the gender inequalities that they express and enforce, Wharton let them be; instead she neutralized masculine public spaces by either feminizing or de-emphasizing them.

The library, like the other rooms, is highly reminiscent of *The Decoration of Houses* (FIG. 6). Floor-to-ceiling bookcases are built into the

FIG. 6 Library, The Mount, c. 1904

wall, bookbindings serve as part of the decoration, and ample writing tables and reading lamps are supplied. Dark wood paneling and comfortable, deep-colored, office-like furniture communicate a masculine gendering of this space in the most stereotypical sense, yet the delicate carving, floral pillows, lamps, and rugs, along with the slender proportions, express a feminine one.[42] Since Edith Wharton was a writer, and friend to many literary figures whom she may have entertained here, the library at The Mount would have been Edith's space much more than her unintellectual husband's. It was thus a space shared between women and men—the dual-gendered space of this "masculine Henry James."

In many of her novels as well as in *The Decoration of Houses*, Wharton seems to have advocated a certain regendering of the library from an exclusively male space to one where men and women could meet on equal grounds. Historically, the library was problematically masculine, in that it was reserved for men, and asexual, in that sexuality did not enter or occupy this room reserved for reading, writing, and the pursuit of knowledge. This gendering of the library seems to be inverted at The Mount, allowing Wharton to enter and occupy the space. The library might be termed "gender-neutral" in that it may be entered and occupied by both women and men, and, in a sense, "sexualized" by the social intercourse that could now take place there. Many have argued that Wharton's library activities—writing, pursuing intellectual friendships, entertaining, and even architectural pursuits—were substitutes for the sexual life that she did not have with her impotent husband.[43] In this light, the "sexualization" of the architectural space of writing and reading becomes emblematic not just of Wharton's appropriation of the male professions of writing and architecture, but, even more importantly, of the metaphorical connection between sexuality and artistic production—the house and books are the children Wharton never had.

Completing this concomitant neutralization and sexualization of space, the sole male room, her husband's den, is to be found in a far corner, in the margins of the dominant public spaces of the floor. While its privacy of place and own bathroom connect it to the male territories described by Kerr, the body enclosed in this space is not the master of the house but Wharton's ineffectual husband. The den thus may be seen as a marginal space for the less-significant gender and is equivalent in this house to the boudoir in the male house.

The stairs to the upper (private) story are placed off the axis of the main public stair; it is thus difficult to gain access to the bedrooms and boudoirs above. On the second level, as on the first, a central hall provides access to every room. Edith Wharton's quarters take up the entire east wing of the house and are divided into four rooms as she had suggested in her book: bedroom, boudoir, dressing room, and bathroom. (*DH*, 170) Here, as in the other bedrooms, there is a separate entrance for the servants.[44] Wharton used her boudoir not only for the "prosaic duties of the household," as described in *The Decoration of Houses*, (*DH*, 170) but also for writing. Placed in the southeast corner, the boudoir was both the most difficult room of the suite to get to and also the one that received the most morning light. Wharton's mornings were spent here undisturbed; no one had permission to enter uninvited while she wrote.[45] The boudoir in Wharton's house suggests comparison to the study in a man's house: it is the privatized power center of the entire house. Almost as if to emphasize this, the newly-empowered, private, feminine boudoir is located directly above the disempowered, marginalized, and masculine den; the desexualized bedroom is above the "sexualized" library, the site of intellectual intercourse between the sexes. Wharton is literally on top physically.

An emphasis on the relationships among gender, power, and space can be found to be at the very center of the design of Edith Wharton's house. At the very least, the design accommodates her needs, as it was in fact her house. The plan assures her privacy while allowing a carefully controlled fluidity to movements within the public sphere. Delving further, one finds that the historically feminine public spaces seem unexaggerated in their femininity while historically male spaces seem to be emasculated either by the integration of feminine occupation and detailing or by spatial marginalization. Private traditionally-feminine rooms seem newly favored in placement, use, and decoration, and are the expression of a house in which the woman is privileged, not as the sign of her husband, but for herself. Inversions of the spatial, sexual order are significant, but also produce a house in which men and women can more easily and equally mix.

Analysis of the exterior of the house shows the degree to which Wharton was trying to create an Americanized European house. The exterior elevation of the house is derived from Belton House in England (1684), although the entrance front is changed due to the gallery and basement entry. The terraced gardens are Italian in inspiration and show correspondences with her book *Italian Villas and Their Gardens*. Finally, the setting and views are American. Over and above the idea of the American Renaissance, Wharton may have been trying to create for herself on American soil a house that allowed her the cultural, social, and artistic freedoms she sensed that the European woman enjoyed, a space in which men and women could interact as equals.

However, this was a fragile construction. In 1913, she divorced her husband, sold The Mount, and moved to France, where she would remain for the rest of her life. These three changes provided those things she strove for at The Mount: sexual and personal freedom as an unrestricted, independent woman; real European houses; and literary recognition. Wharton wrote many of her most acclaimed works while abroad, including the Pulitzer Prize-winning *The Age of Innocence*. In addition to her house in Paris, she had summer and winter villas in the north and south of France. Pavilion Colombe at St. Brice-sous-Forêt was the former home of a pair of seventeenth-century courtesans who murdered their lover, while her house in the south of France, Chateau Ste. Claire, was a former convent. Issues of women's place within society as positioned through architecture continued to fascinate her in France as well.

"The Mount," stated Henry James on his first visit after returning from Europe in 1904, "is unlike other American houses . . . which totally lack *penetralia*. . . . some part . . . sufficiently *within* some other part, sufficiently withdrawn and consecrated."[46] The privacy of *penetralia* is also the publicity of *penetration*: the consecration of Wharton's boudoir is bound to the woman's penetration of the library. The inversions and revisions of gendered space, which create what she may have considered a modern as well as European home—that is, one in which the sexes interacted as equals—must be considered in relation to the kind of homes Wharton described in her novels.

As we have seen, the house of Wharton's novels, and indeed her culture, although identified with the woman, is actually the man's; the woman's power within it is only that which her husband and society allow. This power is centered in the drawing room—a public, accessible, and representational space. The woman has control over her house only through decoration, that is, representation, as she herself, following Veblen, is a representation. As Luce Irigaray argues concerning women and the space of home:

The material-feminine remains the place separated from "her" place, deprived of "his" place. She becomes the place of the other who can't separate himself from her. Threatening therefore—without knowing it or wanting it to be so—with what she lacks: *un lieu propre*. It would be necessary for her to re-envelope herself with herself, and at least twice: as she who is woman and as she who is mother, which implies modifying the whole space-time economy. . . . In exchange—which is not one—paying for a house for her, sticking her inside it, imposing a limit on her, the opposite of the unlimited site where he unwittingly places her.[47]

The potential "envelope" Irigaray cites as the attempted strategy for giving place to displaced woman is make-up, jewelry, fashion, mask—decoration.

Edith Wharton's *Decoration of Houses* occupies a complex position between her own house and the fictional and real houses of her writing and society. In these latter, decoration is a doomed strategy for women. However, the elevation of decoration (the feminine strategy for placing) to the status of architecture (the masculine strategy for placing) in *The Decoration of Houses* provides a theoretical program for equality in gender interaction and space. As a female writer and intellectual, Wharton was outside the norms of her society; she must have yearned for a space in which her feminine nature and masculine interests could coexist in harmony. The Mount was an attempt to create such a space. In the end, however, Wharton found that such physical configurations were futile. "A woman's nature is like a great house," she realized, and the only solution for a woman's happiness was, as she advised Mary Berenson, "to decorate one's inner house so richly that one is content there."

NOTES

1. Edith Wharton, "The Fullness of Life," *Scribner's Magazine* XIV (December 1893), quoted in R.W.B. Lewis, ed., *The Collected Short Stories of Edith Wharton*, vol. I (New York: Charles Scribner's Sons, 1968), 14.

2. Edith Wharton, as quoted in R.W.B. Lewis, *Edith Wharton: A Biography* (New York: Harper & Row, 1975), 413.

3. Quotations from these works are cited in the text with the abbreviations listed below. Page citations are to the reprint editions.

DH: Wharton and Ogden Codman, *The Decoration of Houses* (New York: Charles Scribner's Sons, 1897; reprint, New York, 1902).

HM: *The House of Mirth* (New York: Charles Scribner's Sons, 1905; reprint, New York and London: Penguin Classics, 1986).

CC: *The Custom of The Country* (New York: Charles Scribner's Sons, 1913; reprint, New York: Penguin Books, 1987).

AI: *The Age of Innocence* (New York and London: D. Appleton and Company, 1920; reprint, New York: Collier Books, 1992).

4. For a discussion of architecture and the American Renaissance, see Richard Guy Wilson, *American Renaissance, 1876–1917*, Brooklyn Museum Catalogue (New York: Pantheon, 1979).

5. Her ideas about decoration and gardening were supported by architects at the time; Charles McKim, of the prestigious firm of McKim, Mead and White, previewed her book favorably and even sought out her advice on the White House. See Richard Guy Wilson, "Edith and Ogden: Writing, Decoration and Architecture," in *Ogden Codman and the Decoration of Houses*, ed. Pauline Metcalf (Boston: Boston Athenaeum/David R. Godine, 1988), 152.

6. In *The Decoration of Houses* Wharton notes that hers is the first treatise in English since Issac Ware's *Complete Body of Architecture* (1753) to treat these fields on the same level as architecture. See *DH*, xx–xxi.

7. Lisa Keoningsberg, "Mariana van Rensselaer" in *Architecture: A Place for Women*, eds. Ellen Perry Berkeley and Matilda McQuaid (Washington: Smithsonian Institution Press, 1989), 47.

8. Ibid., 48, 49.

9. One female architect of the period who seems to have escaped such censure was Californian Julia Morgan. The first woman to graduate from the École des Beaux Arts in Paris, Morgan is best known for her work for the Hearst Family (such as San Simeon); she also designed buildings for the YWCA and for cities and fairs, as well as women's colleges, women's centers, and many domestic projects. Personally low in profile, she countenanced little publicity and, although sympathetic to the women's movement, made no effort to publicize herself as a woman architect. Also, since she worked primarily in California and the West, she paid little attention to the East Coast architectural establishment and vice versa. See Sara Holmes Boutelle, *Julia Morgan, Architect*, rev. edition (New York: Abbeville Press, 1995).

10. Henry Van Brunt and a Lady Manager of the Fair, quoted in Robert W. Rydell, "A Cultural Frankenstein?" *Grand Illusions: Chicago's World's Fair of 1893*, ed. Neil Harris et al. (Chicago: Chicago Historical Society, 1993), 155.

11. *American Architect and Building News* 28 (26 November 1892): 134, cited Hayden's "brain fever" as evidence of women's inadequacy for the profession: "It seems a question not yet answered how successfully a woman with her physical limitations can enter and engage in . . . a profession which is a very wearing one. If a building of which women seem so proud is to mark the physical mien of its architect, it will be a much more telling argument against the wisdom of women entering this especial profession than anything else could be." See Judith Paine, "Sophia Hayden and the Women's Building," *Helicon Nine* 1 (1979): 28–37.

12. Louis Sullivan, *Kindergarten Chats* (Cleveland: 1901–1902). Sullivan was later to be censured for the "unmasculine" aspects of his designs, a criticism which may have been leveled as much for his homosexuality as his style.

13. "Some Recent Works by Ogden Codman Jr.," *Architectural Record* (July 1905): 51.

14. Pauline Metcalf, "Ogden Codman Jr., Architect-Decorator: Elegance without Excess" (master's thesis, Columbia University, 1978), 88.

15. Henry Adams, "The Virgin and the Dynamo," (1900) in *The Education of Henry Adams* (Boston: The Massachusetts Historical Society, 1918; reprint, Boston: Houghton Mifflin, 1988), 385.

16. Henry James, Notebooks, 8 April 1883, *The Complete Notebooks of Henry James*, eds. Leon Edel and Lyall Powers (New York and Oxford: Oxford University Press, 1987), 20.

17. Ibid., 73–74.

18. This, of course, was in the upper reaches of society, but it was that world with which Wharton was primarily concerned.

19. See Dolores Hayden, *The Grand Domestic Revolution: A History of Feminist Designs for American Homes, Neighborhoods, and Cities* (Cambridge, MA: MIT Press, 1981), chapters 6–9.

20. Quoted in Sandra Gilbert and Susan Gubar, *No Man's Land: The Place of the Woman Writer in the Twentieth Century* (New Haven: Yale University Press, 1989), 126.

21. Longtime friend Henry James called Wharton "ferocious," while one critic called her a "masculine Henry James," and another a "self-made man"; her family told her she was "unfeminine" and nicknamed her "John." See Gilbert & Gubar, 126, 134. Wharton once even wrote Bernard Berenson, in reference to her love for literary criticism, that she was "getting a little confused about [her] sex." Wharton to Berenson, 4 September 1917, *The Letters of Edith Wharton*, ed. R.W.B. Lewis and Nancy Lewis (New York: Scribner, 1988), 399.

22. Gilbert & Gubar, 129.

23. Ibid., 167.

24. Wharton was living in and decorating The Mount while writing *The House of Mirth*, and the house served as the model for the novel's Bellomont.

25. The Five Orders of Classical architecture were typified by both gender and social class. Vitruvius's *Ten Books of Architecture* discussed the Doric as male, Ionic as matronly, and Corinthian as virginal. Architectural theorists of the Renaissance expanded this theme to the Tuscan and Composite orders and applied class distinctions to elucidate the orders' differences even further. Serlio's Tuscan was a "sturdy (male) laborer," John Shute's Composite, "a courtesan." While the exact relationship between Corinthian and Composite varied with date, country, and author, English writers tended to side with Shute in finding the Composite too florid (and too sexual) and a signifier of a lack of good architectural taste.

26. This can be true in a man's space too if he is the one doing the decorating, as we see in Selden's library. But, as he even admits to himself, it was from his *mother* that he learned his "values . . . of stoic carelessness of material things combined with an Epicurean's pleasure in them . . . the 'knack' of abstinence combined with elegance" which direct his life as well as his decorating. (*HM*, 152)

27. Wharton is even more vituperative against the Hotel, its life, and inhabitants in *The Custom of the Country*.

28. "New Year's Day," in *Old New York* (New York: Appleton, 1924; reprint, London: Virago Modern Classic, 1985), 296.

29. Mrs. Mingott's drawing room, like her character, is unique in its power and architectural arrangement. Her "characteristic independence" had caused her to build her mansion near Central Park, an area untouched at the time by fashionable building. Furthermore, on account of her weight, she placed her private rooms directly *en suite* with the drawing room, all on the first floor. One could see, through a door that was "always open . . . the unexpected vista of a bedroom. . . . Her visitors were startled and fascinated by the foreignness of this arrangement, which recalled scenes in French fiction, and architectural incentives to immorality such as the simple American had never dreamed of." (*AI*, 28) Mrs. Mingott, an enormously wealthy widow, is socially independent and important; she announces this through her house and especially her drawing room.

30. Elsie deWolfe, *The House in Good Taste* (New York: The Century Co., 1913). This book repeats many of Wharton's themes and even uses some of Wharton's phrases word for word.

31. As signs of social transgression and sexuality, smoking and flirtation underscore the interplay of sexuality and gender in Wharton's articulation of space. See Daphne Spain, "From Parlour to Great Room," *Gendered Spaces* (Chapel Hill: University of North Carolina Press, 1992), 26.

32. Ibid., 117.

33. Ibid., 114.

34. Ibid., 114. Kerr also recommended separate bedrooms for husband and wife, as well as the physical separation of rooms for young men and women, including separate staircases for the sexes!

35. See, for example, Magrit Kennedy, "Seven Hypotheses on Female and Male Principles in Architecture," *Heresies* 11 (1981): 12–13.

36. According to *The Decoration of Houses*, the gallery-hall is no place to loiter. (*DH*, 120)

37. For Wharton personally, bedroom and dressing room seem also to have functioned as a place of personal meditation. As a child, she enacted her favorite game of "making-up"—that is making up stories—in the privacy of her dressing room. Edith Wharton, *A Backward Glance* (London: Century Hutchinson Ltd., 1987), 33–35.

38. All the financial information cited is taken from Lewis, *Edith Wharton: A Biography*, 47, 59 and 100–101.

39. *A Backward Glance*, 107. Wharton also commissioned Codman to decorate the interior of her New York house at 884 Park Avenue during the 1890s.

40. Wilson, "Edith and Ogden," 161.

41. Francis L.V. Hoppin (1867–1941) studied architecture at M.I.T. and in France. In 1894, after an apprenticeship with McKim, Mead and White, he and Terrence Koen started their own New York City firm, Hoppin and Koen. They specialized in grand country and city homes, as well as public buildings such as the Police Headquarters in New York City (1907–9). The Mount was one of Hoppin's early prestigious commissions.

42. Although such attributes are common to Codman's libraries, one must remember that he had

been censured for his effeminate interiors, and, secondly, compare these libraries to the weighty spaces of such libraries as McKim, Mead and White's for J. Pierpont Morgan.

43. For example, Wilson, "Edith and Ogden," 138, 177; Gilbert & Gubar, *No Man's Land*, 132; Cynthia Griffin Wolff, *A Feast of Words: The Triumph of Edith Wharton* (Oxford & New York: Oxford University Press, 1971; 2nd edition, Reading, MA: Addison-Wesley, 1995). Although Wharton did her actual writing in the private, feminine space of the Boudoir (see below), historically, the Library is the sign of writing. See Judith Fryer, *Felicitous Space: The Imaginative Structures of Edith Wharton and Willa Cather* (Chapel Hill: University of North Carolina Press, 1986), 27.

44. Indeed, service facilities were given an entire separate wing, far from the Whartons' life. However, no convenience was spared: the house was equipped with an elevator and refrigerator as well as other modern appliances. On the exterior, the servant's porch is given a Doric colonnade—class status too was a part of Wharton's house.

45. Fryer, 65.

46. Henry James, *The American Scene* (New York and London: Harper and Brothers Publishers, 1907), as quoted in Fryer, 65.

47. Luce Irigaray, *L'Ethique de la différence sexuelle* (Paris: Editions de Minuit, 1984) 18–19, trans. and quoted by Elizabeth Grosz, *Sexual Subversions: Three French Feminists* (Sydney, Australia: Allen & Unwin, 1989), 174.

The Story of Hon-Katedral:

A Fantastic Female

MOLLY HANKWITZ

Life . . . is never the way one imagines it. It surprises you, it amazes you, and it makes you laugh or cry when you don't expect it.

—NIKI DE SAINT-PHALLE[1]

Almost everything is yet to be written by women about femininity: about their sexuality, that is, its infinite and mobile complexity, about their eroticization, sudden turn-ons of a certain minuscule-immense area of their bodies; not about destiny, but about the adventure of such and such a drive, about trips, crossings, trudges, abrupt and gradual awakenings, discoveries of a zone at one time timorous and soon to be forthright. A woman's body, with its thousand and one thresholds of ardor—once, by smashing yokes and censors, she lets it articulate the profusion of meanings that run through it in every direction—will make the old single-grooved mother tongue reverberate with more than one language.

—HÉLÈNE CIXOUS, THE LAUGH OF THE MEDUSA[2]

Imagine a woman who felt relegated to circulation space, stairs, corridors, back doors, and could not take up a prominent position in front of the TV, on the bed, or on the globe—who could not move in proper spheres of economy, politics, and social life, but was instead relegated to the role of stepping out of the way of others. Oppressed women, it seems to me, are divorced from the act of living in this way, having learned to take only the bit parts instead of playing the lead.

—MOLLY HANKWITZ, JOURNAL

INTRODUCTION

As an author, I include this particular quote from my journal among the other quotes because there is such a striking contrast in its phrases to both the work of Niki de Saint-Phalle and the quote of Hélène Cixous. I felt it was important because this is a paper not only about de Saint-Phalle but about space, feminism, and pleasure. It seemed therefore appropriate to connect to women who for some reason or another may not have access to these things. Besides, it is my point in this essay that the power of Niki de Saint-Phalle's *Hon-katedral* is its ability to define a different kind of space, the space of leisure, humor, pleasure, and sexuality. This is the work's radical and liberatory content. Therefore, in my heart of hearts, for women artists everywhere, I would hope that such power can be translated culturally through art to all women and not just to the privileged.

Hon (Swedish for "she") is also a pivotal object in Niki de Saint-Phalle's career. *She* was the first major collaboration between de Saint-Phalle and her life partner Jean Tinguely. As you will see, *She* enunciates a moment in the artist's career when de Saint-Phalle went from producing life-sized doll-like sculptures to creating a major work. It has been important to me to look at that juncture because it was a moment when the artist pushed her work in sculpture toward architecture, something that she has continued to do and is still doing

Other architectural projects by Niki de Saint-Phalle: (from Internet URLs: http://gort.ucsd.edu/sj/phalle/Bib.html; http://gort.ucsd.edu/sj/Bio.html; http://www.well.com/user/mvff/Whois.html)

1965   Begins first *nana* dolls.

1966   *Hon-katedral.* Designs sets and costumes for Aristophanes' *Lysistrata* in a production by Rainer von Diez at the Staatstheater in Kassel.

1967   *Le paradise fantastique* with Jean Tinguely, a commission from the French government for Expo '67 in Montreal.
        First retrospective exhibition at the Stedelijk Museum in Amsterdam, for which she creates her first

in her *Tarot Garden* and new work with Mario Botta. Thus, on a personal level and as an object, this work, and its relation to de Saint-Phalle's overall career as a radically different and unorthodox artist, is crucial to contemporary discussions of feminism and architecture. *She* stands as an important example if we are to look at women makers and producers of works and their relationships to art and architecture as whole and complete, not fragmented, marginal, or second best. It is my concern here to show Niki de Saint-Phalle in the best light while also attempting to tie her works to an artistic context, to enlighten us in terms of internationalism in the arts and the politics of the exchange of ideas, which may or may not have affected artists in the late sixties. Surely *She* had a major affect. *She* was written about in every major world newspaper and art magazine. *She* was risqué for her time. *She* was also loved.

In every way, *She* touches on the organic and the sensual in the site of gender, foremost as a sign of both meaning and value for women's bodies. Linked to the possibilities of drama, literature, and imagination, *She* is about space and desire, as is the previously quoted passage from Cixous. *She* is a model. My aim is to illustrate this in a discussion of some of the possible readings and interpretations we can give to this work and its relationship to some tangents of feminism and art history. In doing so, I also focus on de Saint-Phalle as a creative artist—one who has continued to pursue the fantastic and the surreal in architectural form, and one who has rendered permanently, her dreams. This effort on my part is one which, I believe, will open and advance engendered spaces in art[3]—the feminine and the surreal, the fantasy and drama of the grotesque—and their various humorous or tragic appearances in the history of design.

The idea of the woman as monster is not alien to feminism. It seems to emerge often at the point when women artists are beginning to develop in their work, taking power and asserting their themes. The idea of the giantess found in *She* is thus a likely metaphor for women taking space for themselves. And as ugly as a monster can sometimes be, there is something quite beautiful in monstrousness as well. Monstrousness is human. It is political. It is a metaphor for goodness, as in the friendliness of monsters, and also for our dark side.

So, I use further the tiny steps of my path of words in the quote from my journal entry and rather than dwell on the state of possible continual oppression that I have set down, take de Saint-Phalle and Cixous as my leading ladies; from their freedom, I attempt to enlarge the house of women, for myself and for my readers, through the beautiful space of *She*.

CONTEXT

Looking briefly at Western and Eastern art and architectural history, one finds a significant presence of women. There are the often-described organically-formed domiciles such as pueblos, teepees, and tents intuitively built or ornamented by nomadic or agrarian women and girls throughout India, South America, South Africa, Southeast Asia, and Western Africa, where the arts of adobe, beading, building, mud plastering, painting, pottery, sewing, thatching, tile decoration, and weaving have been performed for centuries. These methods and practices operate as systems of exchange wherein symbolic images, colors, methods, rituals, and celebrations are passed on from one generation to another. Mythological fertility goddesses and ideals of harvest, magic, and power abound in many contemporary cultures as well as in prehistory, from which, for example, the voluptuous body of the Venus of Willendorf has become a celebrated artifact. In Greece, delicate mathematical proportions guided classical culture in terms of beauty and codes of femininity, especially in architecture. Figures such as the union of caryatids in the Porch of the Maidens at the Erechtheum supported entablatures and graced the Athenian landscape. These representations of women speak to life's processes.

Among ruling civilizations in Egypt, India, Russia, Turkey, and Western Europe, female royalty often influenced the whole planning of cities.

Nana Dream House, Nana Fountain, and *Nana Town*.

1968 Her first play *ICH (All about Me)* is performed at the Staatstheater in Kassel, co-authored with Rainer von Diez. She designs the sets and costumes.

Exhibits her eighteen-part wall relief *Last Night I Had a Dream* at the Galerie Alexandre Iolas in Paris.

1969 Returns from travels in India and begins work on her first architectural project, three houses in the South of France for Rainer von Diez.

Begins work on *La Tête (Le Cyclope)*, a collaborative project in Fountainbleu forest, initiated by Jean

Castles, fountains, gardens, monuments, temples, and tombs were erected for their pleasure or to honor their memory for all time. Numerous outstanding women make up the visible body of late-nineteenth and early-twentieth-century feminism: activists, artists, suffragists, and writers—women for whom money, occupation, ownership, and political empowerment have been a lived reality. Female architects, clients, and domestic theorists have been written into more and more social histories. The specific needs of an emerging class of working women are seen, for example, in structures created for special populations such as immigrant women, nuns, prostitutes, single mothers, and working women, in works such as the Donaldina Cameron House (Presbyterian Mission, 1907) in San Francisco's Chinatown or the YWCA Building (1918), both designed by Julia Morgan, whose private homes and buildings on the UC Berkeley campus are more often cited.[4]

Women build architecture throughout the world, corresponding to engendered spaces which have opened in academia, film, fine art, history, law, literature, medicine, public politics, and video. These fields burgeon with the voices of creative women, homages to women, and works by and for women. Now, moreover, this same content is being found in multimedia.

To this end—or perhaps it is a beginning—I am delighted to contribute the story of *She*, elaborating on numerous interpretations that have appeared in catalogs and other writings on this work.

She was produced by a recognized woman artist, but equally important is the fact that the statue occupied a main hall of a major European museum, and involved in her making an entire community of women, children, and men. The scope of de Saint-Phalle's endeavor is much of its extraordinary power.

A strong emphasis on festivity, sexuality, and process sets the project apart. It adds to her poetry and to her feminist myth, one which touched many lives. The giantess embodied the newly emerging womanhood of her time—the new woman found in much of the literature of feminism's first wave, for example, the first American printing of Simone de

Beauvoir's *The Second Sex* (1959), and which carried over into later authoritative critical texts such as Robin Morgan's anthology *Sisterhood is Powerful* (1970); the self-health guidebook, *Our Bodies, Ourselves*, first published by the Boston Women's Health Book Collective in 1971; Hélène Cixous and Catherine Clément's *The Newly Born Woman* (1972); and Susan Brownmiller's *Against Our Will* (1975). In short, *She* brings to mind spaces of privilege, politics, and pleasure being won by women everywhere. *She* also suggests a narrative for women, culture-specific to the pop modernity of the sixties as it was played out in "flower power" and "being groovy."

PREHISTORY

As a collaboration by Niki de Saint-Phalle, Jean Tinguely, and Per Olof Ultvedt, *She* is important to the history of the avant-garde within the context of art in the mid-sixties, when a variety of new forms were readily evolving. Frank Popper develops categories for this trope of the avant-garde in his significant work *Art—Action and Participation*: "the disappearance of the *object*, the participation of the public, the architectural factor [monumentality] and the use of entirely new, 'non-solid', plastic materials."[5] These categories are reflected in de Saint-Phalle's *King Kong*, completed at the Dwan Gallery (Los Angeles, 1963), for which she received international recognition, furthering her reputation for being an aggressive woman artist by shooting at paint canisters with her rifle. In this huge non-objective installation, the artist collaged numerous objects onto a wall and proceeded to blow them open, allowing paint to dribble out.[6] Apart from Jean Tinguely, de Saint-Phalle's career evolved through the making of life-sized *nanas*— playful, earthy female figures which she began painting with unique designs in approximately 1965. *Nana* is a French term for a beautiful young

Tinguely and involving a large number of artists.

1971   Designs her first jewelry and begins work on the *Golem*, an architectural project for children in Jerusalem's Rabinovitch Park.

1972   Begins shooting her film *Daddy*. Visits Greece.

1973   Designs a swimming pool for Georges Plouvier in Saint-Tropez.
Builds *The Dragon*, a fully-equipped playhouse for the children of Fabienne and Roger Nellens, in Knokko-le-Zoule, Belgium.

1974   Installs three gigantic *nanas* in Hanover, Germany. Galerie Alexandre Iolas mounts an exhibition of her architectural projects. Begins to discuss her dream

woman, as in *"une belle-nana,"* and the *nana* dolls reflected de Saint-Phalle's interest in female nudes, nymphs, and deities as well as her great love and sense of color.

Per Olof Ultvedt, the sculptor, and Jean Tinguely, the artist and machine-maker, had collaborated on group installations such as *Total Art* (Waxholm, 1960), in which they employed hanging sculpture and a collage-papier technique later used in the fabrication of *She*, as well as a derivation of forms taken from monumental navigational structures and explored through enormous drawings.[7] As early as 1960, Tinguely had installed a huge self-destructing machine at the Museum of Modern Art in New York,[8] and by 1962 had devoted time with Niki de Saint-Phalle to collaborations as part of the Nouveaux Réalistes, the French conceptual art group of which de Saint-Phalle was the only female in the official manifesto.

Thus, in the midst of the 1960s, a handful of experimental artists (though mostly male) were conjuring formal investigations of utopia, motion, and space in the forms of sculpture and installation. Among these manifestations, *Dy-Laby*, an auto-theater, consisted of a series of environments, each created by a different artist, and included the work of K. Pontus Hulten, Martial Raysse, American painter and social activist Robert Rauschenberg, Niki de Saint-Phalle, Willem Sandberg, Daniel Spoerri, Jean Tinguely, and Per Olof Ultvedt. In its various rooms the installations ran the gamut of commotion; some were tipped at an angle or blasting with noise from industrial fans. De Saint-Phalle used real gunfire. Colored light, gratuitous violence and funky, illusionistic objects were introduced à la the Dadaists or Futurists.[9]

This type of temporary destructible art helped to fuel an international dialogue. According to Adrian Henri, *Study for an Exhibition on Violence in Contemporary Art*, held at the ICA in London in 1956, was "a preliminary survey of tendencies that culminated in the 'Destruction in Art Symposium' (DIAS) in 1966 which featured the work of the enigmatic Gustav Metzger."[10]

Early in the decade, artists such as Joseph Beuys, Gustav Metzger, Dieter Rot, and Wolf Vostell had produced disposable art—edible art and art made from trash, TVs, or other deliberately impermanent non-art materials. In Russia, the Dvizjenije group, a fluctuating collective of artists, mathematicians, and poets, experimented in a range of disciplines from art to music to cybernetics and industrial design and especially in kinetic objects. Their projects, *Cosmos* and *Structure of a Diamond*, realized between 1964 and 1968, linked art, technology, and urbanism through collaboration. These projects were followed in 1968 by a curious model for a town designed entirely for children.[11] The collaborations developed into the early seventies.

In Japan, activity in the avant-garde was generated by such groups as the Gutai Theater project and The Institute for Abstract Calligraphy. In New York, important early works were produced, such as Allan Kaprow's *Garage Environment* (1960). John Cage's notions of "alogical theater" were influential.[12] Consistently, after the horrific global extremity of World War II and in the context of the Vietnam War, the recognition of mass spectacle as a human form influenced a wide range of collaborative mixed-media exhibitions and the wholesaling of "total shows" like the Vulgar Show by Sam Goodman and Bruce Lurie (1964). This movement was most effective, perhaps, as political performance in the works of GAAG (Guerrilla Art Action Group).[13]

Some individual artists stand out as having experimented with these ideas. The German-born Wolf Vostell, a maker of books, installations, magazines, performances, sculpture, and video was engaged in a "cathartic use of violence as a form of political allegory."[14] Some of his more disruptive works simulated car crashes and involved disturbances to the customary flow of public space.[15] Brutal poignancy in methods of experimentation and challenge to authority characterize this avant-garde as it was documented and supported by a spate of publications in the same period. In 1959,

of designing a sculpture park and is offered land in Tuscany by Marella Caracciolo's brothers.

1975 Writes screenplay for the film *Un reve plus long que la nuit*. Shoots film and designs many parts of the set.

1976 Spends year in the Swiss mountains planning her sculpture park.

1977 With Constantin Mulgrave, designs sets for the film *The Traveling Companion*.

1978 Begins laying out the *Tarot Garden* in Tuscany.

1979 Spends most of her time in Tuscany laying foundations and inventing new sculptures she calls *Skinnies*. Gimpel & Weitzenhoffer of New York hold an exhibition

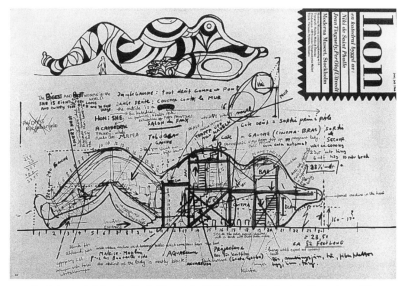

FIG. 1 Preliminary sketches for the built work by Niki de Saint-Phalle, Jean Tinguely, and Per
Olof Ultvedt

Daniel Spoerri's *The Annotated Topography of Chance* (Paris), and Wolf
Vostell's *De-Collage* (Cologne) surfaced to coincide with theoretical texts
from Fluxus and the Situationists.

Violent, sadistic fantasies were overtly manifest in the work of
Hermann Nitsch, whose male-dominated OM Theater regularly exhibited (sexist) live art works which used women as props or with their genitals exposed.[16]

SHE THE OBJECT: PART ONE

Prior to *She*'s conception, the three artists, Niki de Saint-Phalle, Jean
Tinguely, and Per Olof Ultvedt, considered a group of relevant ideas,
including an outstanding one that the work should have something to do
with "Woman assuming Power." In this plan, de Saint-Phalle was to be
animated by her male coworkers.[17] After sketches and discussion, Per
Olof Ultvedt determined that *She* should be an exaggerated *nana* doll, a
temporary installation of mythic proportions celebrating the form of a
huge, sexual Woman (FIG. 1).

TOP: FIG. 2 The giant form of Hon's legs and interior platforms under construction
BOTTOM: FIG. 3 Hon's head in tubular steel prior to being covered in cloth

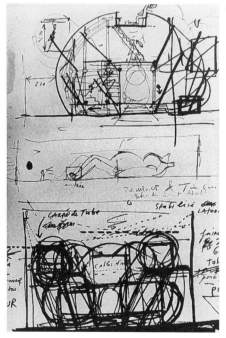

ABOVE: FIG. 4 The view through her massive legs to her entrance. At right are the artists Niki de Saint-Phalle and Jean Tinguely (1967)

LEFT: FIG. 5 Preliminary sketches for the built work by Niki de Saint-Phalle, Jean Tinguely, and Per Olof Ultvedt

In the spring of 1967, permission to build *She* was offered to the artists by K. Pontus Hulten, then director of Stockholm's Moderna Museet (Museum of Modern Art), and construction began with great secrecy and intensity. Accounts in the museum's catalog *Hon—en historia* reflect that the museum became a huge studio space where a crew of ten worked intensively over a period of one month with approximately six tons of tubular steel, timber, chicken-wire, upholstery fabric, glue, and paint[18] (FIGS. 2 AND 3). Finally, there *She* was, lying on her back, to be entered through a sacred vagina-womb (painted green) and filled with an interior of wacky, wonderful spaces for the amusement and edification of an adoring and puzzled public. The spectacle was complete outside and in (FIG. 4).

In a single monumental gesture, *She* occupied the hall of the museum with her enormous raised legs, rolling splayed torso, arms, and head. The form created arches and hills, spaces to move in, under, around, or near. The rounded belly passed close to the museum's pristine ceiling (FIG. 5). In some senses, *She* was the perfect incarnation of fantasy, a primordial experience of passage through a mysterious labyrinth from light to darkness and out to light again. Eventually, one exited either from her side or from a door in her neck. Inside one leg the artists designed a gallery-cum-slide, replete with fake "master" paintings signed with fake signatures. A star-filled planetarium glowed under the dome of an oversized breast. There was a goldfish pond, a pink liquor bar with a neon halo on the ceiling, a sculpted man sitting in a chair, a public address system, and a tiny cinema (Garbo's first film, the surreal *Luffarpetter* [1921], wherein she takes a risqué swim, was projected continuously). An elaborate spiral staircase leading from the belly to a small restaurant atop the abdomen was a central element. Finally, in her head, Tinguely constructed

of the models and photographs for her architectural projects.

The exhibition entitled *Monumental Projects* tours the United States.

1980   Begins first sculptures for the *Tarot Garden*: *The Magician* and *The High Priestess.*

A first edition of furniture by the artist is put into production.

1981   Rents cottage in Tuscany and hires local help.

Paints exterior of a new twin-engine plane for the Peter Stuyvesant Foundation in Amsterdam.

1982   Designs a perfume for an American firm and uses the money to finance her garden.

one of his now famous revolving glass and light machines. (It smashed bottles from beers consumed in the tiny bar.) Drawings and sketches were also exhibited.

"Women especially love it," Niki de Saint-Phalle remarked at her opening. "They seem to understand immediately that it is an *homage* to them."[19]

SHE THE OBJECT: PART TWO

In 1967 Lucy Lippard organized the delightfully weird exhibition *Eccentric Abstraction*. She states in her excellent book on Pop Art that de Saint-Phalle's sculptures had little to do with the intentions of this puzzling genre.[20] Yet when Ultvedt and de Saint-Phalle exaggerated the scale of *She* it became like that of many Pop Art objects. The shift, in fact, addresses from a feminist standpoint elementary issues of what an ordinary object is. For example, *She* was leaned on and entered. Visitors laughed in a cavernous arm, slid through a leg, climbed from the belly, or posed at her side. *She* functioned, it would seem, partially as an enormous piece of prostrate furniture and partially as a building.

In terms of content, the delightful statue draws relationships between figurative art and nature. *She* resonates with the mythology of giants, their grotesque humility and mundane, fundamental ties to the earth. One thinks of ancient Buddhas, reposeful, silent, at peace, reclining in East Asian forests.

The imagination of foothills, elbows of rivers, lakes as lugubrious, water-filled footprints abounds in a metaphorical reading of her body as landscape.[21] Thus *She* is "an object of considerable therapeutic value"[22] for the alienated soul for whom the specter of the loss of childhood, which haunts twentieth-century literary and psychoanalytic discourses, is a central theme laid bare in manifold descriptions of profound sexual desire for the mother or, more abstractly, for a return to connection with the earth.

Inherently a project about feminine power and sensuality, *She* offers us the first and truest pleasure of looking and the space to conjure myth around the imaginary female. It is impossible to look at pictures of her without seeing in them a sexual ideal. In fact the statue is also preposterously *sexist*; her almost hideous and masochistic pose is so object-like. This pose falls into a category for the female nude which John Berger analyzes in his indispensable text *Ways of Seeing*, wherein he suggests that male-defined representations of the female body construct gazes pictorially in a visual language of submission and surveillance.[23] The statue is prone, legs spread, to be invaded, displayed, in a posture symbolic of women's oppression as viewed through public and commercial eyes, a posture laden with the difficult, painful, and theatrical associations of pornographic desire.

Pornographic imagery and the gaze that it constructs, tied to the act of *not touching*, of non*sense*, wherein a body functions solely as an object of the *faculty of sight,* is governed by the seamless silence of sight. It is a body fragmented by the violence of sexist looking, where the eye itself roves across the body frenetically, without recourse to time or thought, but with the objective of owning. It is a body painfully under surveillance, one lodged within sadomasochistic objectification. *She* should also be construed, however, as *open*, colorful and carnivalesque, ready for birth, sex, or a gynecological exam. Unlike a reductivist object or a pornographic sight of pure display, *She* is interactive and explorable, deliberately too large to be taken in and consumed from any one angle. With her spectacular interior, *She* possesses intimacy and connectedness and defies objectification. Both the pornographic and the sensual are at work in her form.

As theorist Jean Gagnon writes in *Pornography and the Urban World*:

Phantasmagoria, apparently . . . the ways in which the author gives voice to fantasy, uses such optical devices and instruments as mirrors, glasses, spyglasses, telescopes and microscopes, just like the cinema, the peep

Work on the *Tarot Garden* progresses. Steel constructions are in place and concrete pouring is in preparation.

1984 Works full time on the *Garden*.

1985 Completes *The Magician*, *The Tower*, *The Empress*, and *The High Priestess*.

1987 First retrospective in America is held.

1988 Fountain for Mitterand is commissioned.
Fountain for the Schneider Children's Hospital on Long Island is commissioned.

1990 Presents a film she has made about AIDS at the Musée des Arts Décoratifs in Paris.

1991 Works on an enlarged model for her Temple Ideal,

show, etc. What we're always trying to do is to see better and further, to see in a different way and to see the other in a configuration that suits our disposition. In phantasmagoria (whether literary or pornographic), optical devices and instruments open another space, an "other scene," where the energy of the instinct to look can be expressed. In this other space, perception becomes uncertain regarding reality and unreality, the status of its object and the position of the perceiver.[24]

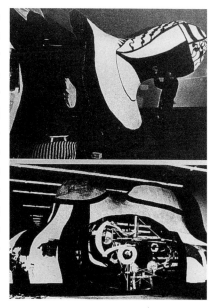

FIG. 6 TOP: The removal of Hon's painted head in the first phase of taking her apart
BOTTOM: Interior showing Tinguely's revolving glass and light machine

In relation to *She*, one is a voyeur, offered the content of female sexuality and ways to reflect upon that experience. *She* thus suggests a synthesis of desire and intellect. Like all good art, *She* triggers unconscious response. Her unusual enormity transforms the act of looking and casts off the surveillance that we have come to connect with nudes. The viewer is affected by her scale and is invited to roam and imagine in her darkened recesses. The vagina is a place of entry into her intimate interior world, displacing the deadened discourse of castration wherein the image of the wound as a twentieth century metaphor for female genitalia is horridly embedded. The cunt in *She* is our doorway, our gate, our point of entry, our common ground. Thus, *She* posits that new 1960s femininity in which the female body is a woman's friend, not foe, and is expressive of a progression to deeper sexuality—the womb— whole, earthly, with a life-spirit, neither cunt nor womb encapsulated in lack, nor stripped of sexuality, as in the "clean" domestic glamour of the 1950s housewife.

Once delivered from sexism, *She* is elevated to architecture, to permanence, to an object of multiple moments, relationships and individuality. *She* is built in the spirit of a *katedral* as a space of human spirituality and grand belief. The architectural process of making her, from start to finish, becomes an allegory for a journey of becoming, of making, of wending one's way through life and art, of enjoyable creativity, and of the creative process, most wonderfully addressed by Claes Oldenburg, who stated of the giant statue, "I wish those who saw and enjoyed *She* whole, could have watched her being taken apart. Three months: birth, life, death. One sixteenth of Europe (to exaggerate) and all of Stockholm getting their heads in. What a fast, full life!"[25] (FIG. 6)

SHE THE OBJECT: PART THREE

When Niki de Saint-Phalle, then living between New York and Paris, created this work in the hall of the museum in Stockholm in 1966, she produced a fantastic artifact. Here is women's empowerment rendered in the form of an enormous Pop Art-like Woman. Here are the contradictions and the excitement of women's sexuality. *She* is profoundly risqué. Her brightly-painted figure, open genitals, and passages of warm, vivid spaces are reminiscent of Bosch's *Garden of Earthly Delights.*[26] In size, posture, and material, *She* was created from an artistic sensibility constructed in the innocent beauty of human desire. Moreover, *She* alludes to femininity as it is constructed by human desire. This is her inherent power. Sexuality is okay and alright, devoid of oppositions. *She* is a big girl with the seductive stature of an *objet d'art. She* is comic. *She* can be vulgar. Most of all, *She* doesn't belong to anyone. *She* erupts. The power of her myth and political allegory conveys something communal and maternal that transcends both real space and time. *She* is a collective experience—a grand myth.

an interdenominational church first planned in 1972.

1995 Noah's Ark project with Mario Botta is underway in Israel.

Who Is the Monster, You or Me? The Life and Work of Niki de St. Phalle (a film documentary directed by Peter Schamoni) is released.

SHE AS ARCHITECTURE

Niki de Saint-Phalle's giant Woman is akin to the architecture of early religion, where sacred cosmogonies of the figural and forms of poetic shelter introduced by the body or the body as house abound. (Feminist performances by Carolee Schneeman of approximately the same period dealt conceptually with some of these same ideas: the creative vagina as history, menstruation ritual, the pleasure of physical touch and the body.)

In terms of form, *She* is clear. *She* is obviously an earth mound and also a sphinx, a universal center, a dignified altar, a corner, and a cave. Metaphors of entering and reemerging from the belly or from the womb are revisited in the cosmogony of her spaces, connecting her to Western and Eastern beliefs where the body, revered as a configuration of the sacred, functions as an iconographic landscape for life's drives and spirit.[27] (The device of scale again lends the sculpture the stature of a cathedral.)

Relationships among art, life, and spirituality are loosely represented in her complex subcutaneous interior. A virtual fun house, *She* is a series of spaces carefully designed to connect to specific parts of the overall form. For example, putting a planetarium inside her breast so that visitors under the infinite sky relate their experience to the comforting bosom is a significant poetic gesture. Just as the breast is used in Afghan shrines and phalluses decorate houses in West African villages, these combinations of rooms articulate complex meanings. *She* is both serious and sacred, frivolous and profane—a work of architecture in the best sense of the word.

And as a work of feminist architecture, *She* is foremost a shelter— a house. Assigned this meaning, the female body of *She* alludes to powerful female identities: Woman as able protector, Woman as an ideal of cultural strength, Woman as central to the community. It connects her to permanence, to the nurturing earth symbolized by the ocean (fish pond), linking her metaphorically to sources of life, to mutability, or again to the comforting mother—to the therapeutic object, to that which is good. Other constructions of the female body as shelter appear and reappear in

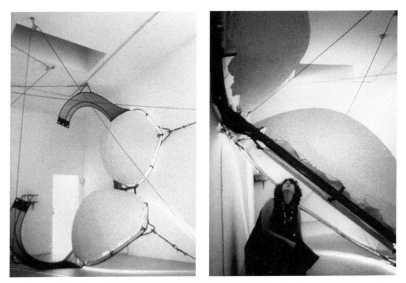

FIGS. 7 AND 8 Vito Acconci, *Adjustable Wall Bra* (1990). Steel, lathe, plaster, cable, lights, audio. 8' x 21' x 3' var. dimen.

architecture, but also in art, significantly in a 1968 project for the Venice Biennale *La Maison est le Corps* (*The House is the Body*), in which Brazilian artist Lygia Clark invited her viewers "to pass through a series of different cells which prefigured the phases of conception: penetration, ovulation, germination and expulsion and in which the complex relationship between the artist's work and sexuality was thus expressed in terms of 'structural' relationships."[28] More recently, Vito Acconci created *Adjustable Wall Bras* (1990), which formed large breast-like shelters for gallery visitors to interact with (FIGS. 7 AND 8). In Acconci's mythical Woman, the American pop symbols of the breast and the brassiere are elevated to a monumental stature and express, beyond their visual power, the peacefulness, sustenance, and solitude to be found there.

As to her permanence in architectural history and design, *She* is (after the Statue of Liberty) possibly the largest completely female figure ever built in Western history.[29] *She* was a monument. At the same time,

She was an antimonument in a time when public art had not yet generally expanded on definitions of public monuments beyond those associated with civic pride, national heroic deeds, or myths,[30] and when public representations of women typically exploited female physical sexuality for commercial pleasure—something that the women's movement took on and challenged. Yet public representations of monumental scale still abound in both Eastern, Western, and primitive cultures. Cities are resplendent with idealized females, civic or literary heroines. Huge billboard advertisements of women objectified as the ultimate stand-ins for commodities are everywhere. Monumental sculpture that functions as art is conceivably different. The antimonument of *She* functions for the abstract creative imagination in a variety of ways and is both utopian and visionary. *She* is fundamentally a challenge to the sexist precepts of public representation, deliberately *not* part of the commercial spectrum or civic rhetoric. *She* is a feminist monument in this context. Against a backdrop of realistic renderings or crass ads, the languorous temporary form of *She* is a statement in which ideas of utopia, leisure, and pride in being female are played out. Her irreverent colorfulness and the elevation of female sexuality in the art object to this powerful, deified plane add to 1960s women's movement art and politics, which supported the physical and professional liberation of the body, distributed and advocated for better birth control and reproductive rights, and which, in pop culture, venerated icons of beauty and success such as Twiggy and Nico. In light of this, it is symbolically ironic that *She*'s head, the only extant piece, was stored in the Ostermölm prison in Stockholm—the modern prison as institution being a place where outspoken women have historically been taken.[31]

SHE—HER INFLUENCE

While de Saint-Phalle's 1967 Woman remains an eccentric figure in the landscape of art, the work is accompanied by a continuing history of similar collaborations between the artist and Tinguely. Such works as the *Stravinsky Garden*, a phenomenological fountain of modish, picturesque pieces designed for the Place Igor Stravinsky in Paris, or the *Fantastic*

Paradise (1971), another surreal landscape of machines, creatures, and dolls created for the French pavilion at Expo '67, are, in idiom and metaphor, similar to *She*. Other offspring of the project are de Saint-Phalle's *Golem*, a huge slide and playground in the form of a monster's grotesque head, built in Jerusalem in 1972, and the complex steel structure of Jean Tinguely's *La Tête*, completed in 1969. *La Tête*, a massive, illogical steel and scaffold building/sculpture, is found deep in the forest of Fountainbleu and is inhabited by spaces for artists, an apartment, and a variety of oddly-functioning machines such as ramps and moving balls. Niki de Saint-Phalle designed a cycloptic face for the project in silvery mosaic. *La Tête* was eventually given to the French Government.

But one cannot comprehend fully the amazing work *She* without discussing (even if only briefly) Niki de Saint-Phalle's continued life's work, the *Tarot Garden* at Garavicchio in Tuscany, which she started at the age of fifty and for which Tinguely acted as her chief engineer. Basing her work on images from cards in the Tarot deck Niki de Saint-Phalle has created an entire garden of fifteen objects and buildings in intricate, decorated reinforced concrete. Tile work, reflecting her interest in Antonio Gaudí, has been fashioned by local Italian artisans.

In her *Garden* is a cottage modeled after the High Priestess. It is replete with a huge bosom, a head, and paws. It is both a workspace and living quarters for Niki de Saint-Phalle. The entrance to this magical cottage is nestled between breast-rooms in a cleavage that reiterates the scale and female form of *She*.

The *Tarot Garden*, wherein the sculptress has developed a magical mirrored mosaic technique for dissolving façades and the material mass of structures,[32] is protected by a gate designed by Mario Botta. It is described with great passion and visual detail in the recent film documentary on de Saint-Phalle's life and work, *Who is the Monster, You or Me?* (1995).[33] The *Garden* is a lifelong synthesis of aesthetic and narrative motifs first developed by the two lovers de Saint-Phalle and Tinguely in Stockholm, amidst the daring construction of *She*.

SHE—FIN

Thus, my paper suggests how the statue's relationship to women and the female form is feminist and undermines the idea of the monumental. It places this remarkable, unusual work within spaces of the pleasurably irrational—those of the hypnotic unconscious, of the psychic—in the heart of human dreams, and with the forbidden and the divine.

For my female family, young and old. . . . Many thanks to Debra Coleman, my patient editor, and to Carol Henderson; to Sandra Cloud for first connecting me to this anthology; to John Campbell for his scholarship and support; to Vito Acconci, Helen Deutsch of Northwestern University, Douglas Garofalo, Lynn Hershman, David Hess, Udo Kultermann, and Mark Linder for their early assistance, suggestions, and ideas on this paper; to Hans Hammarskiöld and Eva Karlsson at the Moderna Museet in Stockholm; to the San Francisco Museum of Modern Art library; to Nick Pasquariello and Betty Traynor; and to Minnette Lehmann, for her strong support and friendship.

Finally, to the artist, for her persistence, her art, her inspiration, and life-energy.

—mh

NOTES

1. Quoted from http://gort.ucsd.edu/st/phalle/html.

2. Hélène Cixous, "The Laugh of the Medusa," *New French Feminisms*, ed. Elaine Marks and Isabelle de Courtivron (New York: Schocken Books, 1981), 256.

3. While women-centered communities of the 1960s and 70s are relevant to the development of feminism and architecture, I am not discussing herein separatist utopias such as those of novelists Charlotte Perkins Gilman or Monique Wittig, nor do I refer to experimental artistic and social communities such as the L.A. Women's Building.

4. David Gebard, Roger Montgomery, Robert Winter, John Woodbridge, and Sally Woodbridge, eds., *A Guide to Architecture in San Francisco & Northern California* (Santa Barbara: Peregrine Smith, 1976), 69, 183.

5. Frank Popper, *Art—Action and Participation* (New York: New York University Press, 1975), 13.

6. Barbara Sylwan, K. Pontus Hulten, John Melin, and Anders Osterlin, eds., *Hon—en historia* (Stockholm: Moderna Museet, 1967), 28–29.

7. Sylwan, et al., *Hon—en historia*, 11.

8. Adrian Henri, *Total Art* (New York: Oxford University Press, 1974), 172.

9. Sylwan, et al., *Hon—en historia*, 17–19.

10. Henri, *Total Art*, 167.

11. Popper, *Art—Action and Participation*, 158–60.

12. Henri, *Total Art*, 86, 93.

13. Ibid., 175–79.

14. Ibid., 170.

15. Ibid., 179.

16. Ibid., 168.

17. Sylwan, et al., *Hon—en historia*, 37. Until the last two decades, the overall impression of male domination in the art forms of sculpture and architecture has been in part a function of the male-dominated field of art history in which the most widely circulated texts describing the history of events are biased toward work by male artists and toward work that defines art within specific conventions of practice customarily occupied by men. This is yet another reason why the work of de Saint-Phalle is impressive from a feminist standpoint. The artist asserted her role among major male artists of her time.

18. Sylwan, et al., *Hon—en historia*, 65, 128. In addition to *Hon—en historia*, the catalog issued by the museum, manifold records of this complex effort were produced. Hundreds of small sketches, working drawings and a dozen or so miniature wire and fabric models, including two full-scale fingered hands and a pair of enormous feet, never used, were left behind. Eighty-two feet long, twenty feet high and thirty feet around, *She* was painted in happy, colorful Pop style by de Saint-Phalle.

19. Ibid., 128. Some 70,000 onlookers visited *She* and participated in traversing the interiors of her limbs and labyrinths.

20. Lucy Lippard, *Pop Art* (New York: Oxford University Press, 1966), 178.

21. Susan Stewart, *On Longing: Narratives of the Miniature, the Gigantic, the Souvenir* (Baltimore: John Hopkins, 1984), 54–55.

22. Richard Boston as quoted in Time Magazine, 17 June 1966, reprinted in Sylwan, et al., *Hon—en historia*, 156.

23. John Berger, *Ways of Seeing* (London: British Broadcasting Network, 1972), 45–64.

24. Jean Gagnon, *Pornography and the Urban World* (Toronto: Jean Gagnon + Art Metropole, 1986), 99.

25. Sylwan, et al., *Hon—en historia*, 201.

26. Gregory Martin, "A Female Gulliver in Stockholm," The Times, 27 June 1967, reprinted in Sylwan et al., *Hon—en historia*, 156.

27. Eliade Mircea, *The Sacred and the Profane: The Nature of Religion*, trans. Willard R. Trash (New York: Harcourt Brace Jovanovich, 1957), 195–97.

28. Popper, Art—Action and Participation, 15.

29. This fact is cited by Arthur Segunda and Jan Thurholm in an essay reprinted in Sylwan et al., *Hon—en historia*, 150–51.

30. The trope of antimonumentalism in the arts deserves to be discussed at much greater length. I touch on it briefly because of its obvious relation to the work.

31. Sylwan et al., *Hon—en historia*, 2.

32. K. Pontus Hulten, *Jean Tinguely: A Magic Stronger Than Death* (New York: Abbeville Press, 1988), 203–6, 242–43, 263–69.

33. Cynthia Robbins, "A Rage for Art," *San Francisco Examiner Magazine*, 17 September 1995. The film documentary is directed by Peter Schamoni and produced by David Hess.

The Lair of the Bachelor

GEORGE WAGNER

The time was adolescence. The place was a wood-frame summer cottage on the edge of a lake in the hills of western Massachusetts. The stud walls of the house were sheathed only on the outside, with horizontal pine boards. This form of construction meant that the walls had no interior. The boys—three of us, a stepbrother and a real one, both about four years older than me—slept on trundle beds in a sleeping loft under the gable and its exposed rafters. These brothers were full of the madness and anxiety of adolescence, and this condition became the atmosphere of that loft. They discovered a knothole in the pine floor, strategically located over the toilet downstairs, which provided hours of viewing pleasure, especially when the grownups had company. What was involving about looking through that knothole was watching people in the bathroom when they thought they were alone. The parents became wiser and had a pine board ceiling installed on the underside of the floor joists in the bathroom. It is only now, after years in the academy, that I can condemn this act as an affront to the material integrity of the house and a purposeful erasure of the infrastructure of its marginal occupation. Adolescents, happily, don't have these words.

These adolescent brothers, in my mind virtual delinquents, acquired a small collection of "literature." Specifically, there was a Harold Robbins novel which had among its virtues a seduction described on page eight[1]—I think that's as far as I got. This book was hidden on a ledge over the door in the water closet. A couple of copies of *Playboy* were kept on the floor inside the storage area underneath the eaves. The *Playboy*s were, as their covers promised, "Entertainment for Men." I must confess to have been fairly unmoved by these selections. Even if I rehearsed an interest in them for the purposes of survival, no one was providing the literature that would allow the hidden attractions of my adolescence to make sense.

What has lingered indelibly in my mind about that loft over the years has been the madness of my brothers as they exercised the parodies of manhood that adolescence provides (or, should I say, the parodies of madness that manhood provides). And one other thing—an article in *Playboy* about a round bed.[2] The bed was Hugh Hefner's, and was placed in the middle of his bedroom at the *Playboy* Mansion in Chicago. It was motorized to rotate and vibrate. Somehow, the idea of this bed was quite memorable to me; this paper has been an effort to figure out why.

That figuring engages aspects of the masculine and the heterosexual in American culture as popularly represented in buildings and interiors. The themes are of fantasy and control in the nineteen-fifties and sixties—for in these decades in North America, as the ideologies of European modernism were digested, consumed, and domesticated, the mass markets flourished. A favored representational mode of ideological modernism was the urban utopia—an elaborate and sober fantasy for the formal and social control of the chaotic city. At the same time, the postwar consumer culture and its extraordinary mass conformity emerged, as products and commodities were woven inextricably into the patterns of everyday life. These products, and the mass-market media that circulated their images, promised individuals the control of ordinary routines and domestic space, an illusion that had previously been seen only in the utopian fantasy for urban space.

The exercise of controls and the projection of fantasies are inherent parts of the function of architecture. Architects make plans, a set of working drawings describes and controls. And yet the idea of control becoming the spectacle of a project, which can occur through manipulations of geometry, contrivances of the visual field and the subject's view, or overt demonstrations of the latent forces of control—the governmental, economic, and bureaucratic—is another matter altogether. It is no secret that architecture is a medium of domination.

Representations of architecture—of buildings, places, and interiors—have been used to trigger, indulge, and focus fantasy. My focus will be on fantasies of control and the function of images that describe the physical characteristics of a world that can be mastered. Public speculation of the ideal and utopian within architecture, both domestic and urban, can be read not so much as proposals for the alteration of reality as vehicles of transcendence, desire, and escape. Pornography is tangentially the subject here, and to invoke it now might leave it silently present within the shadows of this essay, as witness to the strangely passive yet instrumental world of fantasy.

The task, then, is to understand the public speculation of the urban utopia and the private reverie of the domestic fantasy as continuous, but not simultaneous, conditions along the same trajectory of privatization in industrial culture. After the Second World War, the large scale urban plan recedes in importance as the suburban single family house becomes both the test site and hothouse for fantasy projection. We might careen recklessly from the urban to the domestic, explaining that after the war, the masculine fantasies of dominance and control that had been imagined for the city were brought inside, to the newly electronic space of the domicile and the only residential program a man could imagine ruling, the house of the bachelor. On this ride, the grand axis of the City Beautiful boulevard becomes the beam of the hand-held remote control. Further, the bachelor pad, especially as portrayed in *Playboy* magazine, presented a space with an overt program for sexual power, in fact a space for a predator, a program that had been latent within urban proposals as an unspoken but vividly present countertext.

The point is this—to remember that one of the vital functions of architectural representations, especially of popular representations, is to operate as transcendent projections of desire, and that masculine desire, especially of the sexual variety, has thrilled to dominance. And even if that desire has not always been lusty, it has sponsored a similar gaze of longing for the unattainable. Present within the architecture we imagine are the things we do not have, and so every architectural program can be understood as being implicitly critical of reality. Commercial entertainment— publishing and the media—has widely marketed this form of fantasy projection to mass audiences, and so the seat of the gazing subject has evolved from the throne to the armchair.

Before diving into the body of this essay, I ought to reveal what I think I'm doing with reference to the contemporary project of imagining what might be feminist or queer space. I am trying to do two things: first, to recall in our recent history a significant episode in which a set of spaces was popularly seen as gendered, but even more than that, as enthusiastically sexualized. My assumption is that part of imagining spaces of liberation is documenting spaces of oppression, because even if vagaries might surround the exact specifications of a nonpatriarchal space, its other has been well rehearsed. And second, to apply to those episodes a sensibility, explicitly queer, I hope, that might—as a nighttime photo of a garden with a flash—make both the "naturalness" and the dominance of these texts seem bizarre and distant.

Two schemes for American cities—for Chicago[3] and for Fort Worth[4]—help to describe how the urban project has been one paradigm for the imagination of strategies to control and dominate space. People are always trying to impose order on the city, and the question I want to engage is: What kind of image is that order given? Visual, geometrical, architectural, economic, institutional? The formal implications of these strategies are different and are used as ways to describe differing scales of control. After that, I will discuss postwar America and the way in which the prescriptive social reality of that era (the fifties and sixties) established identities and tensions between man and woman, home and office. This will lead to a review of some of the interiors presented in *Playboy* magazine, which is one place where the house of the bachelor was imagined as

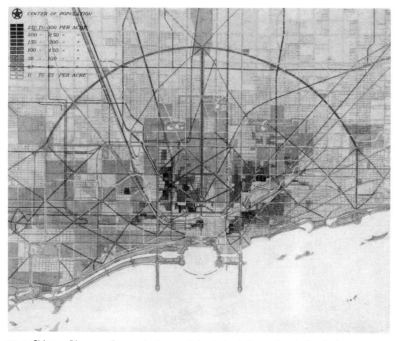

FIG. 1 Chicago. Diagram of general scheme of street circulation and parks in relation to the population, from *Plan of Chicago*, Daniel Burnham

the preferred medium of domestic fantasy. This trajectory, from the urban to the domestic, is meant to follow the development of the domestic as the most intense and gendered site of commodity consumption in the mechanical and electronic era of privatization.

Daniel Burnham's *Plan of Chicago* of 1909 proposed the superimposition of a radial, concentric figure on the grid of the city (FIG. 1). Now, it may seem a little obvious to begin an inquiry into the nature of the masculine with a discussion of Daniel Burnham; it was Burnham, after all, who said, "Make no little plans, they have no magic to stir men's blood."[5] With that remark, Burnham forever inscribed within the dialogues of American architecture the virtues of the ratio of size to quality, and what could be more male than that?

Burnham's *Plan* is usually recognized as the advent of regional planning in the United States, as he sought to align all of the infra-

FIG. 2 Chicago. View looking west, of the proposed Civic Center Plaza and buildings, showing the center of the system of arteries of circulation and of the surrounding country, from *Plan of Chicago,* Daniel Burnham

structural elements needed for Chicago's growth within a radial figure of transportation elements (FIG. 2).[6] There are certain aspects of this plan I would like to identify: first, its reliance on a centered scenographic figure, and the imposition of a singular hierarchy and orientation. Understood within the discourse of control, this figure operates on a number of levels. At the center of the radius, the Civic Center, specifically the domed City Hall, becomes the origin of the geometric construction of the city's new plan. It dominates the field of the city in an heroic and imperial way, as if it had always been there. The history of the city, as represented by its physical form, is rewritten by this figure in a sort of retroactive causality. The control is visual, not simply because the City Hall is so big, but also because its form terminates the space of the new radial avenues. The occupying power is centralized and has an image. Like the panopticon, this plan imposes a identifiable geometrical figure to visually dominate and control the social apparatus that is the city. Domination, representation, transportation, and geometry are aligned. Most every aspect of the city's public life, and significant parts of its private life as well, are affected by this diagram.

The architecture of Burnham's City Hall is extraordinary, first, in its vivid presentations of the economies of a prescriptive architecture—the scale of a controlling object is calibrated in reference to the field it commands—and second, in the resulting form; has a dome ever been quite so vertical? It is anxious and crazed in the self-consciousness of its size (FIG. 3).

FIG. 3 Chicago. Rendered elevation of the proposed Civic Center, delineated by Jules Guérin, 1908, from *Plan of Chicago*, Daniel Burnham

Finally, this plan was laced with a strong sense that the form of the city would directly affect what Burnham called "the intellectual, social, moral, and aesthetic conditions" of Chicago.[7] The *Plan of Chicago* stated that "good citizenship is the prime object of good city planning."[8] Burnham imagined that the restructuring of the city's form would improve the moral tenor of its life. Frederick Law Olmstead imagined the same thing, but through the introduction of the city's other—nature. Louis Sullivan, in his idealization of the city, was simply interested in the optimization of the forces and forms that already existed.[9]

Victor Gruen's *Fort Worth Plan* of 1955 maintains the basic format of the utopian project, presenting a fantasy of idealization through the transformation of the city's form[10] (FIGS. 4A AND B).Unlike the Chicago plan, it is neither geometricized nor burdened by corrective moral agendas or formal absolutes. And unlike its more immediate predecessors,

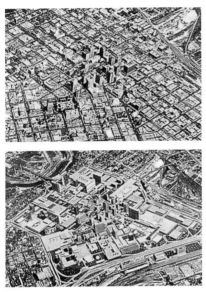

FIG. 4A AND B Fort Worth, Texas, aerial view of downton, before and after Victor Gruen's *Fort Worth Plan*

Le Corbusier's Voisin Plan for Paris or Ludwig Hilberseimer's Plan of Chicago, it does not derive a critical position from the astringent spectacle of extreme reason.

In the *Fort Worth Plan*, the utopian is drained of ideology and saturated with both the strategic motives and delirious effects of the commercial markets. Basically, the plan changes the scale of the center of the city, consolidating and centralizing its services. Its final form is not unlike that of a shopping mall, similarly monolithic and singular in its programmatic, stylistic, and spatial forms, with delivery services for stores located in a series of underground tunnels that interiorize the service infrastructure and essentially transform downtown Fort Worth from a city to a building.

The text of the plan describes the way in which the form of the city is inscribed into the average day of the average man and woman, and in so doing presents clearly the narrow and prescribed social roles in the United States in the 1950s.

Some excerpts from the man's day as imagined for 1970:

> You live in the southwest section of the city and are employed in a downtown office building. You leave your home and enter the freeway shortly thereafter and drive for five minutes at a steady 50 m.p.h. clip. . . . Stepping off the moving ramp which brings you down from the upper level where you parked your car, you walk out in the morning sunlight and stop for a moment to gaze at a panorama that has never ceased to thrill you. . . . It reminds you of Rockefeller Center in New York. . . . Walking to your office building you are only slightly conscious of the morning heat. You no

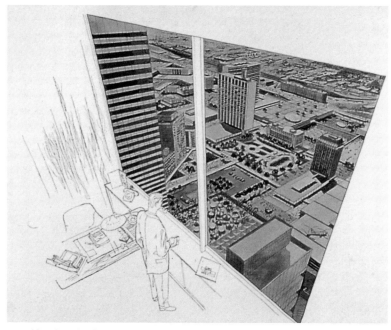

FIG. 5 View from the *Fort Worth Plan*

longer notice the covered sidewalks which have shaded your path from parking terminal to office building. . . . Before leaving for lunch after a busy morning, you look out over the city. Many of the buildings are familiar old friends. But so many new ones have been added that it is difficult to remember the city as it had been in 1956. Some of the new ones are tall and tower like, others are great slabs of glass—all different except you feel the zoning people must have done something because the newer ones are spaced out from each other.[11]

And for another man, a merchant (FIG. 5):

You are standing by a window in your downtown office, looking out over the city. You have spent the morning reviewing quarterly sales figures—and the figures are good. Your suburban stores have more than kept pace with the growth of the downtown store. New office buildings downtown have

FIGS. 6 AND 7 Views from the *Fort Worth Plan*

meant more residents for the city—and more residents for the city have resulted in more business for suburban shopping centers, as well as for downtown. Yes, things have turned out well. All segments of the city have benefited. You turn away from the window overlooking the new Fort Worth, and go back to the plans for your newest unit—an 8,000 square foot suburban store.[12]

The woman's day in the new Fort Worth goes like this (FIGS. 6 AND 7):

You are a housewife living in the greater Fort Worth of tomorrow. As you roll along comfortably on the noiseless electric shuttle car that carries you from one end of downtown to a luncheon appointment at the new tearoom on the other end of the central district, you mentally check over all that you have been able to accomplish in the short period of time since you left your home on the east side this morning.

There had been that real estate business at the bank, then the attorney, then back to the bank again (it was no chore retracing your steps with no parking problems to worry about) a stop for coffee, over an hour of shopping and with all that you were going to be early for your luncheon appointment. There had been a time when things like going to the bank, talking with the lawyer had been handled by your husband, in addition to his full time endeavors of earning a living for the family. Now you are able to take care of these chores for him because it so pleasant to come downtown, and it gives you an added sense of responsibility and accomplishment that you enjoy. After lunch you plan to do a little more shopping, pick up sun suits for the kids, and there will even be time to take in a movie before joining your husband for the ride home together. . . . Your walk to the bank had been brief and enjoyable. You had passed a group of workmen putting up some kind of colorful temporary exhibit. You had seen several of these before and they were always exciting and interesting. . . . You didn't always like to come downtown. You can remember when it was a disagreeable chore. You enjoy it now. And more than that, you're proud that this is a part of YOUR city. Your civic pride keeps asserting itself; as a matter of fact, whenever you visit your sisters in Dallas, Houston, and Abilene. You like to brag about what Fort Worth's got that the other cities haven't. Your sisters enjoy coming to Fort Worth now just to stroll the downtown malls and plazas and browse through the stores. And they bring business with them—for the merchants, gasoline station operators, cafe owners and motel and hotel keepers.[13]

The point of reviewing this plan is to observe the extent to which the proposed controls solidify and entrench existing patterns of consumption. This city is not a diagram of power, but a machine for profit. The project has an image, but it is not geometricized; it is more a kind of visual treatment that unifies, like flowered contact paper, the programmatic life of the city. This is not a scheme with a moral or spiritual agenda; there is no redemption here.

The text of the *Fort Worth Plan* is quite descriptive in characterizing what the film historian Laura Mulvey has articulated in her article "Melodrama Inside and Outside the Home" as the polarized spatial realms of man and woman in postwar America, where "spheres of male space (outside the home) or of female space (inside the home) reflect economic and social aspects of sexual difference."[14]

The tensions are clearly drawn. But it might be useful to turn to a passage by Walter Benjamin, which Beatriz Colamina cites in her piece on the interiors of Adolf Loos. Benjamin says,

> For the private person, living space becomes, for the first time, antithetical to the place of work. The former is constituted by the domestic interior, the office is its complement. The private person who squares his account with reality in his office demands that the interior be maintained in his illusions. This need is all the more pressing since he has no intention of

extending his commercial considerations into social ones. In shaping his private environment he represses both. From this spring the phantasmagorias of the interior. For the private individual the private environment represents the universe.[15]

Mulvey describes a polarization based on gender: woman-home, man-office. Benjamin, who is I think speaking of men, presents different characterizations of the space of home and office based on the psychological tension between the two. Our task now is to superimpose these two readings on each other.

The woman is the manager of the domestic realm, with the home as the site of commodity consumption. The woman, cast as wife and mother, negotiates between the husband's wage and the material world. The house and its interior (and remember that I am speaking of the fifties and sixties) is the site of any number of myths—of progress, of leisure, of normalcy, of fecundity.

The man's world is defined by work, power, and the wage. His dialogue, in Gruen's text, does not extend to any other social relations. The office becomes the complement to the home, but the man must traverse the city in his daily journey from one to the other. Laura Mulvey has written that the only real threat to the repressed sexuality of the home within the landscape of Eisenhower's America was the prostitution hidden within the underworld of the city. It was the city at night, with its shadows and pleasures, that epitomized chaos and uncertainty. The uncontrollable city represented the threat to the enforced normalcy of the suburban. Mulvey points out that the hero of the film noir and detective story was a man who could penetrate this urban chaos and tame it, and that this was a world "to be shunned above all by the bourgeois woman and her family."[16]

Playboy magazine, which began publication in 1953, presented a set of fantasies that allowed the reader to imagine an escape from the conscriptive social order of the patriarchy with no sacrifice of privilege or wealth. These fantasies of bachelorhood were not limited to *Playboy*; they are also well-seen in the media of the time: Ian Fleming's character

James Bond would be one example.[17] These examples stand in contrast to the conformist reality of the era, when the 1960 U. S. census found that 89.1 percent of 40-year-old white men and 85 percent of 40-year-old women were married.

In addition to the erotic photo spreads, there was a mix of material in *Playboy*, with journalism and fiction produced by serious writers, who were paid the highest fees of any magazine of the day. Hugh Hefner's "The Playboy Philosophy," which went on for 25 issues and 250,000 words, was essentially a simultaneous attack on the Puritanical traditions and antisexuality of America and defense of his magazine's sexual explicitness. *Playboy* was always dependent on the spatialization of the lifestyle imagined in its pages, and in its heyday it spawned, besides its own designs for various bachelor pads, publications of built pads, *Playboy* Clubs, *Playboy* Hotels and Resorts, and the *Playboy* Jet, called the Big Bunny.[18]

The *Playboy* man was urban. The first issue in 1953 said,

> We want to make it very clear from the start, we aren't a "family magazine." If you're somebody's sister, wife or mother-in-law and picked us up by mistake, please pass us along to the man in your life and get back to the Ladies Home Companion.
>
> Most of today's magazines for men spend all their time out-of-doors—thrashing through thorny thickets or splashing about in fast-flowing streams. We'll be out there too, occasionally, but we don't mind telling you in advance—we plan [on] spending most of our time inside.
>
> We like our apartment. We enjoy mixing up cocktails and an hors d'oeuvre or two, putting a little mood music on the phonograph and inviting in a female for a quiet discussion on Picasso, Nietzsche, jazz, sex. [19]

The image of the bachelor's life advanced by *Playboy* provided a private fantasy escape for the man whose home had been appropriated as the domain of wife and family and whose office was the site of a definitive reality—the wage. The ideal, imagined reader of *Playboy* magazine was a playboy, and the playboy acquired a fantasized mobility because he was a bachelor. A bachelor is a single man, but some delicacy has always been required in the discussion of why the bachelor is single. *Playboy* espoused the virtue of playing the field, but we know that in the shadows of the cocktail party, the speculation is that the bachelor is a loser, or even worse—he's a queer. And as a result, the decor of the bachelor must be carefully calibrated not to send off the wrong signals.

Emily Post, the president of the Emily Post Institute and celebrated author of *Etiquette: The Blue Book of Social Usage* included in her tract of 1948 *The Personality of a House: The Blue Book of Home Charm* a chapter titled "A House—or a room—for a man" and presented quite directly the delicate question of the bachelor's house.

Ms. Post writes, "That every normal man should be repelled by any suggestion of effeminacy is only natural. But even so, there is no reason why the house of a man living alone should be furnished like the display room of a cement company."[20]

Ms. Post is quite clear about how easily the problem can be derived. Bachelors are single men. Queers are single men. Bachelors are queer. And so her presentation of the masculine house, and the others I will discuss, begins from a defensive position. It is focused around the preservation of the myth that masculinity is the bastion of the natural and the utilitarian. In fact, her reference to the masculine and the cement company is meant to align the masculine with the immediacies of labor and imply the feminine's affiliation with leisure, consumption, and contrivance.

In *The Decoration of Houses*, Edith Wharton and Ogden Codman described men's taste as simple and "uncomplicated by the feminine tendency to want things because other people have them, rather than to have things because they are wanted."[21]

For Wharton and Codman the den (as in lion, the king of the jungle) is a man's room: "The den is freed from the superfluous, is likely to be the most comfortable room of the house; and the natural inference is that a room, in order to be comfortable, must be ugly."[22]

These arguments are laden with clichéd ideas about masculinity: that masculinity is not a construction, but natural, that it constitutes some authentic dimension of human behavior and is free from the codes of artifice that characterize the rest of culture—of femininity, for instance, or the elaborate interstitial codes of homosexuality.

It was Oscar Wilde who said, "To be natural is such a very difficult pose to keep up."[23]

Back to *Playboy* and the defensive position around which the virtues of the bachelor were established: in September 1958, Philip Wylie published an article in *Playboy* titled "The Womanization of America." Mr. Wylie's point was to warn against what he called the encroaching "taffeta tide"—the feminization of the suburban domestic realm. Mr. Wylie says,

> On some not very distant day I expect to see a farmer riding a pastel tractor and wearing a matching playsuit. And as he ploughs, I'll realize with horror it's not a contour job; he'll be fixing his fields so the crops will match an "overall design-feeling" incorporated in his home by the little woman. . . . The only inanimate object I can think of offhand which still has masculine integrity is the freight car, and even some of these are being glamorized.

Obviously this caustic text displays both apprehension and paranoia, but it also quite clearly lays out many of the fears for which the domestic fantasies of *Playboy* are meant to compensate. The humiliation felt at the loss of masculine control is represented by the farmer, whose pantsuit might be color coordinated with his tractor. The freight car, which becomes a venerated icon, is not a space of occupation—except for the vagabond or drifter. Mr. Wylie laments the loss of the man's private domain in the spaces of the city:

> The American male had lost his authority as symbolized by the places where he drank. Sawdust vanished and the stand-up bar was rare; the new saloons were like tea shoppes. . . . America's females pushed and heckled their way into every private male domain.

Wylie describes a spatial and architectural emasculation which occurs not only within the city but also in the home, and is manifest not through behavior or personal interaction, but through design. Men have become spatial expatriates:

> Those domestic improvements which reduce labor—machines that do dishes, dispose of refuse, cook automatically, ventilate, heat, vacuum, clean, air condition, mow lawns, harrow gardens, preserve food and so on—were all of them, invented perfected, manufactured and distributed by males.
>
> The rest of home design fell into the hands of women and decorators who were women or, when not, usually males in form only—males emotionally so identified with the opposite sex they could rout reluctant husbands because their very travesty made men uncomfortable. Sundry special magazines took up the cause. They were identified by women and by women-identified males. These homemaking magazines brought forth a welter of counsel on how to convert normal residences into she-warrens.
>
> Where once man had had a den, maybe a library, a cellar poolroom, his own dressing room, he now found himself in a split level pastel creation. . . . All he knew was that the beloved old place now looked like a candy box without even an attic for his skis, his humidor or hunting prints. . . . The American home, in short, is becoming a boudoir-kitchen-nursery, dreamed up by women, for women and as if males did not exist as males.[24]

If the home is the space of the woman, and if space is either masculine or feminine, what constitutes male space, and what role do women, or homosexuals, play in it?

In the fifties and sixties *Playboy* published a number of commissioned designs for apartments, houses, pads, and penthouses as a way of imagining sites for the *Playboy* lifestyle.[25] One of the most fascinating aspects of this discussion is how tacitly it is assumed that spaces and objects become charged with the conditions of social and economic gender roles, but also with specific ideas about sexuality as well. These spaces can be understood to constitute a strategy of recovery of the domestic realm by the heterosexual male.

By grounding the bachelor's fantasy away from the suburban family, the urban sites of *Playboy*'s apartments engage the dangerous pleasures of the city's shadows. The penthouse sits above but within the city—in it but not of it—and allows the bachelor a controlling gaze of the urban spectacle. The penthouse implicitly evokes the image of the city at night and its illicit pleasures. These apartments are the fantasy sites of seduction, with the bachelor the wily predator and the woman the prey. All of the apparatus that fill these spaces—the remote controls, the furniture, the bar—are essentially prosthetic devices that expand the effectiveness of the bachelor in his seduction, or, put another way, the predator in conquest of his prey.

Playboy's Penthouse Apartment was published in September and October of 1956 (FIG. 8). The article began,

> A man yearns for quarters of his own. More than a place to hang his hat, a man dreams of his own domain, a place that is exclusively his. Playboy has designed, planned and decorated, from the floor up, a penthouse apartment for the urban bachelor—a man who enjoys good living, a sophisticated connoisseur of the lively arts, of food and drink and congenial companions of both sexes. A man very much, perhaps, like you.[26]

The plan of the apartment is fairly simple. It is a penthouse located high in a building of unusual configuration. The plan is open, "not divided into cell-like rooms, but into function areas well delineated for relaxation, dining, cooking, wooing and entertaining, all interacting and yet inviting individual as well as simultaneous use."[27]

There are some things you have to know about the bachelor. He has a lot of friends whom he likes to invite over spontaneously. He has no family; the bachelor is fantasized as a free agent. His apartment is new and facilitates his behavior through a dependency on technology. It is a space of imagined liberation, in which technology serves as an extension of sexual desire.

FIGS. 8 AND 9 The *Playboy* Penthouse Apartment

And speaking of entertainment, one of the hanging Knoll cabinets beneath the windows holds a built-in bar. This permits the canny bachelor to remain in the room while mixing a cool one for his intended quarry. No chance of missing the proper psychological moment—no chance of leaving her cozily curled up on the couch with her shoes off and returning to find her mind changed, purse in hand, and the young lady ready to go home, damn it. Here, conveniently at hand, too, is a self-timing rheostat which will gradually and subtly dim the lights to fit the mood—as opposed to the harsh click of a light switch that plunges all into sudden darkness and may send the fair game fleeing.[28]

The primal theme of the male as hunter is further pursued in the decor: "One entire wall is decorated with bold and vigorous primitive paintings reminiscent of the prehistoric drawings in the caves of Lascaux."[29] (FIG. 9) The seduction continues:

Do we go through the house turning out the lights and locking up? No sir: flopping on the luxurious bed, we have within easy reach the multiple controls of its unique headboard. Here we have silent mercury switches and a rheostat that control every light in the place and can subtly dim the bedroom lighting to just the right romantic level. Here, too, are the switches which control the circuits for front door and terrace window locks. Beside them are push buttons to draw the continuous, heavy, pure-linen, lined draperies on sail track, which can insure darkness at morn—or noon. Above are built-in speakers fed by the remotely controlled hi-fi and radio based in the electronic entertainment installation in the living room. On either side of the bed are storage cupboards with doors that hinge downward to create bedside tables. Within are telephone, with on-off switch for the bell, and miscellaneous bed-time items. Soft mood music flows through the room and the stars shine in the casements as you snuggle down.

At the start of a new day, the chime alarm sounds, morning music comes on and the headboard's automatic controls again prove their value: reaching lazily to the control panel, you press the buttons for the kitchen circuits and immediately the raw bacon, eggs, bread and ground coffee you did the right things with the night before (while the ultrasonic washer was doing the dishes) start their metamorphosis into crisp bacon, eggs fried just right, and steaming-hot fresh java. Now you flip the switch that draws the curtains and opens the terrace doors to let in the brisk morning air.[30]

The woman is never there in the morning, but the eggs and bacon are. We have a picture of the playboy—in the city, but insulated from it by altitude, residing in a space probably not so unlike the office, controlling his world remotely. His actions are not direct, but mediated—he does something that does something to something else. Security, convenience, and desire are electronically intertwined. The world is brought to the bachelor electronically. Everything is reproduced, including the women. The only palpable condition is one of desire, and that for a woman who seems to want to bolt.

The furniture is all new—bought, not inherited. There is no indication of past; the bachelor lives completely within the world of commodities and the market, and enjoys having no apparent fixity to the social order. The bachelor is nouveau riche. The furniture itself should be marked by an "exuberance, finesse and high imagination, to be liberated fanciful and romantic, to reflect good spirits [rather] than high philosophies."[31] The work of high modernists, of Mies, Le Corbusier, and Marcel Breuer was rejected as "a belligerent assemblage of mechanical parts . . . thriving on a dogma that rivaled puritan passion."[32] Preferred designers were Charles and Ray Eames, George Nelson, Edward Wormley.

We should compare the bachelor's house with the apartment for the single woman that Helen Gurley Brown imagined in her 1962 book *Sex and the Single Girl.*

Ms Brown begins,

If you are to be a glamorous, sophisticated woman that exciting things happen to, you need an apartment, and you need to live in it alone! . . .

Being Mama and Daddy's girl and living at home is rarely justifiable either.

Parents who are ill and need you are one thing.

If you are a widow or divorcee with children, living with an older family member may be a blessing.

A beautiful apartment is a sure man-magnet, and not only because he expects to corner you and gobble you up like Little Red riding hood. A wolf can wolf any place.

Think of yourself as a star sapphire. Your apartment is your setting.[33]

Ms. Brown's essay on the apartment is organized with the following headings:

To furnish or not to furnish
What part of town should you be in?
How much to pay?
What to look for in a building?
What color walls?
Inside the castle
How much will it cost
How to get the work done
Decorator fees
To please a man
Gobs of pictures
Travel posters
Television
Books
Hi-Fi
A sexy kitchen
Towel girl
Little Jewel
Something in the Air[34]

The point of going through this rather practical list is as a kind of antidote to the *Playboy* fantasy, which poses the apartment in a way that is essentially idolatrous—one is meant to gaze upon the pictures with wonder and longing. The bachelor pad is an icon of a liberated social position, not simply of material acquisition. Ms. Brown's apartment is fabricated from a life; her guide is practical. *Playboy*'s apartment is fabricated from a wage, the fantasy of a man whose reality is the marketplace. This commerce of the market trades multiples. Uniqueness is absent, or if it is present, it is within the formulaic world of the interior, for example the color accent or feature wall. The *Playboy* Playmate was understood as being the girl next door, a rather generic title. The *Playboy* Clubs employed "Bunnies," named for animals commonly known for their reproductive speed. When Gloria Steinem got herself hired in the New York *Playboy* Club, the woman who interviewed her said, "We don't like our girls to have any background."[35] The bachelor doesn't want any history either. In the summer of 1963, Hugh Hefner announced to the world that Playboy was employing 24 ½ tons of Bunnies with a collective chest measurement of 15,516 inches.[36]

Numerous other *Playboy* designs for bachelor pads were produced.

THE WEEKEND HIDEAWAY (April 1959), designed by James E. Tucker and rendered, with active strokes and a vivid palette that recall Leroy Neiman, by Robert Branham (FIG. 10). The Hideaway, a two-bedroom weekend house, was conceived to solve the problem the bachelor encounters when looking for a country house. He finds "kozy kottages or split-personality ranch houses or gas-station-modern monstrosities. These he discovers are all 'oriented'. . . family oriented, suburb oriented, economy oriented."

The house is organized around a large central living room, with bedrooms facing each other on two sides. "The indoor-outdoor feel of the hideaway is accentuated by the fact that there is no 'entrance door' as such, access being through sliding glass panels facing [the] lake or pool" located on either side of the house. The marital threshold, and all of its associations to suburban iconography, is erased.

*plans for a bachelor's haven
far from the madding crowd*

FIG. 10 The Weekend Hideaway

Below the living area is the rec room, known as the "cave," which features, as does the bathroom of the penthouse, "prehistoric wall decoration" reminiscent of Lascaux. Three large windows to the depths of the pool become "luminous living murals." The master bedroom affords the bachelor control of his domain as it enhances his charms:

> The bedside table contains a master control panel which can be preset to turn on, dim or extinguish lights in various parts of the room, or to tune the hi-fi in or out, draw drapes across the window wall, floodlight the beach or pool. . . . It may even cross your mind, as you bid goodnight to the guest-wing contingent and prepare a final potation to share with your chosen companion, that within these walls, you are, literally, an irresistible host.[37]

The Hideaway maintains the infrastructure of control, but furthers the themes of containment: the woman becomes a zoological specimen, confined and observed within the pool. The bachelor's isolation, the trophy of the penthouse, is sacrificed in the Hideaway. The house itself demonstrates a social agenda—to populate the landscape with swingers.

FIG. 11 The *Playboy* Town House

The bachelor remains in control, as his image is doubled in the guest room, erasing what might otherwise be the site of a child's room in a more typical suburban house. The Hideaway is a country house absent the natural themes of propagation and fertility.

Promising "posh plans for exciting urban living," the PLAYBOY TOWN HOUSE (May 1962) is a project that Hefner commissioned as his own residence, designed by the architect R. Donald Jaye, to be constructed on the north side of Chicago (FIG. 11). This fact explains its relative worldliness among the domestic designs that *Playboy* published. The inclusion of a garage sites the project relative to the city's streets.

A row house of exposed fieldstone party walls with waffle slab ceilings, the town house is organized around a central atrium with a small swimming pool in its center. The town house marks the first appearance of the round bed: "The carousel striped coverlet has been turned down. We've poured a brandy nightcap from the bar concealed in the rotating headboard, propped up our pillow, and push buttoned several hours of balladry to add the proper final notes." The rendering shows but one brandy glass and one pillow. The bachelor is alone tonight.

> The discerning city-dweller of individual ways and comfortable means is turning more and more to the superb outlets for decorative and architectural self-expression inherent in the town house. He is beguiled by its intrinsic advantages of privacy and spaciousness coupled with a metropolitan location just a shift of the gears away from myriad urban attractions. . . . As we turn our high performance *gran turismo* coupe into the driveway, we point out to our comely companion the Playboy Town House's striking exterior. All floor to ceiling glass and masonry, the Town House stands in glamorous contrast to, yet in curiously pleasing harmony with, the post-Victorian brownstones that surround it. . . . Guiding our guest to the right rear of the carport, we unlock the rabbit-escutcheoned teak door (guests arriving later may be screened via closed-circuit TV and intercom before being admitted). . . . Toward the rear of the left-side wall is the houseman's desk located below a central control panel (identical panels are found in the living room and master bedroom; smaller versions are in all the other rooms) which is the omnipresent electronic brain of the house. From this one multibuttoned, many-dialed source, the houseman can open and close the sliding drapes and glass doors, the pool's skylight, control the lighting throughout the house, and precisely regulate the heating and air conditioning.[38]

FIG. 12 The Patio-Terrace

Reflecting Hefner's success, the town house provides more opulent quarters for the bachelor. Provisions are made within the house for servants, while all other spaces open onto the atrium without doors, reflecting the occupation of the house by a single person. The *Playboy* mansion, the purchase of which scuttled the construction of the town house, is visible through the windows in the rendering of the living room. The painting *Duck Pond* by Willem de Kooning, which was owned by Hefner, is shown in the rendering of the living room.

THE PATIO-TERRACE (August 1963), designed and rendered by Humen Tan, is a small roof deck (FIG. 12), forty by thirty feet, a garden for the confirmed city dweller, "an escape hatch from the hurly-burly of city living." Its program, on the other hand, seems decidedly suburban: "No cosmopolite is immune to an occasional longing for some parcel of sky-domed greensward to offset the concrete, chrome, glass and steel that may make city living elegant and convenient, but decidedly non pastoral."

The terrace is comprised of four components: the cantilevered sun deck for "sunning sans suits," the drinking-dining promontory, the tête-à-tête corner, and the romantically sequestered intimate hideaway. A round fountain and a cylindrically enclosed television that rotates 360 degrees complete the party landscape. The formal vocabulary is surreal and futuristic, typified by the biomorphic cantilever of the sun deck and the Kagan-Dreyfuss barstool.

> An upper cabinet against the kitchen wall boasts a stepsaving master-control panel, from which the host can operate a varied assortment of electronic gear—the TV set at the other end of the cabinet, all of the terrace's lighting, the hi-fi, whose portable cylindrical speakers may be place in any area of the terrace where stereo is desired, utilizing the concealed outlets. The control panel also regulates the terrace pool's fountain and the vari-colored lights which play on it in rainbowlike profusion. It operates the counter's awning, which, covering the entire island, is made up of inter-locking porcelain-enameled aluminum slats equipped on each end with steel plates. . . . The panel also holds phone and intercom unit.[39]

Influenced by contemporary Italian design and minimalism, the DUPLEX PENTHOUSE (January 1970) reflects its time, and the sensual turning-inward of the drug culture (FIG.. 13). While the penthouse is still in the city, the urban panorama is more distant, the environment more intro-spective. For the bachelor, the domicile becomes

> an outward reflection of his inner self. . . . A large part of this new urban way of life is responsive to architectural serenity and spatial sculpturing, to gain a sense of quite-private interior vistas, rather than focusing on or rely-ing upon the outward view from the penthouse windows, garden and patio-terraces. . . . The individualization that is ever more important in today's world is most readily achieved, we believe, by working from a validly conceived and pleasingly proportioned architectural matrix for liv-ing, to be imprinted with each owner's choice of colors, textures, works of art and personal *bibelots*, be they heirlooms or recent acquisitions. What you see here are our suggestions; each man will have his own preferences, but may find ours to his liking or stimulating to his imagination. Now—in imagination—we invite you to tour the proposed premises, as a prospec-tive owner would do.

FIG. 13 The Duplex Penthouse

Controls are not forgotten:

The outsize abstract you've been admiring was created with abrasionproof acrylic paints applied to panels that open by remote control to reveal the latest in video and audio equipage.

All of the wall's built-in gear is operated from a master control panel behind the abstract, while a number of the main controls are duplicated in an auxiliary panel that's been placed conveniently at finger-tip reach just behind the couch and to the right of the fireplace hearth. Thus, you can remain seated with your guests while entertaining them with your electronic showmanship.

The environment is tranquilized and serene. More than a collection of machines to foster seduction, it is an environment that projects the desire it shelters, an orgasmatron.

Once the floor-to-ceiling painted panels on the wall behind the head of the bed are flipped back, a battery of projectors connected to the control panel between the headrests can—if you so choose—turn the room into an electric circus of swirling colors that contrast with blinking strobes fired in time to your choice of freaky far-out sounds. Or, if a softly romantic mood is what you're after, the room can glow like an ember, the walls and ceiling pleasantly pulsating, while you're serenaded by sounds more soothingly conducive to matters at hand.[40]

While the earlier projects focused on a set of controls that instrumentally assisted the seduction, the Duplex Penthouse, which was the last in the series of *Playboy* designs, is different. While it also functions as a prosthetic, this Penthouse possesses the characteristics of the mood ring, visually registering the inner life, the nervous system, of the throbbing bachelor.

Some trends do emerge. The kitchen gets smaller and smaller, a process culminating in an article describing the "kitchenless kitchen," a freestanding counter loaded with electric appliances, toasters, blenders, electric frying pans, and deep fryers.[41]But as the kitchen gets smaller, the bar gets bigger, until they are both about the same size.[42] Stereo equipment acquires a greater and greater significance, until it finally becomes part of the architecture, from "Playboy's Electronic Entertainment Wall" of October 1964 to the "Switched on Superwall" of November 1970.

We never see the bachelor, which allows the reader to project himself into the image of the space.

The Taj Mahal of the *Playboy* lifestyle was certainly the *Playboy* Mansion in Chicago, originally designed by the architect James Gamble Rogers and renovated by Ronald Dirsmith for Hefner in 1959. The mansion, with large rooms of heavy beams and dark paneling, was considered, as the Tudor always is, masculine in its decor. Twenty-five Bunnies slept on bunk beds in the attic dormitories. The mansion contained offices for the magazine and numerous guest rooms. Its renovation, in its mix of programs and publics, turned the building into a kind of city.[43]

Hefner's fantasy for the mansion went like this:

I am going to have a house with a massage room, a steam room, a bar, and a bedroom big enough for two 707's. The floor will be covered with a white rug four inches thick, with a polar-bear skin near the hi-fi. And the bed, oh, maneroonian, the bed will be adequate for an exhibition match between the Green Bay Packers and the Los Angeles Rams.

Downstairsville, there is a two story chandeliered, oak paneled living room with teakwood floors and a trap door through which you can drop twelve feet into a kidney-shape indoor pool. "That," I'll tell my visitors, "is where we throw the old discarded girls." At the end of the pool is a water-fall, and you can swim through it twosies into a dark warm grotto which has wide ledges at the sides, softened with plastic-covered cushions. [44]

As this text illustrates, the bachelor's life is quite rehearsed.

The *Playboy* Mansion was the site of the round bed in Hugh Hefner's bedroom (FIG. 14). The magazine described the bed in this way:

Eight and one half feet in diameter, fitting into a bank of curved cabinets, the bed is equipped with motorized controls that enable Hefner to rotate himself—and a dozen passengers, if he wishes—a full 360 degrees in either direction. "It goes 33 ⅓, 45 and 78," Hef says.

When the hinged center panel in the black leather headrest is low-ered, it reveals not only the buttons controlling the rotation of this auto-mated innerspring, but also a set of dials that operate an ingenious three-motor vibrator system. . . . Behind a sliding panel in the stationary walnut headboard is an intercom-phone system that permits direct communica-tion with any room in the Mansion. For outside calls there is a Rapidial telephone which, with the push of single button, will automatically dial any one of the 200 prerecorded numbers anywhere in the country. The head-board also houses remote controls for a video-tape recorder; a rheostat for romantically dimming the bedroom lights; and outlets for two pairs of stereo headphones, with complete controls for the room's elaborate hi-fi system. [45]

A biographer of Hefner's offered this list of what was actually inside

the headboard: "kinky little trin-
kets like dildoes, vibrators,
chains, and studded leather har-
nesses, four white Magic Wand
vibrators by General Electric as
well as economy-size bottles of
Johnson's Baby Oil."[46]

Back to the magazine's description:

FIG. 14 The round bed

A touch of his bed rotating
buttons allows Hef to create, in
effect four distinctly different rooms. With the bed turned toward the east
wall, the bed faces the video hi-fi area: a twin screened Philippine-
mahogany custom TV console, operated from the bed; and a rosewood
Claritone stereo hi-fi. . . . Turned north, the bed faces the conversation
area, created by a long Knoll couch and low marble coffee table. Turning to
the west, the bed faces its stationary headboard, which offers a polished
expanse of walnut that can be used as a desk, a private bar, or a table for
any hour dining. And turning south, the bed faces the romantic glow emanating from the Italian marble fireplace.[47]

Hefner developed some habits that provided for an erratic daily
schedule. As a result, the windows of his quarters in the mansion were
blocked. There was no daylight, severing the interior from the cycles of
the day, but also from the gaze over the city that empowers the bachelor
in his penthouse. The bed with its machines, previously only a fantasy
within the pages of *Playboy*, was the apparatus devised to fill, and control,
the void. Hefner said,

That's what progress is all about—man's ability to control his environment. It's what sets him apart most dramatically from the lower animals.
He's come a long ways since the days of the cave man; his home today is

more than simply a shelter from the elements and a place to eat and sleep. With the inventions of the phonograph, the radio, moving pictures and television, it's a place to be entertained as well. It can become a private world, a place to work and lay, an extension of oneself.[48]

The round bed is that extension. In Burnham's *Plan of Chicago*, the dome of the city occupied the center of the city, controlling its field as the plan of the city radiated from it. In Hefner's bed, an empire is controlled as the occupant pivots around the room, commanding, electronically now, the controls of the empire. It is the electronic panopticon of the sybaritic male.

Tom Wolfe wrote of Hefner and his bed, "Hefner's geographic position, whether he is horizontal, on his feet, sitting down, is a major piece of information inside the house and at the PLAYBOY office."[49]

So far, I have tried to talk about fantasies of control in the space of the city and in the space of the domicile and to explain that those fantasies are strongly connected to assumptions of gender differences and sexual identities. These changes mirror in scale and focus the economic transformations of North America after the war, the advent of intense suburbanization, and a consumer culture revolving around the single-family house. My examples have been from the worlds of Burnham, Gruen, and Hefner. But an elaborate dialogue on the house of the bachelor is waiting to be extracted from the history of architecture, from Hadrian to Gabriele D'Annunzio, John Lautner, Liberace, Paul Rudolph, Philip Johnson and Mies, from designs in which intensity of artifice and singularity of vision outweigh social conventions.

These themes can be examined at Philip Johnson's house, the house of a bachelor and homosexual (FIG. 15). It is frequently overlooked that Philip Johnson has two houses, a house of night and a house of day. The principal text of the Glass House is of course that of the rigors of modernism, of Johnson's struggles with the patriarch Mies. Little is made of the fact that a gay man in 1949 made a bedroom for himself without curtains. In the guest house (FIG. 16), he also made a bedroom for himself without windows, and the classic image seems laden with sexual anticipation to me—the absence of pillows renders the bed more platform than bunk (FIG. 17).

In the Glass House, the bachelor has a controlling gaze, looking down the hill to the pond and its pavilion. The gaze dominates with such force that it has determined the pavilion's scale, reducing it to a defunctionalized product of the bachelor's vision. This vision is active and determining—effecting the bachelor's will over what he surveys. Philip Johnson has said, "In all my recent work I strive for nostalgia, precariousness and sexual yearning. . . . In the lake pavilion for example, the small scale gives the visitor a feeling of all importance, superiority over the environment."[50]

Another example of the imagined power of the bachelor's gaze, here controlling behavior and not simply form, is visible in the photo essay "View from a Penthouse—a contemplation of the urban scene" from *Playboy* in August 1957 (FIG. 18). In this series of nine photographs, a man, whose hands are visible at the rail of his balcony holding a cocktail, observes a woman walk onto the balcony directly below. In the frames that follow, the woman proceeds to undress and strike a Marilyn-like pose on the floor of her balcony. Looking up, she is shocked to see the bachelor, and quickly dresses and retreats. In the final frame, the bachelor has left his drink, and we are left to imagine the rendezvous he has willed.

FIG. 15 Glass House, New Canaan, Connecticut, Philip Johnson, 1949

FIG. 16 Guest House, New Canaan, Connecticut, Philip Johnson, 1949

FIG. 17 Pink Room, guest House, New Canaan, Connecticut, Philip Johnson, 1953

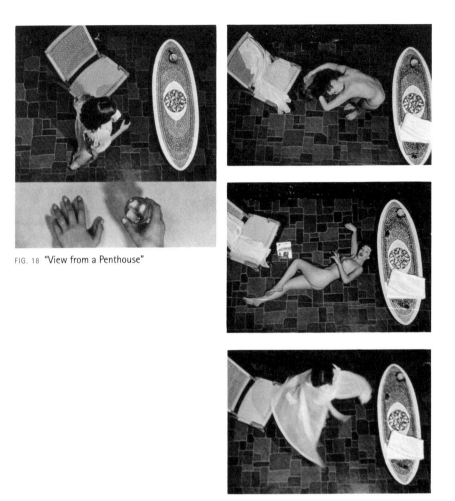

FIG. 18 "View from a Penthouse"

The architectural idealizations of the domestic at Johnson's Glass House (the kitchenless kitchen) and Mies's Farnsworth House can be described as other versions of the domestic fantasy project, as an introduction into the house of the sort of extreme purifications that had characterized the utopian vision of the urban realm. The Farnsworth House was built for a single woman, Dr. Edith Farnsworth, who, Mies biographer Franz Schulze claims, had an affair with Mies during the planning of the project.

Schulze also goes on to say, "Edith was no beauty. Six feet tall, ungainly of carriage, and as witnesses agreed, rather equine in features, she was sensitive about her physical person and may very well have compensated for it by cultivating her considerable mental powers."[51] You get, of course, that he is saying that a developed intelligence in a woman is a compensation for looking like a horse. Not so unlike what Hugh Hefner said in a 1967 interview with Orianna Fallaci: "I don't feel uncomfortable with an intelligent woman. Simply, I do not know what to do with her."[52]

After losing her lawsuit against Mies for cost increases (the house cost $73,000 in 1953) Edith Farnsworth allowed herself to be interviewed by *House Beautiful*. When asked, sardonically, whether the house filled her with implacable calm, she responded, "The conception of a house as a glass cage suspended in air is ridiculous. . . . Do I feel implacable calm? The truth is that in this house with its four walls of glass I feel like a prowling animal, always on the alert. I am always restless. Even in the evening, I feel like a sentinel on guard day and night. I can rarely stretch out and relax."[53]

There are no images in this paper of the *Playboy* Playmates, the revealing shots of the girl next door you can't touch, with which the magazine helped stake its claim to the market. But I expect they have been somewhere not very far back in your mind's eye. And I would like to replace that image now with another one—of a tall, intelligent woman, alone inside a glass house—a cage up off the ground, in fact—pacing anxiously as she imagines the men in the bushes—staring at her.

NOTES

1. "It was cool and clean that night. And there was the smell of the ocean and the surf that came in through the open windows of the small cottage I kept out at Malibu. But in the room there was nothing but the exciting scent of the girl and her wanting.

   "We had gone into the bedroom and stripped with fierce urgency in our vitals. She was quicker than I and now she was on the bed looking up at me as I opened the dresser drawer and took out a package of rubbers.

   "Her voice was a whisper in the night. 'Don't Joney. Not this time.'

"I looked at her. The bright Pacific moon threw its light in the window. Only her face was in shadows. Somehow, what she said brought the fever up.

"The bitch must have sensed it. She reached for me and kissed me. 'I hate those damn things, Joney. I want to feel you inside me.'

"I hesitated a moment. She pulled me down on top of her. Her voice whispered in my ear. 'Nothing will happen, Joney. I'll be careful.'

"Then I couldn't wait any longer and her whisper changed into a sudden cry of pain. I couldn't breathe and she kept crying in my ear, 'I love you, Joney. I love you, Joney.'

"She loved me all right. She loved me so good that five weeks later she tells me we got to get married. (Harold Robbins, *The Carpetbaggers* [New York: Pocket Books, 1961], 8.)

2. "The Playboy Bed," *Playboy* (April 1965): 88.

3. Daniel Burnham and Edward H. Bennett, *Plan of Chicago* (Chicago, 1909) reprint ed. (New York: Da Capo Press, 1970).

4. Victor Gruen, Gruen Associates, *The Fort Worth Plan*, 1955.

5. Thomas S. Hines, *Burnham of Chicago, Architect and Planner* (New York: Oxford University Press, 1974).

6. See Mario Manieri-Elia, "Toward an 'Imperial City': Daniel H. Burnham and the City Beautiful Movement," in *The American City*, ed. Georgio Ciucci, et al. (Cambridge: MIT Press, 1973).

7. Daniel Burnham and Edward H. Bennett, *Plan of Chicago*, 120.

8. Ibid., 117.

9. See George Wagner, "Freedom and Glue: Architecture, Seriality and Identity in the American City," in *Harvard Architecture Review* 8 (New York: Rizzoli, 1992): 66; see also Garry Wills, "Chicago," in *New York Review of Books* XL, no. 17 (21 October 1993): 15.

10. The Plan was commissioned by J. B. Thomas, president of Texas Electric Service Co. ("Don't think I'm Santa Claus. I'm not that altruistic. I'm a businessman, and my business is supplying electricity. If the city grows, my business grows." *Fort Worth Press*, 11 March 1956, 21.)

11. *Fort Worth Plan*, 6.

12. *Fort Worth Plan*, 9.

13. *Fort Worth Plan*, 10.

14. Laura Mulvey, "Melodrama Inside and Outside the Home," in *Visual and Other Pleasures*, (London: Macmillan, 1989), 70. For additional reading on the gendered spheres of city and suburb, see: Margaret Marsh, *Suburban Lives* (New Brunswick: Rutgers 1990); Martin Wachs, "Men, Women, and Urban Travel: The Persistence of Separate Spheres" in *The Car and the City*, ed. Martin Wachs and Margaret Crawford (Ann Arbor: University of Michigan Press, 1992), 86; and Susan Saegert, "Masculine Cities and Feminine Suburbs: Polarized Ideas, Contradictory Realities," *Signs: Journal of Women in Culture and Society* 5, no. 3 (Spring 1980): 96.

15. Walter Benjamin, "Paris, Capital of the Nineteenth Century," in *Reflections* (New York: Schocken Books, 1986), 154–56, cited by Beatriz Colamina, "Intimacy and Spectacle: The Interiors of Adolf Loos," *AA Files* 20, 15.

16. Mulvey, "Melodrama Inside and Outside the Home," 70.

17. An article "Blessings of Bachelorhood," published in *Life* (26 January 1959): 95, provides an insight into the cult of the bachelor:

> William Niall Mitchell of Atlanta, Ga. is a bachelor. By dictionary definition a bachelor is "any male animal (esp. the young fur seal) without a mate." But to Billy Mitchell, healthy, intelligent and unattached, and to millions of non-fur-bearing Americans like him, bachelorhood is more complicated than that. It has special privileges mainly involving freedom—freedom from responsibility, freedom to switch jobs, to move fast and do as you please. It also means being the prey of husband-seeking American females. Its problems, aside from income tax disadvantages, really boil down to one word: loneliness.

Several books chronicle the swinging life of this era, a life that was not only available to the bachelor, but also to adventurous couples: Frank Robinson and Nat Lehrman, eds., *From Playboy: Sex American Style* (Chicago: Playboy Press, 1971); and Joe David Brown, ed., *Sex in the 60's: a candid look at the age of mini-morals*, (New York: Time-Life Books, 1968). See also the film *Pillow Talk*.

18. For a feminist perspective on *Playboy* and their philanthropic foundation, see Catherine MacKinnon, "'More Than Simply a Magazine': Playboy's Money," in *Feminism Unmodified: Discourses on Life and Law* (Cambridge: Harvard, 1987). For histories of *Playboy* magazine see: Surrey Marshe with Robert A. Liston, *The Girl in the Centerfold: The Uninhibited Memoirs of Miss January* (New York, Delacorte, 1969); Stephen Byer, *Hefner's Gonna Kill Me When He Reads This . . .* (Chicago: Allen-Bennett, 1972); Frank Brady, *Hefner* (New York: Macmillan, 1974); and Russell Miller, *Bunny: The Real Story of* Playboy (New York: New American Library, 1984).

19. *Playboy* 1, no. 1 (December 1953): 2.

20. Emily Post, *The Personality of a House: The Blue Book of Home Charm* (New York: Funk and Wagnalls, 1948), 410. See also "The Masculine Graces," in *Amy Vanderbilt's New Complete Book of Etiquette: The Guide to Gracious Living* (Garden City, N.Y.: Doubleday & Co., 1952).

21. Edith Wharton and Ogden Codman, *The Decoration of Houses* (New York: W. W. Norton and Co., 1978), 17.

22. Ibid., 152.

23. Oscar Wilde, *An Ideal Husband*, as cited in Susan Sontag, "Notes on Camp," in *A Susan Sontag Reader* (New York: Farrar Strauss, 1982), 110.

24. Philip Wylie, "The Womanization of America," *Playboy* (September 1958): 51–52, 77–79.

25. Between 1956 and 1970, *Playboy* published five commissioned designs for the bachelor's quarters. These spreads featured complete texts describing the 'lifestyle' of the bachelor and also displayed contemporary furniture. Throughout the same period the magazine also published a larger number of houses and apartments, including Charles Moore's house in New Haven ("A Playboy Pad: New Haven Haven," *Playboy* [October 1969]: 125–8, 186).

26. "Playboy's Penthouse Apartment," *Playboy* (September 1956): 54.

27. Ibid., 60.

28. Ibid., 59.

29. "Playboy's Penthouse Apartment—A Second Look," *Playboy* (October 1956): 70.

30. Ibid., 68–70.

31. "Designs for Living," *Playboy*, (July 1961): 48.

32. Ibid.

33. Helen Gurley Brown, *Sex and the Single Girl* (New York: Random House, 1962), 119–20.

34. Ibid., "The Apartment," Chapter 7, 119–37.

35. Gloria Steinem, "I Was a Playboy Bunny," in *Outrageous Acts and Everyday Rebellions* (New York: Holt, Rinehart, and Winston, 1983), 35.

36. Miller, *Bunny: The Real Story of Playboy*, 94.

37. "Playboy's Weekend Hideaway," *Playboy* (April 1959): 49–56.

38. "The Playboy Townhouse," *Playboy* (May 1962): 83–92.

39. "Playboy's Patio Terrace," *Playboy* (August 1963): 102.

40. "Playboy Plans a Duplex Penthouse," *Playboy* (January 1970): 155–61, 233–35

41. "The Kitchenless Kitchen," *Playboy* (October 1959): 53.

42. The bar, and the bachelor's mastery over its technique, has been a favored subject in the pages of *Playboy*:"Pre—and Post—Prandial Potables and Paraphernalia" (January 1958): 17, and "Gentleman's Home Bar" (February 1960): 65. See also Thomas Mario, *Playboy's Host & Bar Book* (Chicago: Playboy Press, 1971).

43. "To me," says Harvey Kurtzman, "this house is almost dangerous. When you walk in, you're not so much walking into a house; you're walking into Hefner's world. I don't know anyone more personally involved in his home than Hef is. Its really his personal 21st Century Disneyland—for adults only!" "The Playboy Mansion," *Playboy* (January 1966): 200.

44. Ibid., 106–7.

45. Ibid., 202.

46. Stephen Byer, *Hefner's Gonna Kill Me When He Reads This . . .* (Chicago, Allen-Bennett, 1972), 119.

47. "The Playboy Mansion," *Playboy* (January 1966): 202.

48. Ibid., 207.

49. Ibid., 202–203.

50. Philip Johnson, "Preface," in *Philip Johnson: The Glass House*, ed. David Kipnis and Jeffrey Whitney (New York: Pantheon Books, 1993), viii.

51. Franz Schulze, *Mies van der Rohe: A Critical Biography* (Chicago: University of Chicago Press, 1985), 258.

52. "Orianna Fallaci Interviews Hugh Hefner," *Look* (10 January 1967): 56.

53. Joseph A. Barry, "Good and Bad Modern Houses," *House Beautiful* (May 1953): 266. This interview with Dr. Farnsworth appeared in the considerable wake of *House Beautiful*'s article in April 1953 "The Threat to the Nest America," which demonized International Style modernist architecture at the moment of intense anticommunism in the United States in quite similar terms.

A Revolution in the Woman's Sphere:

Grete Lihotzky and the Frankfurt Kitchen

SUSAN R. HENDERSON

The years between 1890 and 1918 were pivotal in the struggle for the rights of German women. The feminists of this radical period worked primarily within the political parties of the left, where they argued for total social and political equality for women. Women like Clara Zetkin, the leader of the women's branch of the Social Democratic Party, and communist Rosa Luxemburg were ultimately responsible for forcing the agenda of equality on their reluctant parties.[1] While the male majority of socialist opinion only recognized a "helpmeet" role for women, the leadership officially supported a limited progressive plank in the concept of separate-but-equal spheres. Thus, when the Social Democrats unexpectedly came to power in 1918, they fulfilled the political promises of the revolutionary days more from political embarrassment than conviction. The Weimar Constitution declared women to be the equals of men and granted them the vote.

Ironically, these legal victories were followed by a period of profound retrenchment within the feminist movement. The women who had achieved the great victories of the previous decade were entering their

FIG. 1 The modern dancer, Gert Valeska, epitomized the Weimar spirit of the New Woman.

mature years, and young women, apparently feeling that political activism in the postrevolutionary period was passé, no longer joined the movement. As a result, the ranks of organized feminists fell precipitously in the Weimar years. Those stalwarts remaining faced overwhelming opposition, much of it from their own sex.

On the other hand, the introduction of new constitutional rights was paralleled by the advent of the New Woman, a complex and contradictory figure. Young women, it seemed, attempted to match the rising cult of modernity and their new freedoms with a model of contemporary woman of their own making (FIG. 1). Their ideal was shaped by the images of women in advertisements and American films as sexually and socially liberated free spirits as much as by the growing numbers of young working mothers.

Even as an idealization, the New Woman was a phenomenon that seemed to portend a problematical fulfillment of constitutional promises. Though in her many incarnations she was not an overtly political being, in her style—the short hair and the "unfeminine" lines of her dress—and in her social behavior—working, often single, with no interest in a large family and little enthusiasm for homemaking—the New Woman embodied an independence and a modernity that was an anathema to the many self-appointed conservators of the home. Socialists and conservatives alike believed that she represented a force for change that would destroy the family, and with it the moral fabric of the country, leading the working classes down a path to revolution that would end in Germany's economic and spiritual ruin.[2]

Supporting their fears were alarming demographic shifts. Postwar male joblessness was high and in sharp contrast to the rapid increase in the number of working women.[3] The figures for women in the professions and the universities were on the rise. In 1917, as a result of war casualties, women attending universities outnumbered men by 2.5 million.[4] At the same time a so-called "birth strike" retarded population growth among the working classes. Experts blamed the dramatic drop in the birth rate, down to 3.9 births per household by 1925, on young women's selfish preoccupation with acquiring material comforts.

Still reluctant when it came to its feminist commitments, the newly empowered Social Democratic Party now felt pressures from the right to assert the concept of the woman's sphere. The middle class was alarmed at the declining number of women available to work as servants, while industry wanted women available both as cheap labor and to produce a new generation of workers. Critical observers recognized the strain that such conflicting roles inevitably produced. This conflict was at least partially to blame for the drop in the birth rate. And it was noted that women who combined long hours on the job with responsibilities at home had a much higher mortality rate than men in their age bracket.[5]

This combination of factors—the veiled misogyny of the New Woman scare along with class and economic issues—resulted in a state policy called "female redomestication." With it, the effort to improve the lot of German women quickly narrowed its focus. Rather than striving to apportion women the same "basic duties and rights" as men, as the constitution promised, a loose coalition of interest groups sought to reassert the woman's sphere, at the same time bolstering it as the ideological equivalent to the male professions and distinguishing it from factory jobs, which were simply work.

As part of this program, state agencies and the liberal wing of the women's movement forged an ideal of the household as the "professional workplace" of women, one that needed the same studied research as the production line did for men. In one of the ironies of this history, they proposed that an aggrandized status for woman's sphere would be achieved

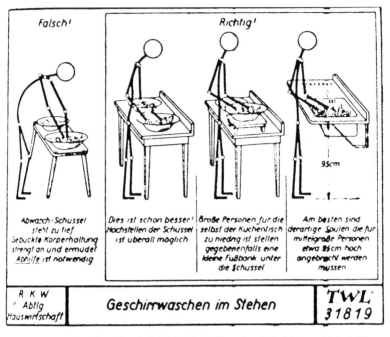

FIG. 2 *Reichskurtorium fuer Wirtschaftlichekeit* in its *Hauswirtschaft* division published Gilbert and Taylor's research on the ergonomics of housekeeping in 1929.

by making it more like men's. The Weimar Republic became known not as an era when women joined the world of men, but as a time of modernization in the household sphere.

The strategic solution and promise of domestic reform was the elimination of drudgery. The "new housekeeping" took less time, was reputedly less tedious, and freed the housewife for more uplifting endeavors. Even feminist Clara Zetkin saw the issues in these terms:

> Rooted and active in the world and in the family she is able to make the husband completely at home in the house again. From her own rich, wide circle of influence there grows in her an untroubled understanding of his aspirations, his struggles and his work. She stands by his side no longer as a faithful and solicitous handmaid, but rather as a convinced, warm

guardian of his ideals, as a companion in his struggles, as a comrade in his efforts and his exertions, giving and receiving intellectual and moral support.[6]

According to the experts, professionalization in the domestic sphere would be realized through simplified household design and the introduction of labor-saving appliances. Guided by the principles of scientific management that operated in modern industry, designers and reformers reshaped the household. Time and motion studies and the dogma of efficiency confirmed the efficacy of their work (FIG. 2). The end product was quantifiable: an increase in productivity and less "wasted effort," resulting in a stable home life, a contented husband, and more and healthier children. Middle class women could now envision themselves pursuing housework with ease and grace, while working women could be expected to maintain two jobs with dexterity (FIG. 3).

FIG. 3 The cover of the Dutch translation of Frederick's *The Thinking Housewife* (1928) contrasts modern housekeeping with old-fashioned drudgery.

American women in the mid-nineteenth century had introduced the first reforms in household self-sufficiency and time-saving techniques. In *The American Woman's Home* (1869), Catharine Beecher and Harriet Beecher Stowe initiated American women in mechanical production as the means to professionalization.[7] In their pursuit of the "Christian Household," Beecher and Stowe urged women to economize time, labor, space, and expense "so as to secure health, thrift, and domestic happiness to persons of limited means."[8] Christine Frederick urged the same message in the twentieth century and became the torchbearer of scientific

management in the home and the official founder of "domestic science."
In *Household Engineering: Scientific Management in the Home* (1919),
Frederick attached to homemaking a new, worldly imagery that, although
not actually altering women's isolation in the home, associated it with
heroic themes of modernization and social progress.[9]

> I . . . really liked housework. . . . But now it was a daily struggle to "get
> ahead" of household drudgery. . . .
>
> Just about this time my husband's work brought him in touch with
> the new movement called "scientific management," and he came home
> with glowing accounts of what it was accomplishing in the various shops,
> offices and factories. . . . In fact, he and his friends talked of nothing but
> this new "efficiency idea." Because I had an intuition that perhaps in this
> new idea was the life-preserver for which I had been so earnestly searching
> in my own problem, I listened eagerly to their discussion.[10]

Using time charts, meal plans, and inventories, women would
become plant managers as Frederick rearmed the kitchen to become the
woman's factory work station.

Frederick's works had a seminal influence in Europe. In Germany,
the bourgeois women's movement embraced household reform in a campaign dubbed *Mütterliche Politik* (motherly politics). The ranks of the
Bund Deutscher Frauenvereine (BDF) (Federation of German Women's
Clubs), a coalition of bourgeois women's organizations, grew exponen-
tially on the wave of patriotic sentiment and conservative reaction that
followed the First World War. By the 1920s, the BDF had more than
6,000 member groups, totaling more than one million women. It was the
nation's largest and most influential women's association, and it was this
group that took up Frederick's banner in an alliance with the professionals among the state bureaucracy.

With its sudden expansion, the composition of the BDF became
increasingly conservative; in order to appeal to a broad base, it opened its
membership to women's groups either neutral or actively opposed to

feminism. The conservative wing was largely represented by the *Reischsverband Deutscher Hausfrauenvereine* (RDH) (Federal Union of German Housewife Associations). Comprising half the total membership of the BDF, the RDH was initially founded by women coping with the "servant problem."[11]

Following the war, the BDF used its extensive influence—influence originating from social and familial ties as much as institutional ones—to play a major role on national and industrial advisory boards. The collaboration between the state and the BDF was largely concerned with the formation of a new federal educational policy. In the primary schools, the important curricular innovation was the institution of compulsory home economics courses for girls, while the effort to preserve a servant class spurred the creation of women's vocational secondary schools that trained women as "professionals" for service jobs as seamstresses, laundresses, and day-care and nursery-school attendants. Although Weimar schools were remarkable for their many progressive innovations, the rise of the BDF spelled an era of retrenchment in women's education. At the college level as well, women's programs, which had opened up to a broad range of fields during the war, returned to an almost exclusive preoccupation with the social service professions: domestic science, teaching, social work, and nursing.[12]

Meanwhile, the RDH had adopted the legal status of a professional association with an official expertise of housewifery, and assumed a major role within the state research branch, the *Reichsforschungsgesellschaft* (RfG) (Reich Research Organization). Their members worked with industry, education, and housing authorities in the design of new programs and products to modernize housekeeping.[13] Together the RDH and the RfG produced their own literature, exhibitions, and conferences, and, in some cases, their own products. In June of 1928, for example, a special edition of the RfG organ, the *Reichsforschungsgesellschaft für Wirtschaftlichkeit im Bau- und Wohnungswesen E.V.* (Federal Research Society for Economy in Building and Housing), entitled *Die Küche der Klein- und Mittelwohnung* (*The Kitchen of the Working- and Middle-*

Class House) included articles ranging from the particulars of kitchen design to a general exhortation on the virtues of the modern kitchen and its tie to Christian morality.[14] The issue was an extension of an exhibit held by the RfG in Berlin in 1928 entitled *Die Ernährung*.[15] Primary among the displays was a series of RfG model kitchens. The designs dealt with such matters as convenient furniture arrangement and "professionally" detailed kitchen equipment largely inspired by Frederick's work.

On a local level, the RDH network established collaboration among women's organizations, municipalities, and housing authorities to bolster a sense of shared goals and citizen involvement. Across the country, its women's clubs consulted with the Bureau of Standards on appropriate home equipment and advised industry on suitable household products. Industry, in turn, made the alliance a promotional forum and a participatory form of advertising. One such collaboration resulted in the *Haus der Ring der Frauen* (*House of the Circle of Women*) of 1931. The exhibition pavilion, designed by Peter Behrens and Elsa Oppler Legband, represented its feminine subject with a great central cylinder, encircled by smaller ones.[16]

The most influential propagandist in this alliance was Marie-Elisabeth Lüders. Lüders came to prominence during the war as an advocate and admirer of women's involvement in war work. She refocused her studies on household professionalization under the aegis of the Weimar state following the 1918 Revolution. To the public, Lüders identified herself as a housewife, but both in her writings and her activities she stood forth as the new, conservative professional woman, ready to join with the state to redefine and strengthen the notion of the woman's sphere. She frequently acted as an advisor to industry and designers, and served on the *Reichstag* committee that funded the Bauhaus and experimental projects in product rationalization. In regard to the household, Lüders advocated a complete rethinking "in a manner conforming to health, morals, and culture."[17]

Erna Meyer was the other important semiofficial spokesperson on the woman's sphere. A professional housewife, like Frederick, and a prolific writer, Meyer commented extensively on new household

equipment and furnishings and was
insistent on the importance of collaboration between architects and housewives to develop good products.[18]

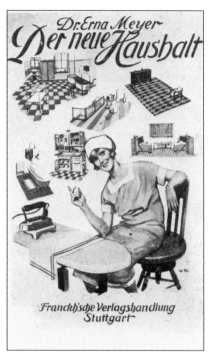

> Whether she is typically a Cinderella
> or a bad-tempered hysteric . . . or one
> who masters her tasks with a steady
> hand and happy eyes and is aware of
> her own worth. . . . [W]hether she is
> the slave to her plight or its creative
> master . . . the house makes a vast dif-
> ference for her, her family and there-
> fore for society as a whole. . . .
>
> Before anywhere else change
> must occur here, and the way there
> lies clear enough before us if we will
> only see it! Systematic collaboration
> between architect and the housewife
> must command the solution.[19]

FIG. 4 The cover of Erna Meyer's *Das neue Haushalt* (1926)

Her book, *Das neue Haushalt* (1926), went into twenty-nine editions in the first two years[20] (FIG. 4).

The work of women like Lüders and Meyer gave political credibility
to redomestication as a feminist program. Their activities supported the
notion that the transformation of the woman's sphere was being forged
through a participatory process—that women, working together with
professionals, the state, and industry, were themselves creating the world
best suited for them, from the base of their intimate experiential knowledge, and that this process was for women the fulfillment of the egalitari-
an social contract of Weimar.

The advisory boards also provided a legitimizing liaison between
the design profession and the female public. On the one hand, they outlined women's needs in design journals; on the other, they collaborated

on professional exhibitions that instructed women in "better living practices." While architects emphasized the influence on them of women
"experts," these same "experts" chided lay women to recognize their
ignorance of modern techniques and to accept what the designers had
developed with them in mind:

> The architects need to educate the housewife in how to use the space and
> in why the small kitchen works . . . that there is only one purpose for the
> room. . . . Most people do not know how to furnish them . . . . [T]he
> housewife must also be educated in taste.[21]

> Many criticized its [the RfG's] model kitchen's small spaces . . . but it is to
> be hoped that the housewife will not reject it simply because it is unfamil-
> iar.[22]

Responding to such specific objections as constrained space, the
"expert nonprofessionals" called upon women to "readjust their demands."[23]

Designers' interest in the woman's sphere was galvanized by Irene
Witte's 1922 translation of Frederick's *The New House-keeping: Efficiency
Studies in Home Management.* A group of young industrial designers
immediately took up her book as a manifesto, and a flood of works that
supported and embellished Frederick's notions followed: Bruno Taut's
Die neue Wohnung: Die Frau als Schöpferin (*The New House: The
Woman as Creator*), Grete and Walter Dexel's *Das Wohnhaus von Heute*
(*The Dwelling of Tomorrow*), and Ludwig Neundörfer's *So wollen wir
wohnen* (*This is How We Want to Live*).[24] As Frederick herself recognized, the advent of rationalization offered a major opportunity for
would-be modernizers of household culture. In the 1920s, the prospects
for mass-produced housing, housewares, and furnishings beckoned the
members of an overwhelmingly male field toward the reconfiguration of
domestic culture and the private sphere. Inevitably, the result was the erosion of a tradition of female practice in favor of the scientific and modern.
As evidenced in the many new professional manuals, this most subjective

and personalized realm was rethought as an objective, technological problem.

In the modernist model, technology and the cult of rationalization were the methodological linchpins that ensured that progress was being made. And always in the back and forth between domestic scientists and architects was the presumption that the best social purpose of managerial and technical expertise was to bolster the existing model of the family and woman's role within it. These various currents effectively coalesced in 1927 at the Werkbund Exhibition in Stuttgart. Erna Meyer authored the household section, *Siedlung und Wohnungen* (*Settlement and Housing*), and displayed two demonstration kitchens of her own design, one in collaboration with architect J. J. P. Oud. Their kitchen became one of the best-known and frequently reproduced kitchens of the Weimar period (FIG. 5). Though it is generally attributed to Oud with no mention of Meyer's contribution, at the time, its validity depended on the participation of an expert homemaker.

FIG. 5 J. J. P. Oud and Erna Meyer's kitchen at the Weissenhof Settlement (1927)

THE NEW FRANKFURT

Only twenty miles from Stuttgart, the city of Frankfurt am Main had gained international recognition for developing the social ideal of the *Neues Leben* (New Life) within a belt of modern settlements.[25] In 1927, the city architect Ernst May invited the thousands flocking to see the Weissenhof Settlement, the complex of modern housing built at the Werkbund Exhibition, to take tours of the new parks and housing estates of Frankfurt.

Ernst May viewed the woman's sphere primarily in terms of housekeeping. Its prominence in his program was largely due to the importance he accorded to *Wohnkultur* (domestic culture) in the program as a whole. The study of domestic life received unique emphasis in Frankfurt: May initiated research and published it in the journal *Das Neue*

Frankfurt (*The New Frankfurt*), which extended from the household to the kitchen, from the consumer market in household products and appliances to the design of home economics classrooms. His design team studied psychology, material and product evaluations, and, of course, scientific management principles as applicable to the home. They scrutinized every aspect of household design to produce efficient and content housewives: color brightened the housewife's world, making housework more tolerable; enameled surfaces made for easy cleaning; and furniture with smooth lines eliminated dusting in hard-to-reach places.[26]

The modern Frankfurt household was to be based on this happy combination of a "scientifically" designed house and rationalized furnishings and equipment. While life in the new settlements offered the most complete array of conveniences, consumers living in older quarters could match some of its efficiency by purchasing items from *The Frankfurt Register*, a line of household furnishings by various manufacturers recommended by the municipal housing authority and published regularly in *Das Neue Frankfurt* and elsewhere[27] (FIG. 6).

Modernizing efforts focused on the kitchen above all. The center of household labor, it became the professional "office" of the housewife and the subject of endless technological improvements. During the program's five years, several different designs were installed in the settlements, including Franz Schuster's all-purpose cupboard kitchen of 2.3 square meters and Anton Brenner's foldout model, both for use in small flats. Undoubtedly the best known project, however, was Margarete ("Grete") Schütte-Lihotzky's 1926 Frankfurt Kitchen (FIG. 7).

MARGARETE SCHÜTTE-LIHOTZKY

> And, again, I was part of a group that stood up for certain principles and architectural ideas, and fought for them uncompromisingly.
> —GRETE SCHÜTTE-LIHOTZKY ON COMING TO FRANKFURT IN 1926[28]

Grete Lihotzky was the only woman architect on May's design team, but she gained international recognition for her design of the Frankfurt

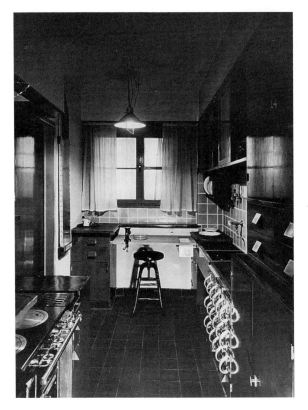

TOP LEFT: FIG. 6
*Das Frankfurter
Register* #11 is the
Belco Camera Bath,
a *Sitzbad* and shower
designed by Ferdinand
Kramer and installed
in the Frankfurt set-
tlements.
BOTTOM LEFT: FIG. 7 The
Frankfurt Kitchen
(1927)
TOP RIGHT: FIG. 8 Grete
Schütte-Lihotzky in
1915

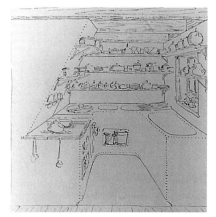

FIG. 9 Lihotzky's design for a concrete kitchen (1921)

Kitchen[29] (FIG. 8). Lihotzky was a socialist activist who dedicated her professional life to the embetterment of the working classes, beginning with her student days during the war.[30] After completing her studies at the *Wiener Kunstgewerbeschule am Stubenring* (Vienna School of Arts and Crafts), now the *Akademie für angewandte Kunst* (Academy of Applied Art), she began work in 1920 under Adolf Loos when he assumed the leadership of the Vienna Housing Authority. For the next five years, she worked for the city designing housing and new domestic facilities.[31]

With Loos, Lihotzky shared both a political outlook and an interest in the economizing strategies of rationalization—the reduction of living spaces to their smallest functional component. It was the same work that was being undertaken, more-or-less systematically, by professionals across Germany and Austria.

Ernst May and Lihotzky first met when May arrived in Vienna to visit Adolf Loos and to see his worker housing estates.[32] As Loos's assistant, Lihotzky acted as guide and emissary. She especially impressed May with her discussion of the work being done in household rationalization, an area May was concurrently exploring in the backwaters of Silesia, where he headed the *Schlesische Heimsttäte* (Silesian Rural Housing Authority). In 1921, he asked her to become a contributor to the journal he was then publishing, *Schlesisches Heim* (*Silesian Home*). In the first article of her career, Lihotzky published a modular kitchen—a concrete, factory-assembled model, installed on site by crane, just as the Frankfurt Kitchen would be[33] (FIG. 9). In 1925, May invited her to become part of his design team in Frankfurt, where he would direct one of the largest housing programs in the country.

Lihotzky's Frankfurt Kitchen became one of the most acclaimed creations of the Weimar housing programs.[34] In its gleaming metal surfaces,
its high imagability, the specificity of its
interlocking parts, its modular totality,
and its largesse of technical fittings, it
epitomized the transformation of everyday life in the modern age. Above all,
Lihotzky's kitchen created an immediate photographic impact. Intricately
coordinated and tightly configured, the
Frankfurt Kitchen was the realization of
the kitchen as machine.

Lihotzky's points of reference
were far removed from the woman's
sphere: ship galleys, the railroad dining
car kitchen, and the lunch wagon.[35] As

FIG. 10 The Frankfurt Kitchen

models, these commercial kitchens, developed to produce hundreds of
food servings within short spaces of time, reduced domestic culture to a
meals-per-minute equation. Thus, with Lihotzky, the kitchen came to full
maturity as a piece of highly specialized equipment—a work station
where all implements were a simple extension of the operator's hand. Its
tiny plan of 1.9 by 3.44 meters was "scientifically" calculated as the opti-
mal dimensions by which every movement was totally efficient and every
operation coordinated (FIG. 10).

Though several different versions were designed, including two larger ones for middle-class families with either one or two servants, the standard demonstration model was fully operable by one person. Continuous
counter space encircled the worker/housewife; at the short end of the
room was the cutting board fitted with its own small waste bin and directly lit by a window, and on one end a wooden plate holder, attached to the
underside of the glass-faced cupboards, allowed wet dishes to drip in the

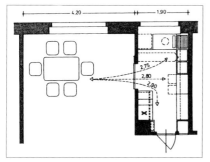

FIG. 11 The plan of the Frankfurt Kitchen ana-
lyzed in relation to the dining area

drainage tray and sink below. Above, a row of hooks provided easy access to an array of special tools, and to the side eighteen labeled metal drawers stored flours and other staples. A square of open circulation space in the center of the kitchen was adjacent to the sliding door that led into the living room. Thus, as the housewife moved the meal to the table, her ambulatory movements were neatly confined to this small area. Light from the end window filled this cube of space, which Lihotzky freed from cabinets on the upper walls to create a feeling of spaciousness[36] (FIG. 11).

Although in the rest of the house, plaster and enameled wood gave a homey quality to the scene, here (and in the bath) the machine age resonated in gleaming surfaces of tile, glass, and metal as Lihotzky experimented with new materials and simple, strong colors. The white of the plaster fabric on the walls and the ventilator hood reflected the light, while the aluminum sink, its splash tiles, and the aluminum storage bins were metal gray. The linoleum work surfaces, the stove top, and the tile floor were black, and the enameled cabinet fronts were a deep blue, a color that Lihotzky understood repelled flies.[37]

That the kitchen was no longer a room, but rather a "niche," was also key. The woman's sphere was thus prevented from intruding on the serenity of other coexisting spheres within the already-reduced household quarters. In order for the home to provide calm and a respite from labor in the outside world—understood to be that of the husband—the household tasks had to be isolated and, indeed, invisible. Again, this was argued in terms of efficiency and health issues: the niche kept the living space free of cooking odors, steam, noise, and equipment.

There was yet another reason for the unique power of Lihotzky's design: among all the various proposals for kitchen modernization, hers was the only one that transformed the kitchen into a consumer product. The Frankfurt Kitchen was a factory-assembled module delivered to a building site and lifted into place by crane. Ten thousand were installed in the Frankfurt settlements alone, but individual units were also sold commercially as an item available from *The Frankfurt Register*. In contrast, Meyer and Oud's collaboration at the Weissenhof Settlement, or Georg Muche and Adolf Meyer's model kitchen at the *Haus am Horn* in Weimar seem fragmentary and unresolved.[38]

This conceptualization of the kitchen as a consumer product underscores the progressive commodification of household culture and the expansion of determinant market interests into the private domain. Lihotzky's design process depended on collaboration with industry—in this case Georg Grumbach, the manufacturer—and consultation with clients—women from middle-class *Hausfrauvereine* (housewives' clubs). May and Lihotzky regarded this collaboration as one of the singular successes of the Frankfurt Kitchen, a model of the ideal working relationship between the corporate structure and the welfare state:

> It is especially gratifying to see how closely in tune industry is with the practical concerns of the housewives.[39]

Thus the private patriarchy represented by the family was gradually given over to a public patriarchy dominated by industry and government. Increasingly, within the municipal housing programs like those headed by Ernst May in Frankfurt or Bruno Taut and Martin Wagner in Berlin, the lines between private and public were indistinct; indeed, the heroic nature of modernism depended on such comprehensivity, on a universal vision that overrode social and gender differences.

Lihotzky's kitchen was first demonstrated at Frankfurt's annual international trade fair of 1927, coincident with the Werkbund exhibition in Stuttgart. Like Meyer, Lihotzky set her kitchen within a larger context called *Die neue Wohnung und ihr Innenausbau* (*The New Housing and Its Interior*), an exhibit she designed that focused on Wohnkultur in the Frankfurt settlements.[40] Around a central display of Frankfurt housing and product samples, including a full-scale, concrete-plate model of a typical Frankfurt row house, photographs and models illustrated the work of Walter Gropius, Taut, Adolf Rading, Le Corbusier, P. Jeanneret, and Franz Schuster's work in Vienna and set the Frankfurt work in the larger context of the *Neues Bauen*.

Local housewives' clubs worked with Lihotzky to develop a subsection of the exhibit entitled *Der neuzeitliche Haushalt* (*The Modern Household*).[41] A didactic introduction to modern kitchen and household design, the display offered an array of technically sophisticated alternatives presented like museum period rooms. In conjunction with the exhibit, the housewives' clubs also sponsored a special lecture series addressing the practical arrangement of kitchen plans and living rooms; the labor-saving kitchen; the hygienic, problem-free bath; the latest in practical, inexpensive furniture; and the advantages of gas and electricity for a clean and efficient home.[42]

It was at this exhibit that the Frankfurt Kitchen first gained international recognition. In 1928, the French Labor Minister Loucheur proposed to purchase as many as 200,000 for his housing program, and it was such a critical success at the Stockholm exhibition of Weimar housing that within the year a Swedish version was put into production.[43] Subsequently, any professional critique of kitchen design in Germany was obliged to include it. Sociologist Ludwig Neundörfer discussed it in his professionally popular book *So wollen wir wohnen*, and in April 1929, the Department of Standards produced a special issue dedicated entirely to it, one that enlisted housewives' opinions. The reviews were generally admiring but mixed, even advocates of professionalization being somewhat alarmed by its absolute rigidity. Neundörfer, for example, criticized it as overdetermined, quipping "all you have to do is use it properly," and regretted that its small dimensions precluded two people working together.[44] Similarly, undazzled by its technical virtuosity, Erna Meyer complained that the Frankfurt Kitchen left too little to chance.[45] But even among critics, the Frankfurt Kitchen was widely acknowledged.

One of the chief innovations of the Frankfurt Kitchen and projects like it was the absolute embrace of modern technology. The postwar expansion of utility networks in Germany had already presupposed

FIG. 12 The western half of Römerstadt in 1927

expanded private and commercial uses, and designers tended to view these opportunities as manifestations of progress. Largely as a result of the reciprocal relationship they developed with industry, new housing settlements became the proving ground for a commodity-oriented rethinking of the single-family home.

In Frankfurt, the expansion of utility networks began shortly before the war; the city enlarged existing power plants and built new ones. At the East Harbor, it added new electrical generating equipment to the gas plant and merged local servicing with the municipal heating network. By the war's end, the city had an energy production capacity far beyond the existing market, one readily filled by the introduction of new energy-consuming sources in the home.

Those who made the trip from the Weissenhof exhibition to visit Frankfurt were offered tours of the city's most famous settlement of Römerstadt (1927). Römerstadt offered not only a lush, modern version of the Garden City, it was the first completely electrified settlement in Germany (FIG. 12). As its renown spread, appliance manufacturers used its image to advertise their products. Covering the opening of the settlement, the newspaper *Frankfurter General Anzeiger* saw the electricity as

FIG. 13 Inside the *Gaspassage*, designed by Adolf Meyer in 1928

its most notable feature. It led with the headline: "America at the Gates: The electric stove. The permanently installed water heater. Everyone can hear the radio without an antenna."[46]

> The main thing is the electricity. Naturally, in the new current of 220 volts. In the new home it is "the servant girl who performs all tasks": it cooks the soup, grills the meat, bakes the cake, heats the bath and the cooking water—and, of course, lights the house.[47]

While the Frankfurt Kitchen was the locus for most of these innovations, the electrified communal laundry, complete with washers, dryers, mangles, and irons, was also hailed for its labor-saving potential. Lihotzky calculated that this facility, built in all the major new Frankfurt settlements, reduced a typical laundry day from fifteen to five hours.[48]

Frankfurt's public utility office was a major force behind these developments and actively pursued public education projects in modern housekeeping. Franz Tillmetz, the director of Frankfurt's utility division, sponsored a permanent exhibition space to display all the wonders of new kitchen technology. The scheme was implemented by architect Adolf Meyer, then one of the Frankfurt design team.[49] Meyer transformed the old shopping arcade "Kaiser-Wilhelm Passage" in the city center into the *Gaspassage*, a permanent forum for demonstrating the latest in gas appliances (FIG. 13). Banking services located in the middle of the hall insured constant traffic through the space. Meanwhile, the passage itself was shorn of its nineteenth-century ornament in favor of Meyer's strong industrial forms, here concrete frames in a rectilinear grid. Heating equipment, including gas and electric ovens and stoves, hot water heaters, and various modern kitchen apparatus flanked the passage.[50]

Tillmetz's office also worked in cooperation with the local school authorities to create a model kitchen to occupy the front window. Designed by Lihotzky, it was used for daily demonstrations of the latest in cooking techniques. Courses in cooking and baking actively propagandized on the virtues of gas appliances.[51]

SCHOOLING FOR THE MODERN HOUSEWIFE

The goal to rationalize housework will come to total fruition only in the next generation. The more we achieve widespread instruction within the Mädschenschulen on questions of labor-saving household operations, the more comprehensive this realization can become.

The most important teaching tool in domestic economy instruction is in the school kitchen. The transformation . . . of the kitchen . . . must be reflected in the arrangement of instruction rooms in which cooking is learned. Recently many labor-saving layouts and devices have been applied to the instructional kitchen. The entire planning of the space results from an analysis of the labor transaction.

—GRETE SCHÜTTE-LIHOTZKY[52]

In the schools, redomestication began with the institution of required courses for young girls in domestic science and the allied household arts.

FIG. 14 Instruction at the Professional Teachers' Institute (1928)

In order to assert the new professional expertise over motherly example, classroom techniques, and indeed the classrooms themselves, replicated the aggrandized sphere of the domestic engineer, and the teacher gained a new authority in her command of a technology generally unavailable at home. The "laboratory" installed in new and remodeled schools around the country consisted of a complex of lecture, sewing, laundry, and dining rooms, with the kitchen as the centerpiece (FIG. 14).

Initially, professionalization and hygiene were the two great themes in this pedagogical revolution, but as the German industrial economy slowly regeared toward peacetime production, training young women to be modern consumers gained equal importance. The kitchen classroom, like the *Gaspassage*, typically introduced the array of consumer choices; gas and electric appliances of German manufacture in a variety of models let the student appraise their particular advantages. In her design for the Professional Teachers' Institute in Frankfurt, for example, Lihotzky provided eight kitchen cubicles: five had gas stoves, two electric, and only one was of the old-fashioned coal-burning type (FIG. 15). At the

FIG. 15 The kitchenettes at the Professional Teachers' Institute

Varrentrapp School in Frankfurt, the electric cooker—a modern "miracle"—sat next to the teacher's demonstration table. Other more mundane designer features, like an overhead cupboard with its hanging utensils easy-to-hand, developed student awareness of the potentials of wise consumer choices in furnishing the home.

Lihotzky designed fourteen homemaking instructional facilities for the public schools of Frankfurt.[53] Her schoolroom kitchenette was a miniature version of the Frankfurt Kitchen, then being installed in new housing throughout the city. At Römerstadt, every unit had a Frankfurt Kitchen; at the same time, Martin Elsaesser and Wilhelm Schütte installed Lihotzky's kitchenettes in the domestic science "laboratory" at the local public school. A girl trained in the Frankfurt kitchenette could move into the new world of the Frankfurt settlements with full confidence in her modern homemaking skills.[54]

In comparing her kitchenette-equipped classroom with those in older schools, Lihotzky credited her analyses of "systematic labor" in

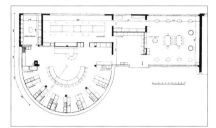

FIG. 16 The Professional Teachers' Institute, designed by Max Cetto and Grete Lihotzky in 1928

FIG. 17 The demonstration table at the Professional Teachers' Institute

generating the arrangement of utensils. The plan was a product of the path-diagram technique promoted by Frederick and Alexander Klein, intended to produce efficient circulation. Other contemporary examples like Otto Haesler's school at Celle, despite sharing the same consideration for light, cleanliness, and stylistic modernity, exhibited neither the precision of Lihotzky's kitchen designs nor the clear distinction between practice and study areas.[55]

At the Professional Teachers' Institute, designed by Max Cetto in 1928, Lihotzky was free to engender a more dynamic plan in the school kitchen and use the most deluxe equipment (FIG. 16). In the rarefied air of this modern laboratory, the woman's sphere was characterized by sleek lines and sophisticated technology, and was peopled with uniformed girl-technicians in starched, white aprons (FIG. 17). Reportedly, this rather complete embodiment of the domestic science ideal was greeted warmly by the school; it not only exemplified modern practice but lightened the work of the teachers as well. Above all, it was reported, the students engaged in their work more joyfully than before, since so little of their time was now given over to the drudgery of cleaning and maintenance.[56]

While the new housekeeping had important social objectives in better public health and hygiene, and fostered hopes for the rejuvenation of the German economy, the predominant message to students was imparted by the "scientific" atmosphere and a pedagogy dominated by rationalization concepts. The domestic science classroom represented a key moment in the challenge to women's authority over their traditional sphere.

CONCLUSION

> Recently, the subject of the house as workplace has again been taken up and researched, primarily by parts of the women's movement. On the one hand, one viewpoint advocates moving away from rigid house plans since they only strengthen stereotyped social roles. The champions of this position have thereby also viewed the Frankfurt Kitchen as a synonym for the oppression of the housewife, banished to the isolated kitchen, whereas (they believe) the new Wohnküche really can be liberating. Others, on the other hand, defend the opinion that the dissolution of the sex-specific practices of role behavior can in no way be expected from such an architectural/spatial transformation.
>
> —GRETE SCHÜTTE-LIHOTZKY, 1980[57]

Throughout her career, Lihotzky's belief in the importance of eliminating household drudgery through rationalization remained firm. In more recent times, she has proposed that with the reemergence of the "country kitchen," women have sacrificed efficiency and practicality to the whimsy of fashion and have left themselves with even a longer list of tedious chores.[58]

In the 1920s, however, the issue was much greater than a design fashion and concerned the technical and social transformation of an entire society. It is ironic that a politically engaged Lihotzky seemed to view the kitchen as the motor for change, rather than as a manifestation of larger redomestication issues.

Whether Lihotzky's Frankfurt Kitchen actually lessened the workload of the housewife is unclear—with women assuming jobs outside the home and becoming isolated in smaller family units, all indications are that their burden was growing rather than diminishing, and this in spite of labor-saving devices. At the same time, the professional dignity that the Frankfurt Kitchen was to confer on the role of housewife does not bear scrutiny. The work station was not borrowed from the professional world, but from the factory, from labor characterized by single, repetitive, and mind-numbing operations. The notion of creativity was anathema to

FIG. 18 A workstation in a soapmaking factory in 1931

this model—it was for the manager/ designer, the Taylorizer of the space, to blot out free action by delimiting an imperative "one best way" (FIG. 18). That this was not a situation compatible with household labor, with its myriad tasks and practices and varied member composition, was largely irrelevant to the overriding ideological notions of efficiency and scientism.

Indeed, household labor itself was revealed in the parallel made between the factory worker and the housewife to be a degraded process, as the persistent references to it as "drudgery" confirm. To all accounts, the "professional" housewife was admittedly committed to a life of grinding labor from which she could only be freed for brief moments through the application of techniques invented by authorities in the professional world. In the 1920s, there were few critics of this limited policy—few among the powerful women's groups, and fewer still within the ranks of the Social Democrats.

The backlash against the women's movement that followed World War I echoed this general erosion and devaluation of women's contribution to culture. At the same time, the positivist and male-defined architectural culture produced new artifacts of domesticity that fostered the development of the market in household goods. It also facilitated a new professional role for designers, one that might emerge only after the home had been newly consecrated as a professional realm and was largely shorn of its feminine attributes.

Lihotzky herself viewed this work primarily as part of a broader socialist enterprise, independent of any notion of feminist politics:

My work was based on the idea of women who worked and not in cooking itself. I had never concerned myself with cooking in my life. Nowadays this is seen as feminist but it was not feminist at all.[59]

This last remark, that basing her research on women who worked was "not feminist at all," reflects the situation of would-be professional women in an era of limited options: either to embrace patriarchal culture as a New Woman, as Lihotzky did, or to support it from the vantage point of the helpmeet, as did women in the ranks of the RDH. Lihotzky's ideal, both personally and in her work on behalf of women, was clearly to reject the confines of home in favor of participation in the public world of men. Even backed by modernized domestic facilities, for most German house-wives there was no such choice. The Frankfurt Kitchen may be taken as a kind of emblem of this cultural conundrum: a brief, if uncomfortable, res-olution between women's culture and the ideal of a technological utopia.

NOTES

1. On the history of the German women's movement see Barbara Aschoff-Greven, *Die bürgerliche Frauenbewegung in Deutschland, 1894–1933* (Göttingen: Vandenhoeck & Ruprecht, 1981) and Ute Frevert, *Women in German History. From Bourgeois Emancipation to Sexual Liberation*, trans. Stuart McKinnon-Evans (New York: St. Martin's Press, 1989).

2. As originally coined, the "New Woman" was a concept dating from the fin de siècle. Of her, Elaine Showalter writes, "The New Woman, university educated and sexually independent, engendered intense hostility and fear as she seemed to challenge male supremacy in art, the pro-fessions, and the home. Politically, the New Woman was an anarchic figure who threatened to turn the world upside down and to be on top in a wild carnival of social and sexual misrule." Elaine Showalter, *Sexual Anarchy: Gender and Culture at the Fin de Siècle* (New York: Viking Press, 1990), 38. On the New Woman in Germany see Atina Grossmann, "The New Woman and the Rationalization of Sexuality in Weimar Germany," in *Powers of Desire: The Politics of Sexuality*, ed. Ann Snitow et al. (New York: Monthly Review Press, 1983), 156–58; and Claudia Koonz, *Mothers in the Fatherland: Women, the Family, and Nazi Politics* (New York: St. Martin's Press, 1987). In *Screening out the Past: The Birth of Mass Culture and the Motion Picture Industry* (New York: Oxford University Press, 1980), 200–37, Lary May describes the development of the New Woman in American silent films, one of the most influential mediums disseminating con-cepts of modernity. Germany had by far the largest number of cinemas among the European

countries, and the "insidious" influence of American film, both culturally and as a market encroachment, was widely discussed. For a general discussion of the Weimar woman see Renate Bridenthal and Claudia Koonz, "Beyond *Kinder, Küche, Kirche*: Weimar Women in Politics and Work," in *When Biology Became Destiny: Women in Weimar and Nazi Germany*, ed. Renate Bridenthal et al. (New York: Monthly Review Press, 1984), 33–65.

3. The major shift in the number of women working outside the home actually occurred between the 1880s and 1907 when it jumped 300 percent. Although many observers predicted the destruction of family life, government programs to reverse the trend were not implemented until after the First World War. Robyn Dasey, "Women's Work and the Family: Women Garment Workers in Berlin and Hamburg Before the First World War," in *The German Family: Essays on the Social History of the Family in Nineteenth- and Twentieth-Century Germany*, ed. Richard J. Evans and W.R. Lee (London: Croom Helm, 1981), 222.

4. The first women enrolled in German universities in 1900; by 1910 they numbered only 1,867. Yet by the end of the war, women had not only moved into the professional fields of dentistry, political science, and law, but had grown to comprise a large part of the student body. At some universities such as Heidelberg, where they comprised 52 percent, women were in the majority. In the postwar years, the number quickly fell, until by 1930 it was near its prewar level of 10 percent. Hugh W. Puckett, *Germany's Women Go Forward* (New York: Columbia University, 1930), 200–201.

5. Arthur E. Imhof, "Women, Family and Death: Excess Mortality of Women in Child-bearing Age in Four Communities in Nineteenth Century Germany," in *The German Family*, ed. Evans and Lee, 153.

6. From *Die Gleichheit*, quoted and translated by Richard J. Evans, "Politics and the Family: Social Democracy and the Working Class Family in Theory and Practice Before 1914," in *The German Family*, ed. Evans and Lee, 271.

7. Catharine Beecher and Harriet Beecher Stowe, *The American Woman's Home* (1869; reprint, Hartford, Connecticut: Stowe-Day Foundation, 1975). On the life of Beecher and for a discussion of her collaboration with Stowe, see Kathryn Kish Sklar, *Catharine Beecher: A Study in American Domesticity* (New York: W.W. Norton & Company, 1973).

8. Beecher and Stowe, *The American Woman's Home*, 24.

9. See Christine Frederick, *Household Engineering: Scientific Management in the Home* (Chicago: American School of Home Economics, 1919). *Household Engineering* first appeared in 1915 in a short version that was billed as a correspondence course at the Chicago-based American School of Home Economics. The subject was "the application of the principles of efficiency engineering and scientific management to the every day tasks of house-keeping."

10. Ibid., 8–9.

11. On the history of the BDF and the RDH see Renate Bridenthal, "'Professional Housewives': Stepsisters of the Women's Movement," in *When Biology Became Destiny*, ed. Bridenthal et al., 153–73, and Frevert, *Women in German History*, 168–204.

12. Thomas Alexander and Beryl Parker, *The New Education in the German Republic* (New York: The John Day Company, 1929), 276–77.

13. Examples are illustrated in Marie-Elisabeth Lüders, "Erste die Küche—dann die Fassade," and Wilhelm Lübbert, "Rationelle Küchengestaltung," both in *Die Küche. Der Klein- und Mittel-wohnung Reichsforschungsgesellschaft für Wirtschaftlichkeit im Bau- und Wohnungswesen E.V. Sonderheft* 2, Group II 6, No. 2 (June 1928) Year 1, 6, and 23–24, respectively.

14. Clara Mende, "Alte und neue Küchen," *Die Küche der Klein- und Mittelwohnung Reichsforschungsgesellschaft für Wirtschaft-lichkeit im Bau- und Wohnungswesen E.V. Sonderheft* 2, Group II 6, No. 2 (June 1928) Year 1, 9; Gertrud Lincke, "Wohnungsbau und Hausfrauen," *Die Frau 33* (July 1926): 609.

15. An exact translation is difficult. Strictly speaking *Die Ernährung* refers to provisioning; the title thus implies all that is necessary to provide sustenance for a family.

16. See the illustration in *Bauwelt*, no. 22 (1931): 753.

17. Marie-Elisabeth Lüders, "Easy Management of the House as the First Consideration of the Builder," *Wohnen und Bauen* (July/August 1930): 149. This article forwards one by Lihotzky, "What is being done for the Women and Children in the new Residential Quarters and Colonies?" 152–68. The latter deals with labor-saving and child-supervisory facilities in the household and the community.

18. See Erna Meyer, "Zweckmäßige Küchmöbel," *Bauwelt*, no. 9 (1927): 240–42, which details kitchen furniture requirements and specifications.

19. Erna Meyer, "Wohnungsbau und Hausführung," *Der Baumeister 25 Beilage* (1927): 89. Author's translation.

20. Nicholas Bullock, "First the Kitchen—then the Facade," *Journal of Design History* I, nos. 3–4, 182.

21. Edith Jacoby-Oske, "Frauenanteil an der Lösung der Wohnungsfragen," *Die Frau 33* (September 1926): 719–20. Author's translation.

22. Lincke, "Wohnungsbau und Hausfrauen," 607. Author's translation.

23. Ibid.

24. Grete and Walter Dexel, *Das Wohnhaus von Heute*; Erna Meyer, *Das neue Haushalt* (Stuttgart: 1926); Ludwig Neundörfer, *So wollen wir wohnen* (Stuttgart: Franckhische Verlagshandlung, 1931); Bruno Taut, *Die neue Wohnung. Die Frau als Schöpferin* (Leipzig: Verlag Klinkhardt and Burmann, 1928).

25. Works on Ernst May and the Frankfurt housing program include Susan R. Henderson, "The Work of Ernst May, 1919–1930" (Ph.D. diss. Columbia University, 1990); and Christoph Mohr and Michael Müller, *Fünktionalität und Moderne. Das Neue Frankfurt und seine Bauten, 1925–1933* (Cologne: Rudolf Müller Verlag, 1984).

26. The precepts of labor-saving house design came into currency in America before the war and were the subject of great interest among women's groups. Max Heidelberg, a New York architect who chaired the Feminist Alliance's Committee on the Socialization of the Primitive Industries of Women in 1914, was one who attempted to eradicate household drudgery through design: "There would be no wallpaper and no picture moldings. All corners would be rounded, all bath-tubs would be built in, all windows would pivot, all beds would fold into the walls, and all hard-ware would be dull-finished." The currency of such ideas is evidenced in the striking parallels

between these and May's strategies. Dolores Hayden, *The Grand Domestic Revolution. A History of Feminist Designs for American Homes, Neighborhoods, and Cities* (Cambridge: MIT Press, 1981), 200.

27. A supplement entitled "Das Frankfurter Register" appeared in each issue of *Das neue Frankfurt* beginning with no. 1, 1928 through no. 4/5, 1931. There were seventeen entries to the register in all, including items such as the Kramer Oven, the Frankfurt Bed, Christian Dell lamps, Adolf Meyer lighting fixtures, and Bauhaus wall coverings and fabrics. May said the purpose of the register was to influence the public to purchase "good and price-worthy" household furnishings. Joseph Gantner, the editor of *Das Neue Frankfurt*, presented it as an overview of the best of mass-produced furnishings for the modern house.

28. Quoted from Burkhard Rukschcio and Roland Schachel, Adolf Loos. *Leben und Werk* (Vienna: Residenz Verlag, 1982), 575. Author's translation.

29. The only other major female contributor to the program was Grete Leistikow, who, with her brother Hans, designed many *Das Neue Frankfurt* covers. The photographer Grete contributed the images, and her brother designed the layouts. They produced nearly all the covers between no. 2 of 1929 and no. 9 of 1930.

Though never directly employed by the Frankfurt Hochbauamt, Lilly Reich was also on the scene. From 1925 to 1927, Reich worked as the coordinator of the yearly Werkbund Exhibition at the *Frankfurter Meße*. See Deborah Dietsch, "Lilly Reich," *Heresies 3* (1981): 73. Ferdinand Kramer attested to Reich's importance in bringing the latest issues to the attention of many of the young Werkbund exhibitors. Ferdinand Kramer, an interview with the author, Frankfurt, 22 June 1984.

30. Lihotzky is indeed an inspiring figure. She studied architecture against the best encouragement of her male teachers in Vienna and was the first woman graduate in her atelier. In 1930, she accompanied Ernst May in his voluntary exile to the Soviet Union, where she stayed to work for the state through 1937. In 1940, she left her work, then in Turkey, to join the Austrian resistance movement. She was arrested within weeks, narrowly missed a death sentence, and spent the subsequent four and a half years imprisoned. She continued an active career in Vienna through the 1970s and has since been working on various projects concerning her career and memoirs. Throughout her career Lihotzky remained a dedicated communist party member.

31. Lihotzky worked on *Winarskyhof* (today *Otto-Haas-Hof*) in Vienna in 1923. A collaborative effort, the coworkers included Peter Behrens, Josef Frank, Josef Hoffmann, Adolf Loos, Oskar Strnad, Oskar Wlach, and Franz Schuster. However, Loos, Schuster and Lihotzky's joint contribution— several adjoining blocks along *Kaiserstraße*—is characterized by the extreme *sachlichkeit* that marked Loos's early Heuburg Settlement (1920). Loos left the project in midstream to attend to other commitments, handing his responsibilities over to Lihotzky. Both Schuster and Lihotzky joined the Frankfurt team in 1925 and seem to have had a great influence on the evolution of May's modernist style. Rukschcio and Schachel, *Adolf Loos. Leben und Werk*, 574–75.

32. Margarete Schütte-Lihotzky, *Erinnerungen aus dem Widerstand. 1938–1945* (Berlin: Verlag Volk und Welt, 1985), 13. This source also contains the basic biographical material on Lihotzky. Other reminiscences were published in Lore Kramer, "Biografie/Biography: Margarete Schütte-

Lihotzky," in *Women in Design. Careers and Life Histories since 1900* (Stuttgart: Design Center Stuttgart, 1989), Exhibition Catalogue, 160–69; and Günther Uhlig, "Margarete Schütte-Lihotzky. Textcollagen aus und zu ihrem Werk," *Um Bau*, no. 5 (December 1981): 27–36.

33. Grete Lihotzki [sic], "Einige über die Einrichtung österreichischer Häuser unter besonderer Berücksichtiger Siedlungsbauten," *Schlesisches Heim*, no. 8 (August 1921): 217–22. Lihotzky's several articles for *Schlesisches Heim* were primarily concerned with kitchen design and garden huts. See her "Die Siedlungs—, Wohnungs- und Baugilde Österreichs auf der 4. Wiener Kleingartenaustellung," *Schlesisches Heim*, no. 10 (October 1922): 445–47; and "Wiener Kleingarten- und Siedlerhüttenaktion," *Schlesisches Heim*, no. 4 (April 1923): 83–87. Her resume, however, proves the bulk of her work to be concerned with other than explicitly women's design issues. Indeed, when she agreed to travel with May to the Soviet Union, one of her preconditions was that she not have to design any more kitchens.

34. For example, in the special RfG publication on kitchen design, Paul Mebes singled out Lihotzky's kitchen (for which he credited May) as the best solution to date for those without servants. Paul Mebes, "Gedanken zur Küchengestaltung," *Die Küche der Klein- und Mittelwohnung Reichsforschungs-gesellschaft für Wirtschaftlichkeit im Bau- und Wohnungswesen E.V. Sonderheft* 2, Group II 6, No. 2 (June 1928) Year 1, 10; Anton Brenner, "Die Frankfurter Küche," *Bauwelt*, no. 9 (1927): 243–45. Lihotzky, of course, did other design work for the *Hochbauamt*, although none of it was widely hailed. Among this work is the Praunheim Kindergarten (unexecuted) and the garden sheds of the Nidda Valley garden colonies.

35. It was not a new idea. An earlier home efficiency expert, Catharine Beecher, was intrigued by the lunch wagon in the nineteenth century: "The cook's galley in a steamship has every article and utensil used in cooking for two hundred persons, in a space not larger than this stove, room and so arranged that with one or two steps the cook can reach all he uses." Beecher and Stowe, *The American Woman's Home*, 33. The parallels between the designs of Beecher and Lihotzky are also remarkable: "The flour-barrel just fills the closet, which has a door for admission and a lid to raise when used. . . . On the other side next the sink, to hold the dishes, and grooves cut to let the water drain into the sink." Stowe, 35.

36. Kramer, "Biografie/Biography: Margarete Schütte-Lihotzky," 165.

37. The best and most complete description of the Frankfurt Kitchen is in Grete Schütte-Lihotzky, "Arbeitsküche," *form + zweck*, no. 4 (1981): 22–26.

38. Oud's Weissenhof kitchen appears in nearly all the major discussions of the kitchen after 1927. See, for example, Dexel and Dexel, *Das Wohnhaus von Heute*, 131–32; Erna Meyer, "Wohnungsbau und Hausführung," *Der Baumeister* 25, Supplement (1927): 90–92. *The Haus am Horn*'s kitchen was also widely published. See Taut, *Die neue Wohnung. Die Frau als Schöpferin*, 41.

39. Lihotzky, "Die neuzeitliche Haushalt," 112. Author's translation.

40. "Vom neuen Bauen in Frankfurt am Main III. Ausstellung 'Die neue Wohnung und ihr Innenausbau' und 'Tagung der Baufachleute' am 28. und 29. März 1927," *Der Baumeister 25 Beilage* (1927): 107.

41. Dexel and Dexel, *Das Wohnhaus von Heute*, 125–26. Descriptions of the exhibition can be found

in Grete Lihotzky, "Rationalisierung im Haushalt," *Das Neue Frankfurt*, no. 5 (1926/27): 120–22; and Werner Nosbisch, "Die neue Wohnung und ihr Innenausbau, der neuzeitliche Haushalt," *Das Neue Frankfurt*, no. 6 (1926/27): 129–33.

42. Wilhelm Schütte, "Von neuen Bauen in Frankfurt am Main. II. Das Wohnungsprogram," *Der Baumeister* (1927): 121.

43. "Das Programm Loucheur," *Das Neue Frankfurt*, no. 9 (1928): 161; Lore Kramer, "Rationalisierung des Haushaltes und Frauenfrage—Die Frankfurter Küche und zeitgenössische Kritik," *Ernst May und Das Neue Frankfurt*, 1925–1930, Exhibition Catalog (Frankfurt am Main: Deutsches Architekturmuseum, 1986), 83. The French government suspended negotiations for the kitchen in 1929 when the intention to credit payment to a reparations account was called into question. "Frankfurter Normenbauteile für Frankreich," *Das Neue Frankfurt*, no. 1 (1929).

44. Neundörfer, *So wollen wir wohnen*, 55–56. Author's translation.

45. Erna Meyer, "Wohnungsbau und Hausführung," *Der Baumeister* 25, Supplement (1927): 93.

46. "Die elektrische Römerstadt: Amerika vor den Toren," *Frankfurter General Anzeiger*, 18 August 1927. For more on the importance of electricity see Mende, "Alte und neue Küchen," 8.

47. Ibid. Author's translation.

48. Grete Schütte-Lihotzky, "What is being done for the Women and Children in the new Residential Quarters and Colonies?" *Wohnen und Bauen* (July/August 1930): 158.

49. Adolf Meyer was an early partner of Walter Gropius's. They worked together on such projects as the Fagus Factory (1911) in Alfeld an der Leine and the Model Factory (1914) at the Werkbund Exhibition in Cologne. In 1926 he joined Ernst May's team in Frankfurt. His distinguished career was cut short by his premature death by drowning in 1929.

50. "Umbau der Frankfurter Gasgesellschaft in der Kaiserpassage. Frankfurt a. M.," *Das Neue Frankfurt*, no. 5 (1928): 83–84; *Frankfurt am Main* (Frankfurt: Werner Rades, n.d.): 102–3.

51. "Umbau der Frankfurter Gasgesellschaft in der Kaiser-passage," 84.

52. Grete Schütte-Lihotzky, "Neue Frankfurter Schul-und Lehr-Küchen," *Das Neue Frankfurt*, no. 1 (January 1929): 18. Author's translation.

53. Lihotzky's kitchen cubicles were used at the Römerstadt *Volksschule*, at the *Eschersheim Ludwig-Richter-Schule* designed by Martin Elsaesser, and the *Niederursel Volksschule* designed by Franz Schuster. The semicircular plan of the *Berufspädago-gischen Institut* was also repeated in the scheme for the unexecuted *Gewerbe-und Haushaltungsschule* designed by Elsaesser and Wilhelm Schütte (1930). On the three schools, see *Frankfurter Schulbauten 1929*; the *Gewerbe-und Haushaltungsschule* is published in *Martin Elsaesser. Bauten und Entwürf aus den Jahren 1914–1932* (Berlin: Bauwelt Verlag, 1933), 189–91.

54. She could also move back out into the work world: "One of the reasons for the stream-lining of the household was surely so that women could be moved into the factories on a moment's notice, just as the preoccupation with the health of the workers had military implications." Helene Röttiger, "Erfahrungen nach dem hauswirtschaftlichen Volljahr," *Die Frau* 32 (1925): 235. Author's translation.

55. Lihotzky, "Neue Frankfurter Schul- und Lehr-Küchen," 18. See Otto Haesler's school at Celle in

N. L. Engelhardt, "Planning High School Buildings for Better Utilization," *Architectural Record* 66 (1929): 281.

56. Lihotzky, "Neue Frankfurter Schul- und Lehr-Küchen," 21.

57. Grete Schütte-Lihotzky, "Frauen, Räume, Architektur, Umwelt," *beiträge* 4 (Munich: Verlag Frauenoffensive, 1980), quoted in Uhlig, "Margarete Schütte-Lihotzky. Textcollagen," 31. Author's translation.

58. Kramer, "Biografie/Biography: Margarete Schütte-Lihotzky," 168.

59. Lihotzky, "Arbeitsküche," 26. Author's translation.

MANUELA ANTONIU is currently at the Architectural Association in London. She received her architectural training in Canada, and her work has been exhibited in Europe and the U.S.

VANESSA CHASE is a graduate student in architectural history at Columbia University. She received a bachelor's degree in Art from Harvard and Radcliffe Colleges, a master's degree of Art in Art History from the University of London, and a master of Philosophy degree from Columbia University. She is currently researching her doctoral dissertation "Gender and Architecture in Renaissance Venice: The Casa Delle Zitelle della Giudecca."

DEBORAH FAUSCH teaches architectural theory and history at Parsons School of Design in New York, and has practiced architecture in New York and Minnesota. She is an editor of *Architecture: In Fashion* (Princeton Architectural Press, 1994). Her articles have appeared in *Archithese* and *ANY*.

MOLLY HANKWITZ is a theorist living in San Francisco. She writes about art, architecture, urbanism, feminism, and the internet. She can be reached at mhankwitz@aol.com.

SUSAN HENDERSON is an associate professor of Architecture at Syracuse University, where she teaches architectural history. She received her bachelor's degree in Environmental Design from the University of Washington, a master's degree in Architecture from MIT, and her Ph.D. in Architectural History from Columbia University. Her articles about aspects of German modernism have appeared in *Planning Perspectives*, *Journal of Decorative and Propaganda Arts*, and *Architecture + Culture*. The article "Ernst May and the Campaign to Resettle the Countryside" is forthcoming in the *Journal of the Society of Architectural Historians*.

LIQUID inc. is an Atlanta-based artistic/architectural collaborative team that produces objects, installations, and architectural design. Amy Landesberg and Lisa Quatrale studied architecture at Yale University, and each has since taught at Georgia Tech. They have lectured and exhibited widely, and their multidisciplinary projects have appeared in *Art Papers*, *Assemblage*, and *ANY*.

CHRISTINE MAGAR teaches at SCI-Arc and at Iowa State University. She has an office in Los Angeles where she designs for commercial, institutional, and residential clients. She has also taught at the University of Southern California where she received her bachelor's degree in Architecture. She received a master's degree from Yale University. Her publications include the art books the *Cosmetic Case* and the *Wandering Whole*, and she is coeditor of the web-project "Womenhouse."

MARY MCLEOD is an associate professor of architecture at Columbia University, where she currently teaches architectural history and studio. She has also taught at Harvard University, University of Miami, University of Kentucky, and the Institute for Architecture and Urban Studies. She is coeditor of *Architecture, Criticism, and Ideology*, and *Architectu-re-production* (both from Princeton Architectural Press), and is currently writing a book on Le Corbusier's architecture and politics between the wars (Princeton University Press). Her articles have appeared in *Assemblage*, *Oppositions*, *Art Journal*, *AA Files*, *Lotus*, *Domus*, *Places*, and *Design Book Review*, and in a number of anthologies including *Architecture: In Fashion* (Princeton Architectural Press) and *Americanisme et modernité* (Flammarion).

GEORGE WAGNER is associate professor of Architecture at the University of British Columbia. His writing has been published in *Harvard Architectural Review* 8, *Center*, and *Canadian Architect*. He has edited two monographs: *Thom Mayne: The Sixth Street House*, and *Stanley Saitowitz: A House in the Transvaal*.

ILLUSTRATION CREDITS

EVERYDAY AND "OTHER" SPACES | MARY McLEOD 1, 3: Peter Eisenman. 2: Bernard Tschumi Architects. 4: collection of the British Library, rpt. in Robin Evans, *The Fabrication of Virtue: English Prison Architecture, 1750–1840* (Cambridge: Cambridge University Press), 289. 5: Jean I. Marot, *L'Architecture française (Le Grand Marot)* (Paris, 1683). 6: Serge Nazarieff, *The Stereoscopic Nude 1850–1930* (Cologne: Benedikt Taschen, 1993), 132. 7, 8, 21, 28, 29: Mary McLeod. 9: Zaha Hadid. 10: Andreas Papadakis, *Deconstruction: Omnibus Volume* (New York: Rizzoli, 1989), 220. 11: Selfridge Archives, rpt. in Rachel Bowlby, *Just Looking: Consumer Culture in Dreiser, Gissing and Zola* (New York and London: Methuen, 1985), 21. 12: Mary Evans Picture Library, rpt. in Bowlby, 153. 13: Elisabeth Sussman, ed., *On the Passage of a few people through a rather brief moment in time: The Situationist International 1957–1972* (Cambridge, Mass.: MIT Press, 1989), 42. 14: Sussman, 53. 15: David Robbins, ed., *The Independent Group: Postwar Britain and the Aesthetics of Plenty* (Cambridge, Mass.: MIT Press, 1990), 99. 16, 17: Alison and Peter Smithson. 18: Venturi, Scott Brown and Associates. 19: photograph by George Pohl, courtesy of Venturi, Scott Brown and Associates. 20: *Architects' Journal* 137 (16 January 1963): 127. 22, 23: Josef Astor. 24: *U. S. News and World Report* (18 July 1988). 25, 26: Karl Hulten, *Tinguely* (Paris: Centre Georges Pompidou, 1988), 243–44. 27: National Parks Service. THE KNOWLEDGE OF THE BODY AND THE PRESENCE OF HISTORY | DEBORAH FAUSCH 1, 2: Jeff Brokaw. 3, 8, 9: Deborah Fausch. 4, 5: Mary Miss. 6: Venturi, Scott Brown and Associates. 7: Tom Bernard, courtesy of Venturi, Scott Brown and Associates. 10: Bibliothèque Nationale. 11, 12: Mark Cohn, courtesy of Venturi, Scott Brown and Associates. PROJECT MANUAL FOR THE GLASS HOUSE | CHRISTINE S.E. MAGAR Footnotes by Philip Johnson from the article "House at New Caanan, Connecticut," *Architectural Review* 108, no. 645 (September 1950): 152–59, reprinted courtesy of *Architectural Review*. (Credits for images within this article are as follows: 1: H. Girsberger, Zurich. 8: Hedrich Blessing Studio. 10: Museum of Modern Art, New York. 13, 17, 20: Arnold Newman. 14, 15, 16, 18: Ezra Stoller. 19, 21: McCallum, Arphot. 22: André Kertész.) Additional images: p. 75. Farnsworth House: Werner Blaser, *Mies van der Rohe Furniture and Interiors*, trans. Roger Marcinik (Italy: Barron's Educational Series, Inc., 1982), 108. pp. 76, 77. Partial plans of IIT: John M. Jacobus, Jr., *Philip Johnson* (New York: George Braziller, 1962), 54. p. 78. Parthenon: Le Corbusier, *Towards a New Architecture* (New York: Dover, 1986), 135. p. 80. Casino in Glienicke Park: *Schinkel* (New York: Princeton Architectural Press, 1989), pl. 138. p. 81. Maison des Gardes Agricoles: *Ledoux* (New York: Princeton Architectural Press, 1984), pl. 254. p. 83. Glass House Fascia: Kenneth Frampton, "The Glass House Revisited," *Catalog* 9 (September/October 1978), illustr. 54. p. 84. Ludwig Mies van der Rohe, Library and Administration Building, Illinois Institute of Technology, Chicago, Illinois, 1944; Perspective of southeast corner; Pencil on illustration board, 44 x 34": The Mies van der Rohe Archive, The Museum of Modern Art, New York; and Vertical and Horizontal sections; Ink on illustration board, 30 x 40": The Mies van der Rohe Archive, The Museum of Modern Art, New York; Gift of the Architect, ©1996 The Museum of Modern Art, New York. p. 85. Ludwig Mies van der Rohe, Plan and perspective for a court house or, possibly, the proposed Hubbe House, Magdeburg: *Mies Reconsidered: His Career, Legacy, and Disciples* (New York: Art Institute of Chicago & Rizzoli, 1986), 119. p. 89. Glass House plan 1947: Frampton, "The Glass House Revisited," illustr. 35. p. 90. Ludwig Mies van der Rohe, Ulrich Lange House, 1935; Two Elevations; Pencil on tracing paper, 9 ¾ x 20 ½": The Mies van der Rohe Archive, The Museum of Modern Art, New York, ©1996 The Museum of Modern Art, New York. p. 94. Erechtheum: Le Corbusier, *Towards a New Architecture*, 206. p. 98: Ludwig Mies van der Rohe, Museum for a Small City: *Architectural Forum* 78, no. 5 (1943): 84–85; p. 102. Johnson's Apartment: Henry-Russell Hitchcock, Jr. and Philip Johnson, *The International Style: Architects Since 1922*, rev. and enl. (New York: W. W. Norton, 1966), 191. All other illustrations and photographs by Christine S.E. Magar. EDITH WHARTON, THE DECORATION OF HOUSES, AND GENDER | VANESSA CHASE 1, 2, 5, 6: The Yale Collection of American Literature, Beinecke Rare Book and Manuscript Library, Yale University. 3A, 3B: Codman Collection, Avery Architectural and Fine Arts Library, Columbia University in the City of New York. 4A, 4B: Hoppin Collection, Avery Architectural and Fine Arts Library, Columbia University in the City of New York. THE STORY OF HON–KATHEDRAL | MOLLY HANKWITZ 1, 2, 5: Moderna Museet, Stockholm. 3: Lutfi Özkök. 4: Hans Hammarskiöld. 6: Hans Hammarskiöld and the Moderna Museet, Stockholm. 7, 8: Vito Acconci. THE LAIR OF THE BACHELOR | GEORGE WAGNER 1–3: Daniel H. Burnham and Edward H. Bennett, *Plan of Chicago* (New York: Princeton Architectural Press, 1993). 4A-7: Gruen Associates. 8-14, 18: *Playboy* magazine. 15-17: George Wagner.